W9-DGN-906

PROVEN WORD BOOKS

- Have *proven* themselves where it counts—among the thousands of readers who have made them best-sellers, who have found these books meaningful in the arena of real life

- Were best-sellers in hardcover and are now made available at more affordable prices in deluxe paperback bindings

- Offer new, built-in study guides with questions to encourage private pondering and group discussion

- Meet the widespread needs of people everywhere who are searching for answers to the pressures and problems of living in the modern world

PROVEN
WORD

THE
BUSH IS
STILL
BURNING

Other books by Lloyd John Ogilvie

Making Stress Work for You
Acts, Volume 5, Communicator's Commentary
Congratulations, God Believes in You
When God First Thought of You
Drumbeat of Love
Life Without Limits
Let God Love You
The Autobiography of God
Loved and Forgiven
Lord of the Ups and Downs
If I Should Wake Before I Die
A Life Full of Surprises
You've Got Charisma
Cup of Wonder
God's Best for My Life
The Radiance of Inner Splendor
Gift of Friendship
Gift of Love
Gift of Caring
Gift of Sharing

Lloyd John Ogilvie

THE BUSH IS STILL BURNING

The Christ Who
Makes Things Happen
In Our
Deepest Needs

With Built-In Study Guide by
Andrea Wells Miller

PROVEN
WORD

WORD BOOKS
PUBLISHER
WACO, TEXAS

A DIVISION OF
WORD, INCORPORATED

THE BUSH IS STILL BURNING
Proven-Word Edition
Copyright © 1980, 1985 by Word, Incorporated
1800 West Waco Drive, Waco, Texas 76703

Unless otherwise noted, all Scripture quotations are from the Revised
Standard Version of the Bible, copyrighted 1946, 1952, © 1971, 1973
by the Division of Christian Education of the National Council of
Churches of Christ in the U.S.A., and are used by permission.
Quotation marked KJV is from the King James Version of the Bible;
quotation marked LB is from *The Living Bible, Paraphrased* (Wheaton:
Tyndale House Publishers, 1971) and is used by permission. Quotation
marked Phillips is from *The New Testament in Modern English* (revised
edition), © J.B. Phillips 1958, 1960, 1972, and is reprinted with
permission of Macmillan Publishing Co., Inc. Quotation marked NAS
is from *The New American Standard Bible* © The Lockman Foundation
1960,1962, 1968, 1971.

Library of Congress catalog card number: 79-055924
ISBN 0-8499-3031-6
Printed in the United States of America

7898   RRD   98765432

To Mother and Dad Jenkins
Loving and Faithful Encouragers
Through the Years

Contents

Preface

LAST YEAR, I did an inventory of the deepest needs of the American people. The basic question I asked throughout the nation was, "What is the one thing which causes you the greatest difficulty in your daily living? State your deepest need." The survey was sent out to a cross section of people in various parts of the country. The question was asked of people in conferences wherever I spoke. On successive Sundays, I asked worshipers in my Hollywood congregation to complete the statement, "My deepest need in living is . . ." Several thousand cards were collected.

All of the needs expressed then were sorted, sifted, and categorized. The raw nerves inside people were expressed in what they shared. I felt the pulse of the hurts and hopes of all of us.

At the same time, I was doing a devotional study of the "I am" statements of Jesus. The deeper I penetrated into these powerful self-disclosures, the more excited I became. Each of the "I am" promises matched one of the deep needs which headed the list I had collected.

Listening to people and to the Lord at the same time gave birth to the vision of doing a contemporary exposition of the "I am" affirmations as the Lord's healing answers for the aching needs of people. My studies in the original Greek text revealed several pointed "I am" claims of Jesus which have been blunted in all the English translations. Therefore, my list of "I am" ascriptions is expanded beyond most traditional compilations. What

Jesus said about himself and what he offers to do in our lives today become a solid biblical basis for emotional healing. The Lord can turn our struggles into stepping stones!

Each of the chapters in this book was spoken on my church's national television program, "Let God Love You!" The responses of people were gratifying. Their shared insights about the Lord's healing power in their struggles greatly assisted me in the revision of the material for publication. I am also indebted to the Hollywood Presbyterian congregation for the dialogue between pastor and people. Through the media and opportunities to speak extensively, the Lord has given me the privilege of feeling our nation's deepest needs. We are fellow strugglers who are discovering the Lord's stepping stones together. This book is offered in praise to the "I am" who can make things happen in our lives today.

LLOYD JOHN OGILVIE

1

A New God for Old Struggles

The God Who Makes
Things Happen

"Before Abraham was, I am!"
John 8:58

IT HAD BEEN A LONG DAY listening to people share their struggles. The last appointment, late in the afternoon, made my day! I had talked with the man often before and I felt that prolonged listening had earned me the right to ask a penetrating question.

"What do you now feel is the deepest need in your life, and what can I do to help?"

His response was immediate and direct. "I need a new God!" he replied urgently.

My face must have shown a mixture of delight and excitement. He went on to explain with intensity what he meant.

"During the past few weeks we've been talking about what to do with the struggles in my life. You've tried to tell me that God loves me, is for me, and has the power to help me in my struggles. That's been difficult to hear because of what I've known about God from friends, my family background, and our culture. I've thought a lot about what you've said and read the Bible verses about God's power you gave me—even memorized a few. Then, the other day, it hit me that the reason for my struggles is that I have had a wrong idea about God.

"I've thought of him as a judge, or a heavenly police-man. He has been up there or out there somewhere. I couldn't believe that he either knew or cared about me and my struggles. I guess I've picked up a lot of fuzzy thinking about God. Most people believe in God, but he's like an absentee landlord—aloof, distant, and nonexistent as far as daily problems are concerned. My God has been a conglomerate of that conditioning and not the compelling God of love and action you've talked about. My greatest need is to find this new God—not new in the sense that he never existed before, but new to me."

I was on the edge of my chair! The man's words set a torch to the gathered kindling of a growing conviction. I thought of little else for weeks afterward. The man had articulated an answer to a question I'd been asking for a long time.

People are my life. The famous and the frustrated, the successful and discouraged, the rich and poor, young and old, single and married. What life does to them and they do to life is my daily and passionate concern. And most have two things in common: they believe in God and yet have persistent struggles in their lives. Strife. Strain. Strenuous effort against difficult pressures. Why? The man had given me the key. "That's it!" I said to myself. *The reason so many of us struggle is that we need a new God.* Most of the struggles we endure are the result of a profound misunderstanding of God's real nature and of what he is ready and able to do in our lives.

Struggles are the stuff of life for most of us. What are yours? I have mine. Few of us consistently feel good about ourselves; we all have times of insecurity and self-doubt, times when we lack self-esteem. Anxiety is a stranger to none of us. Fears and frustrations track us like angry dogs. We've all had periods of discouragement, disap-pointment, and feelings of depression. Every one of us has memories which haunt and unfulfilled dreams which hurt.

Who hasn't felt the loneliness which has little to do with the absence of people? We need love and yet persist in

doing unlovable things. Broken relationships, misunderstandings with people, and distorted communication trouble all of us. Worry raps at the door of every heart and is
entertained as an unwelcome tenant for what seems to be
an endless visit.

Not all our struggles are internal. We all face difficult
situations at work or in society. Progress is slow; conflict
seems inevitable. Everyone has his or her share of impossible people. We listen to the news or read the daily paper,
and our nerves are jangled by what's happening in the
asphalt jungle around us. What could we do about things
if we tried? A feeling of impotence engulfs us. We wring
our hands in powerless frustration.

All because we have settled for a diminutive god of our
own making. We need a new God for our old struggles.
The true God who knows and cares and intervenes and
acts, who is present and powerful, who makes things
happen!

That was Moses' greatest need as he tended his father-
in-law's sheep in the Midian Desert. It had been forty
years since he had discovered that he was not the son of
the Pharaoh's daughter, but a Hebrew like the slaves of
Egypt. He had known little of the God of his people, but
felt deeply the anguish of their servitude. His anger and
rage had prompted his early attempt to play deliverer of
Israel by murdering an Egyptian taskmaster. He had
taken things into his own hands, failed, and been forced
to flee to the desert.

It had been a sharp descent from the splendor of the
Pharaoh's palace to the stark solitude of the wilderness.
Now the struggles of Moses' people were matched by the
struggles of his own heart. He knew he belonged to the
God of Israel. His brief encounter with his people had
introduced him to their fierce loyalty to the God of
Abraham, Isaac, and Jacob. Where was that God now?
Did he know what was happening to his people? Did he
care? Why didn't he do something?

Forty years in the desert is a long time to ponder
questions like that! And yet it was there in the wilderness,

with its hostile crags, its interminable silences, and its blistering sun, that the very God who seemed so aloof and distant was preparing Moses to be the deliverer of His people. The old Moses, self-assertive and brash, was fading from his soul like color from cloth exposed to the wind and sun. In its place, humility and dependence were growing. God was hammering out a deliverer whose only strength would be in Him and whose only weapon would be an intimate knowledge and experience of His true nature.

When Moses was ready and the right time had come, an empowering encounter with God occurred. One day the lonely shepherd was completely astonished by an acacia bush that burned and was not consumed. An ordinary fire would have left the bush in gray ashes in a flash. Moses was irresistibly drawn to the blazing brightness. It was then that he heard the voice which was to become the source of his hope and courage. The voice of God was incisive and impelling. "Moses! Moses!" The long years of preparation were expressed in Moses' obedient reply, "Here am I."

God told Moses that he knew of the suffering of his people, that he would deliver them out of the bondage in Egypt and lead them to a land he had promised them. And Moses himself would lead the deliverance. The assurance was clear: God would be with him, and his authority would come from the fact that he was sent by God.

The frightened shepherd's response was predictable: "Why will they listen to me?" "If I come to the people of Israel and say to them, 'The God of your fathers has sent me to you,' and they ask me, 'What is his name?' what shall I say to them?"

The answer Moses received introduced him to a new God for his own and his people's struggles. God said to Moses, "I am who I am. . . . Say this to the people of Israel, 'I am has sent me to you'" (Exod. 3:13–14). Here is a new name for God revealing his essential nature. In Hebrew it is *Yahweh*. This powerful new name for God has a special meaning. It is based in the Hebrew infinitive *hayah*, "to be, or to cause to happen." When Ya is added, it becomes third person singular in the masculine, future tense. Thus the new name meant, "He who will make things happen." The Hebrew word *Yahweh* stands for the Lord's divine self-disclosure—he is Lord of creation, Lord of our destiny, Lord of our circumstances, Lord of victory in our struggles. That's exactly what Moses and his people needed to know. "I am" would help them. He would act on their behalf as a God of liberation and deliverance.

That knowledge sent Moses back to Egypt knowing that all things were possible because "I am," Yahweh, was with him. In the midst of the conflict with Pharaoh and the frightened reluctance of the Hebrews, God came to Moses again to be sure he and his people understood who was the source of their hope. And God [Elohim] said to Moses, "I am the Lord [Yahweh]. I appeared to Abraham, to Isaac, and to Jacob, as God Almighty [El Shaddai], but by my name the Lord I did not make myself known to them. . . . Say therefore to the people of Israel, 'I am the Lord, and I will bring you out from under the burdens of the Egyptians, and I will deliver you from their bondage'" (Exod. 6:2–3, 6).

A new God, indeed! No longer was he just El Shaddai, the all-powerful God of the mountains, but Yahweh, the Lord, the "I am," who would make things happen in the valley of human struggle. The Lord would do exactly what he promised. He delivered the suffering people out of bondage. He was a God of activity and liberation.

The same Lord is alive and at work today. We were never meant to struggle alone. The promise made to Moses is made to us: I will be with you; I will make things happen. Most of the struggles of our lives come because we have painted ourselves into a corner of impossibility. We can't imagine that things will change. Our own efforts seem futile. Then God comes, and he says, "Go back into the problem, your Egypt, and you will be amazed at what I will do!"

It is fascinating to note that hundreds of years later, in

the third century before Christ, when these Exodus
passages were translated into Greek in the Septuagint for
the Jews scattered throughout the then known world, the
verb meaning "to be, to make happen," was translated
into the present tense. This was a theological annotation
which affirmed the translators' experience of God acting
in the present. In Greek, the divine name, Yahweh, is *egō
eimi,* present tense. "I am" the One who makes things
happen *now.* He is Lord of the past, the present, and the
future. Because he makes things happen now, in the
present moment, we can trust him to forgive the past and
we can surrender the future to him. All because of the
nowness of his intervention.

That's exciting! We are not alone in our struggles. We
can talk to the God who makes things happen—tell him
how we are feeling, share the anguish and the frustration,
feel the presence of unlimited power for our needs.

But knowing the fact that God can make things happen
is of little help until we know him personally. Through the
years of history the Hebrew people knew of Yahweh and
yet did not trust and love him with all their hearts. They
still struggled with failure, fear, and frustration. The
name of Yahweh became so sacred and awesome that it
was considered a sin to say it aloud.

That's why Yahweh had to come into history and live
among us. Jesus Christ, Immanuel, "God with us."
Strength for life's struggles comes from a love relationship with One who affirms and accepts us, and who
enables us to trust all of our affairs to him. God has come
in flesh in his own Son so that we can know him
intimately: "And the Word became flesh and dwelt among
us, full of grace and truth; we have beheld his glory, glory
as of the only Son from the Father. . . . For the law was
given through Moses; grace and truth came through Jesus
Christ. No one has ever seen God; the only Son, who is in
the bosom of the Father, he has made him known" (John
1:14, 17–18).

Do you realize what that means for us and our struggles? Jesus Christ is none other than Yahweh, the creative

Word of God. He is the glory of God, in all his excellence and majesty, in time and space. He is grace, unmerited favor, from God himself. He is truth about God's essential being for us to behold and know. Jesus Christ is God with us in all our struggles.

But listen to Christ himself as he speaks about who he is and what he came to do. Twenty-two times in the Gospel of John we hear Jesus assume divine authority over our sin, sickness, and sadness. The bold self-disclosure is "I am!" The Greek words are the same. *Egō eimi.* Yahweh. The God who makes things happen is our Lord Jesus Christ! He came to confront the taproot source of our struggles and to conquer. Each one of Jesus' "I am" statements is his answer to one of our aching needs. The same words spoken to Moses by God are used by Jesus to declare who he is and what he can do. He is the preexistent Lord of all; he comes to you and me to save us from our sins and to free us from our burdens so that we can live the abundant life.

That's what we all need to know in our struggles. To endure, we don't need advice, admonitions, or guilt-producing accolades. We need power from an ultimately reliable source. But most of all we need to know that the God who lived among us as the Lord, the "I am," who revealed life as it was intended to be lived, who defeated the demons of despair which deplete us, and who vanquished death and all its power—is alive! Here and now. With you and me at this moment.

But our response is often like that of the leaders of Israel during Jesus' ministry. They, too, needed a new God for their old struggles. But they found it difficult to accept Jesus as the true Messiah. This prompted the most dramatic of Jesus' "I am" self-disclosures. It came at the conclusion of a heated dispute with the Pharisees (John 8:32–33, 58). Jesus asserted, "If you continue in my word, you are truly my disciples, and you will know the truth, and the truth will make you free." That brought the angry response, "We are descendants of Abraham, and have never been in bondage to any one. How is it that you say,

'You will be made free?'" Then followed a series of
messianic claims which concluded with the astounding
statement, "Truly, truly, I say to you, before Abraham
was, I am." That is the fulcrum "I am" of Jesus's message!
Jesus was claiming to be the very author of Abraham's call
and promise; his was an undeniable claim that he was the
preexistent God.

The assertion left the leaders with two alternatives:
believe in him as the expected Messiah, or totally reject
him and plot his demise. Our choice is not very different.
Either Jesus was who he said he was, or he was a megalo-
maniac caught in a complex of assumed omnipotence and
self-aggrandizement. But if we accept him as God, the
ultimate "I am," the uncreated creator, then all of the rest
of his "I am" statements flash like diamonds of truth.

Linger on the immensity of this basic assertion, "Before
Abraham [before anything or anyone existed] I am." If we
can say, "My Lord, my God" in response to that, then we
are on the way to making our struggles into stepping
stones. When he is our Lord, we can allow him to come
into our fears and say "I am, have no fear"; into our
darkness, blindness, and need for direction and assert "I
am the light of the world"; into our hungry hearts with
the fulfilling "I am the bread of life; he who comes to me
shall not hunger"; into our pressures with equalizing
power. He can come into our self-destructive patterns
with divinely inspired self-esteem; into our anxieties with
the comfort of "I am the good shepherd"; into our lust for
life with the assurance, "I have come that you may have
life, and may have it in all its fullness"; into our worries
with the promise, "I will never fail nor forsake you." He is
the Christ who comes into our uncertainties and affirms,
"I am the way, and the truth, and the life"; into our
impatience and offer, "Take my yoke upon you and learn
from me"; into our anguish over death and sets us free by
the liberating hope, "I am the resurrection and the life; he
who believes in me, though he die, yet shall he live, and
whoever lives and believes in me shall never die"; into our

impotence and offers an indwelling power, "I am the true vine. . . . Abide in me, and I in you"; and into our loneliness with an eternal friendship, "Lo, I am with you always."

The "I am" affirmations of Christ and his promises are inseparably linked. What he promised he can do is based on who he is.

I have known Christ for thirty years. In those years I have never faced a struggle in which Christ and his promises were not the answer. My problem has not been trusting him with a specific struggle and finding him inadequate or unresponsive, but rather not trusting him soon enough. I have spent twenty-five years listening to people and to their struggles. There has never been a need, a sin, a broken relationship, a problem, or an emotional ailment that Christ could not heal or solve. The issue is always: Will we allow Christ, *egō eimi*, the "I am" who can make things happen, to be the Lord of our struggles?

Allow me to share four basic questions. How we answer them makes all the difference in how we handle life's struggles.

1. Do you believe that Jesus is who he says he is? Is he truly God with you and therefore Lord over all of life's circumstances—able to marshal all power in heaven and earth to meet your needs?
2. Do you really believe that Jesus performed miracles in the physical, emotional, and spiritual struggles of people?
3. Do you dare to believe that he can and will perform these same miracles today in your life? Can he who is creator, sustainer, and innovator of all that happens make things happen in your life?
4. Are you willing to ask him to be the triumphant "I am" in your specific struggles?

I find that most people can say yes to the first two but become uncertain and reluctant about the last two. And

I'm convinced the reason is that our idea of what Christ can do today is debilitated by layers of distorted thinking. One layer is formed by the idea that we should be able to handle life ourselves without asking for help. The next layer comes from thinking of our Lord more as a judge of our failures than as an enabler who loves us in spite of what we've done or been. A deeper layer is formed by self-depreciation; we think, how can the Lord care about me when there are millions of people with greater needs? But by far the thickest and most impenetrable layer results from thinking of the Lord in impersonal, historical terms; we live in two worlds—the world of bold beliefs about what he said and did, and the world of bland agnosticism about what he can and will do today.

Under all the layers are the real you and me—feeling alone, often troubled by life, constantly battling for security and peace. Christ wants to penetrate through those layers to find us right now. He wants to know us as we are and have us love him as he is: present, powerful, promising new possibilities. The Lord who makes things happen wants to move us out of immobility, out of the cycle of strain, stress, and struggle.

Here's how to let him do it.

First, identify the struggle that represents your deepest need right now. Press deeper to the real cause of the problem. Why are you struggling? What do you do to cause the struggle? What are the basic assumptions on which the struggle is based? What ideas or feelings cause your reactions to what's happening to you?

Second, imagine how Christ would have dealt with someone with this struggle during his earthly ministry. What would he have said? Now hear him say, "I am the Lord who makes things happen." If you were that person, what would you tell him about your need, and what would you ask him to do?

Third, affirm the fact that he knows, cares, and has come to you right now. Tell him all about the struggle. Leave nothing out or hidden. Tell him that, more than a solution to the struggle, you need him. Turn the struggle over to him completely. Leave the results to him.

Fourth, expectantly anticipate the way he will make the struggle a stepping stone. Instead of asking, "How can I get out of this?" ask "What can I get out of this?"—to grow, to become stronger, to be more sensitive to others who struggle.

Fifth, praise him that he can unleash resources, people, and unanticipated potentials which you could never have imagined possible to help you. That's the excitement of the adventure of the Christian life. When we least expect it, Christ breaks through with blessings—perfectly timed, magnificently suited to our needs.

Like my friend, most of us need a new God. But not a god of human limitations and prejudices, negativism and reservation. Not an El Shaddai, powerful but unreachable. We need the Yahweh who was the "I am" in Jesus Christ, who is with us now to do in us and around us what we thought impossible.

The bush is still burning; do you see it? I do! The voice of Yahweh is calling your name, do you hear him? I do! He came in Christ for you, the triumphant "I am" to defeat anything which would keep you struggling; do you believe it? I do! Death could not hold him nor the grave defeat him. He's alive! He's there with you now. Will you give him your struggle? I will! Let's share the adventure together!

2

Someone Knows and Understands

The Lord Knows All About Us

> *"I am speaks to you."*
> John 4:26

HAVE YOU EVER PLAYED the game, "I'll give you a penny for your thoughts"? I have. There are times when I am suddenly, sometimes painfully, aware that a loved one or friend has deep thoughts or feelings that are hidden from me. I should not be surprised. Often I have inner reflections, attitudes, or memories that I am reserving for my private inner world. Most of us would give lots more than a penny to penetrate inside another person. And there are times we wish we had the kind of friend or confidant to whom we could entrust our guarded skeletons or cherished dreams.

But the warning flags are up in the safe harbor of our inward hearts. They tell us that it's dangerous out there on the sea of human relationship. Most people can't be trusted with our inner hearts. We've had enough near wrecks with people who misuse the things we've shared.

In response to my inventory on life's deepest needs, one man wrote, "My greatest need is to have someone know me—really know me—and not go away." We all need friends like that. A true friend is one who knows all about us and believes in us in spite of what he or she knows.

24

How many people do you know who, if they knew all about you, would not go away or would not stay to make life uncomfortable with the leverage of what they know about you?

We learn the power of secrets early in life. A child's first sense of independence and individuality dawns when he realizes that he can have a life of his own in his garrisoned memory or imagination.

I remember a happy, singing child building amazing images out of sand on a beach one day. She was lost in her own world. "What are you building?" the little girl's mother asked. "I'm not going to tell you," the child replied indignantly. "It's a secret!" "But you must always tell your Mommy everything," the mother responded, showing the first sign of panic that her little girl could wield the scepter of personal freedom so powerfully.

The child's private world of vision had been invaded. She stopped what she was building so creatively and dashed the sand off her hands. Her question was a good one: "Mommy, will I always, even when I grow up, have to tell you everything I'm thinking? Will everyone always have to know what's inside?"

Do you remember the first time you decided not to tell your parents something that happened? I do. One day I was walking home from school through Lincoln Park in Kenosha, Wisconsin, with my best friend, Arthur. Arthur was carrying a spelling paper on which was written the teacher's "A" of approbation. He couldn't contain how good he felt. But a gang of toughs, who didn't like the recognition my friend had received, met us on the path and tore Arthur's paper into little bits. Indignation and rage burned inside my little boy's heart. I tore into the whole gang of ten with blind anger. Arthur was too distraught to help. You guessed it. I was beaten badly— bloody nose, torn knickers, and a bruised ego.

I can still remember the feeling that came over me as I limped home. I didn't want my parents to know that I'd been fighting again or, most of all, that I hadn't fulfilled my self-image of a "Jack Armstrong, all American boy" hero.

"I won't tell them!" I mused to myself. "I'll keep it all to myself." I washed my face over the park bubbler and tucked the torn part of my knickers into my "high cuts." "They'll never know!" I vowed.

At dinner that night, the usual parental concern flowed. "How was your day?" my Dad asked. "Just great!" I replied dishonestly. Wondering about the bruise under my eye, my mother inquired, "What happened today?" "Ah, nothin'," I lied.

It worked! They didn't press me. I went to bed that night feeling a great sense of personal uniqueness and separateness. I knew something my parents did not know about me. The defeat of the day was somehow balanced. And yet, my secret gave me a turbulent mixture of independence and loneliness. I knew something they didn't, but I had to nurse all alone my hurt for myself, and for Arthur who had no paper to display at home. How strange—Arthur had a good secret about an "A" he wanted to tell; I had a painful secret about a defeat I would not tell.

The growing years are the same for most of us. We soon learn that we can control our relationships and circumstances by how much we let people know the real person inside. We live in two realms: the personal region of our minds and emotions, and the interpersonal area of what we want people to think and assume we are. And all we need is a few statements like, "I would never have thought that about you!" from people with whom we have shared out tender, inner hearts to close us up and encourage us to stay behind the guarded wall of our polished images.

The result is that we are resigned to live in two worlds. And into the private world we cram the fantasies, fears, and failures, hurts and disappointments, insecurities and jitters about the future, that we desperately hope no one will ever uncover. We paint masks to be placed upon our faces for every changing challenge in life's relationships and responsibilities.

"How's it going?" people ask. Our conditioned response is "Great!" with a few successes which can be told thrown in. "How are you really?" loved ones inquire. "Never better!" is our patterned equivocation, fortified by fear that if they truly knew we would topple from their hero's throne (erected from the selected data provided them in our cautious sharing of ourselves).

Actually, in some ways it's a good thing that we have private sanctuary of the inner self. We need that for sanity in a very sick world. But there are some real dangers. We begin to feel that we alone have the problems we feel inside. We can't imagine anyone else ever felt the way we do. We become more closed as the years go by; the surface becomes more varnished.

Furthermore, our protective measures finally rob us of warmth and openness. People put up fronts with us that match our own stagecraft. Life becomes a clashing of shields and a crossing of spears. Most dangerous of all, our inner life begins to show through in the form of personality tics and compulsive behavior. And we are left to deal with our inner world alone. It becomes a breeding ground of remorse and regret—a snake pit of broken hopes, slights, rebuffs, angers, and "what might have beens." F. W. Boreham, the Australian preacher and devotional writer, was right: "There are two worlds: one is the world within, the other the world without; and of the two, the first is always the harder to conquer."

It's when we are alone that we realize how much unresolved tension there is inside. In the quiet, what's below the tip of the iceberg we show others becomes an obstruction to deep peace of soul. The bow of our smartly sailing Titanic is ripped open by a collision with the real person we have submerged below the surface, away from the observation of others.

Know what I mean? I know you do. I've talked to too many people about what's behind the moat bridges of

their castled hearts to assume that any one of us is an
exception. And most distressing of all are the hidden sins
we hope no one will ever discover. We've tried to cover
our tracks. The imprints may be washed by time from the
paths of our outer lives, but the impressions in our
memories are the size of a ten-league boot. There are little
failures which have been magnified by private rumina-
tion, and grosser sins which no amount of self-protective
rationalization will make right.

The law of human nature is that we will not be healed
or free until someone knows us absolutely and utterly. It is
a law as irrevocable as nature's law of gravity. But who can
be trusted? Who is ultimately reliable?

The Samaritan woman Jesus met by the well of Jacob
(John 4:7–42) needed that kind of friend. She had come
from her village of Sychar (Shechem) to draw water from
the Patriarch's historic watering place. In the distance she
could see Mount Gerizim, the holy place where her people
believed God was to be worshiped. But that God was
painfully distant from the inner turmoil of her private
heart. The memory of fractured, broken relationships
tumbled about in her complex of hidden hurts. It was
high noon. And she was alone. Women usually drew
water together early in the day or at sunset. Had her
checkered life made her unacceptable to others, or had
she rendered a verdict on her own value that made
companionship with her unacceptable? We do not know.
What we do know is that she met another solitary figure at
the well who would change her life.

Jesus and the disciples were on their way north from
Judea to Galilee and stopped by the well. The disciples left
Jesus by the well while they went into the village to seek
food for their noon meal. They had selected the route
through Samaria, seldom traveled by Jews because of
their hatred for the Samaritans.

The rift between the Jews and the Samaritans dated
back to 722 B.C., when the Northern Kingdom had fallen
to Assyrian conquerors. The people who had not been
carried off into exile remained, and many had intermar-

ried with the occupying Assyrians. They had become abhorred half-breeds. At the end of the exile, they had been rebuffed in their efforts to help rebuild the temple in Jerusalem, and had adopted Mount Gerizim as their site of worship. Though both the Jews and Samaritans were descendants of Abraham, they had sharp differences over both history and Scripture. The Samaritans rejected the prophets' writings and differed with the Jews about the coming of the Messiah, whom they believed would be a new Moses, a deliverer.

All this background helps us understand the startled surprise of the lonely, introverted, self-incriminating woman when Jesus asked her for a drink. She felt rejected by her own people. Now here was a Jew not only speaking to her but asking her help. "Another man wanting a response from me with no continuing responsibility?" she wondered. Her puzzlement was also based on other customs and dicta. Not only did Jews not speak to Samaritans, but no man spoke to a woman in public. The Hebrew rabbinical precept was practiced inviolably: "Let no one talk with a woman in the street, no, not with his own wife." Jesus had broken the national and sexist barriers.

No wonder the woman asked, "How is it that you, a Jew, ask a drink of me, a woman of Samaria?" But no person was off bounds for Jesus. And he discerned a deeper barrier in the woman than either her sex or nationality. With all his divine, incarnate power to perceive the inner hearts of people, he saw a person in need. The woman blistered with defensiveness, and yet Jesus went to the core of her need.

Note how he did it. He wants to do the same for each of us right now.

The Lord moved in with an astounding offer and an amazing self-disclosure. "If you knew the gift of God, and who it is that is saying to you, 'Give me a drink,' you would have asked him, and he would have given you living water." To a person hiding her secrets, Jesus offered to share a secret he'd shared with no one thus far in his ministry. He prepared her to ask, "What is this gift, and who are you?"

The woman was intrigued. "Sir, you have nothing to draw with, and the well is deep; where do you get that living water? Are you greater than our father Jacob, who gave us the well, and drank from it himself, and his sons, and his cattle?" Jesus hoped she'd ask. Her question was legitimate. Jacob's well was a cistern type of well about a hundred feet deep. It was filled with water which seeped through from the earth and was collected from the rain. Jesus had offered living water, which means running water. Running water would normally come from a subterranean spring, flowing with artesian resourcefulness. No wonder the woman asked, "Where do you get that living water—where do I find water like that?"

The conversation plunged to a deeper level as Jesus revealed more of himself to the guarded woman. He discerned the thirst of her parched inner soul. "Every one who drinks of this water will thirst again, but whoever drinks of the water that I shall give him will never thirst; the water that I shall give him will become in him a spring of water welling up to eternal life."

The woman eyed Jesus intently. Who is this? Who could make such a claim? "Sir, give me this water, that I may not thirst, nor come here to draw." The Lord had touched her deeper thirst for life. She responded beneath the level of her words with a desire to receive the intangible power she felt flowing from him. Her heart with all its hurt was still hidden. But Jesus knew. Divine omniscience!

"Go, call your husband, and come here." Cruelty or compassion? I say compassion. Jesus knew her life was an endless string of unfulfilling relationships. He understood the woman's problem and that the water of eternal life could not assuage her true thirst until she invited him to penetrate her inner world. The Lord is never willing to deal in depth with surface needs.

The woman was undone. She dared to trust the Lord with a layer of herself. "I have no husband," she confided, still withholding her anguish with a dissimulating dishonesty. True, but also very false. Now Jesus cut deeply. "You are right in saying, 'I have no husband,' for you have had five husbands, and he whom you now have is not your husband; this you said truly."

What could the woman do? What would you have done? Or better, what are you doing right now as Christ puts his finger on the raw nerve in you? He knows everything! There's no secluded place to hide from him.

The woman tried—as we all do. Her defense was an offense. She launched into a theological argument. Anything to take the focus off her hidden heart. Quickly she mustered up all the old shibboleths of the conflict between the Jews and the Samaritans over whether Jerusalem or Mount Gerizim was the place to worship God. She tried to side-step Jesus' offer to bring refreshing water to the parched places of her soul.

Jesus would have none of it. He loved the woman too much for that! He could have spent hours arguing theology and left her as bound up in her secrets as before. Think of how often we argue religion, when our deepest need is to experience the God about whom we are splitting hairs!

Instead of yielding to the woman's attempts to dissuade his surgery of her soul, Jesus immediately told her about a God who loved her, who was greater than the geographical limits of either Jerusalem or Mount Gerizim. Hear his authority. Sense the intense warmth of his revelation of God. "Woman, believe me, the hour is coming when neither on this mountain nor in Jerusalem will you worship the Father. . . . But the hour is coming, and now is, when the true worshipers will worship the Father in spirit and truth, for such the Father seeks to worship him. God is spirit, and those who worship him must worship in spirit and truth."

A woman in desperate need prompted one of the most awesome and assuring statements about God and about us that has ever been made. He is not limited by man-made religions, his past performance in any time or place, nor restrictive theories about him. He is a Spirit, and can be known in truth only in the spirit of a person. The Greek New Testament uses two words for "spirit" in this passage. The word referring to God is *pneuma,* and the word for spirit of a person, the deepest portion of our nature, greater than intellect or will, is *pneumati.* Truth is the condition of Spirit-with-spirit encounter and abiding relationship. It is in the secret heart of our spirit that God comes.

Now Jesus completely undoes us with the assertion that God is searching for us. "For such the Father seeks to worship him" is one of the most gracious affirmations of the Lord's message—an autobiographical disclosure from God himself through Immanuel. Jesus is God incarnate in relentless search for us. In response to that we can sing,

> I sought the Lord, and afterward I knew
> He moved my soul to seek Him, seeking me;
> It was not I that found, O Savior true,
> No, I was found of Thee.

That's what the woman by the well experienced. Jesus' disclosure of the immensity and intimacy of God set her rocking back on her heels. Who was this? Could he be the Messiah? Her response betrayed her suspicions. "I know that Messiah is coming (he who is called Christ); when he comes, he will show us all things." Jesus had done just that for her. He had shown her himself and the true God. It was as if her reply was, "The Messiah is coming. You've done for me what he's expected to do. Are you the one?"

Now Jesus and the woman were eye to eye and heart to heart. His voice resonated with authority and power. "I who speak to you am he." The actual rendering of the Greek is, "I am speaks to you." *Egō eimi.* The Greek words for Yahweh, "I am." Yahweh speaks to you! This is the first of the dynamic *egō eimi* self-disclosures recorded in John's Gospel. The first unveiled declaration that Jesus is the Messiah. The Word of God about himself. He is Spirit—impinging, invading, infusing the spirit of any person who will be truthful about his or her inner, hidden heart.

Is it any wonder the woman ran back to her village to tell everyone she could find that she had met a man who told her all that she ever did? She could not contain her excitement. "Come see! . . . Can this be the Christ?"

The people rushed out to meet Jesus and to invite him to remain with them. After two days of Jesus' personal ministry with them, the people affirmed the once rejected and misused woman with a chorus of conviction. "It is no longer because of your words that we believe, for we have heard for ourselves, and we know that this is indeed the Savior of the world."

We are left to ponder this alarming and assuring "I am" disclosure of Jesus, and what it means to us today. It comes alive for us with personal intensity in the context of this encounter of Jesus and the woman. It means five liberating things to me, all because Jesus is *egō eimi,* the all-powerful, all-knowing Yahweh.

The first is that the Lord knows me better than I know myself. There is nothing I can tell him he doesn't know already. The Lord's omnipresence—his everywhereness— is linked to his omniscience—his all-knowingness. What the Lord did to the woman, he does to us. He reveals that he knows all about what we've done and said. There are no secrets hidden from the great "I am." He who knew "the hearts of all men" (Acts 1:24) knows what's inside of us.

And yet, the twist of our self-deception is that we assume we can think and act without his knowledge. We have been given the power to resist him and hold him at arm's length because of the freedom entrusted to us, but we cannot keep him from knowing what we do while we hold him at bay.

The Psalmist knew what we must rediscover again and again: "O Lord, Thou hast searched me and known me. Thou dost know when I sit down and when I rise up; thou dost understand my thought from afar. Thou dost scruti-

nize my path and my lying down, and art intimately
acquainted with all my ways. Even before there is a word
on my tongue, Behold, O Lord, Thou dost know it all.
Thou hast enclosed me behind and before, And laid Thy
hand upon me. Such knowledge is too wonderful for me;
It is too high, I cannot attain to it" (Ps. 139:1–6, NAS).

What the Psalmist could not attain, Jesus Christ came to
incarnate. He who created us for himself came in person
to help us open our hidden hearts.

The second stirring implication of this *egō eimi*
statement of Jesus is that our Lord can forgive us and
reconcile us to God *and* to ourselves. He not only knows
all that we have done, but he also has the authority to
release us from self-condemnation. Martin Luther said,
"What will Almighty God say about it in the end?" My
question is, "What will he say about it now?" The Lord's
life, message, and atoning death on the cross is our
answer: "You are forgiven!" We don't need to carry the
baggage of remembered failure. The "I am" God with us
says, "Neither do I condemn you; go, and do not sin again
(John 8:11).

Josiah Royce in the *Hell of Irrevocables* put it directly:
"To find real forgiveness, to know the strange power of a
love that will not let us go, and to know a new sense of
cleanness within, this is what it means to be saved. To be
saved from all that separation from God means." The
Lord who knows all about us forgives us once and for all!

That leads to the third discovery. As much as we need
forgiveness, we also need to know the potential person
within us who is greater than our difficulties. We need
someone who believes in us. Jesus communicated that to
the woman by the well. She found a source for self-esteem
in Jesus. It was a new beginning, one which gave her the
courage to go back into her village with an enthusiasm
which had lifted her out of self-depreciation. We all need
someone with Jesus' "I am" authority, the power of God,
to say, "My dear friend, your real problem is not your
secrets about what you've been, but your unrealized secret
of what your life can be!"

That's based on the fourth discovery. Jesus Christ is the only reliable diagnostician of our real needs. What we discern to be our deepest need may only be the symptom of a much more profound emptiness in us. Whatever we would analyze as our impediment may only be a sign of our real sickness. Our fears, anxieties, insecurities, and loneliness are all rooted in a need for Christ. The woman thought her broken relationships were her problem. But the Lord showed her that the wound was deeper than she thought. It could not be bandaged; it needed radical surgery.

What this means to you and me is that we can ask our Lord to tell us what our aching need really is. "Lord, help me to know the one thing in me that debilitates me, that keeps me from being whole. Heal me at that level so that I can get on with the adventure of living."

But we can't grasp that alone. The fifth triumphant impact of this passage of Scripture is that we can receive power in the inner heart from the Spirit of God himself. He is seeking us. His Spirit can invade our spirit. The same *egō eimi* who made all things also made each of us. If we worship him in truth, which means being honest with him not only about our past, but also our future, the "I am" who told the woman all she ever did can tell us all that we are able to do by his indwelling power. When we put him first in our hearts, he will help us sort out our priorities and move on to becoming the persons he intended us to be. He has sought us out; he knows the longings we all feel to maximize the days of our lives. We can dare to dream again.

Someone knows and understands. *Egō eimi.* The inner selves we keep so carefully guarded are really meant to be his dwelling place. When we allow him to take up residence, he takes control, forgives the past, sorts out the present, and guides the future. We don't need to hide any longer. The persons he has freed us to be inside can be the persons we dare to be on the outside. There will be congruity, consistency, freedom, and joy.

3

I Don't Need My Fears Any More

The False Security of
Many of Our Fears

"I am, fear not!"
John 6:20

SHE WAS MISS PUT-TOGETHER—a very attractive, carefully coiffured, smartly dressed, intelligent, and seemingly confident woman. She projected an image of adequacy and assurance at work and among her friends. No one would have known that fear dominated her every waking moment and frightening dreams invaded her sleep.

One afternoon recently, she came in to see me. We played conversational hide-and-seek for a long time, and then she blurted out the panic she felt inside. Fear raged in her heart. Some of her fears were legitimate; others were fantasized, but all were very real to her. None had been helped by her traditional belief in Christ, she said.

During several visits we tried to distinguish the real from the imagined. Then we went for the jugular vein— the cause of the illusionary fears. When we had a firm hold on that, I told her about what a personal relationship with Christ could do in her conquest of fear. She had never made a commitment of her needs to the Lord, but at the end of the visit we prayed together and she surrendered her frightened heart to the love and acceptance of Christ. She left my office radiant. But something made me feel uneasy about her. I knew it wouldn't be long before she would be back to see me again.

I was not surprised when she appeared a month later. Fortified by her new and growing faith in Christ, she was ready to get down to business. She confided a profound discovery. "You know, I've gotten so accustomed to my fears that letting go of them is more scary than clutching on to them. I fall back into a mood of fear with no discernible cause. The terrible thing is that it feels good because it's familiar. I'm so used to my fears that even though I give them over to the Lord in one hour, I grasp them back in the next. How long will I have to go on this way?"

"As long as you need to and want to!" I replied firmly. That alarmed her. She was on the edge of one of the greatest discoveries of her life. Like so many of us, she was cuddling the monster of fear. That was her conditioned response to reality. Familiarity with fear had not bred contempt for her fears, but security in them. She had given her life to Christ, but had not allowed him to displace her fear with the new feeling resulting from her faith.

"You mean I have a choice?" she asked.

"Yes!" I responded urgently. "You have the power to choose how long you want to coddle fear." She was shocked. "As soon as you are ready to give up the security of your fears, the Lord can help you. But you need to get to know him better than your fears. You need deep companionship, prolonged meditation on his love and indwelling power."

"How?" was her predictable response.

"Know how you feel inside when you trust him completely? Isn't that better than the anguish of fear?" I asked.

"Of course!" she said, recapturing the feeling of peace she had experienced the few times she had opened herself to the Lord's infusing love and his power to deal with the memories which jabbed her with fear. We talked at length about the capacity of her intellect to comprehend what

Jesus said and did, and what he enables and does today. Those thoughts could control her emotions. And with her will she could obey Christ's will for her life.

Fellowship with Christ requires obedience. Having the power to be selective about which emotions will dominate us is inseparably related to obeying Christ's will for us in all of life. The volitional muscle of obedience must be strengthened. The woman had never considered that. She left that day less radiant on the surface than after her first visit, but determined to come to a decision about how long she wanted to keep her fears.

When I saw her the other day, I was delighted by what she said. "Who needs it!?" she exclaimed. "I've decided I don't need my fears anymore!"

What happened to this woman can happen to all of us. We all have fears. Some of them are creative; they alert us to real dangers and help us avoid harm with a healthy measure of safety and caution. All God's creatures have been endowed with the reaction of fear for an encroaching peril. The juices of the adrenal gland flow to meet the danger. Then we can choose the alternatives of fight or flight and realize victory or escape. But only mankind has the capacity of imagination—the breeding ground of imagined fear. An imaginary fear may be unreal, but a fearful imagination is very real: ask the man or woman who owns one!

We all have experienced imagined danger, harm, conflict, rejection, or failure. The spiraling syndrome of fear sucks us into its whirlpool until our emotions are dominated by fear. Soon we become so accustomed to fear that it feels good to feel frightened. As one man said, "I'm so used to being tense that when I'm calm I get nervous." That's the kind of fear we want to confront and conquer in this chapter.

When I run late at night for my exercise I awaken all the watchdogs of our neighborhood. They bark wildly and I run all the faster. What if one of them got loose? It's then that I think about the watchdogs of fear that prowl about in our hearts. They leap awake at the least sign of danger and stir up our emotions and our nervous system.

We begin life as babes with a fear of loud noises. We grow as children fearing the darkness or falling. We reach adolescence with a load of conditioned fears imposed by parents to protect us from strangers, physical dangers, and the consequences of being reckless or foolish. But by the time we are barely into our teens, we catch the infection of imagined fears so epidemic in most families and our society. An exaggerated response of fear, motivated by what happened to us or around us in growing years, becomes our emotional condition.

What makes you afraid? What is the focus of irrational fear in you? What or who has the capacity to unleash the wild watchdogs to prowl, bark, and growl in your heart?

Many of us feel a fear of the unknown which eclipses our boldest dreams. We fear the untried, the strange, the unfamiliar. We don't regard the future as a friend. Bad memories are a breeding ground for the fear that someone will find us out. We fear being in physical pain and ill health, being too young to be respected or too old to be useful, being inexperienced or specialized and out of a job.

Financial fears are common to many of us. The hidden scars of money problems from our childhoods can be crippling. We either have too much and are afraid we'll lose it, or we have too little and are afraid we won't make it. A woman said, "Why is it my husband and I argue every time we talk about money? There's never enough for the simple pleasures of life. Yet he keeps stashing it away for a rainy day and not even a monsoon would loosen up ol' money bags. Funny thing, we both came from poor families. It's made me want to spend and him want to save."

Many of our fears come from our relationships. Some of us fear the cost of loving and others feel the fear of being loved. Fear of rejection makes some solicitous and others surly. We are afraid that we will be misused by others. We fear being alone, and yet we are panicked by people pressure.

Beneath it all are the ghosts of remembered people of the past. They keep reappearing in different costumes and with new names. We react to people in the present on the basis of how people like them acted in the past. Parents, friends who hurt us, rejected or rejecting lovers, significant others who never seemed to appreciate *our* significance—they keep bobbing up with new faces, but the fear reaction is the same.

The one thing we all have in common is fear. Not just little fears, but floating fear that is ready to fasten itself like a leech on any situation or person. There is undiagnosed fear, pervading dread of life. Angelo Patri, the American educator and writer, said, "Education consists of being afraid at the right time." But our emotional conditioning makes us afraid most of the time.

We're in good company. The disciples who had spent months with Jesus, heard him talk about the power of faith in God, witnessed his miracles, and felt his love, were afraid. It was a good thing; it prompted one of Jesus' most healing "I am" self-disclosures: "I am; have no fear." Let's consider the context of this incisive imperative.

The Lord had multiplied the loaves and fishes and fed five thousand people. When the multitudes saw the miracle, they exclaimed, "This is indeed the prophet who is to come into the world!" (John 6:14). They wanted to take him by force and make him king. We can imagine that the disciples were delighted and excited by that. They had waited for Jesus to declare himself and welcomed the opportunity to rise to power and recognition with him. They were astonished, if not disgruntled, when he refused to be one more king among the kingdoms of the world. When we check the Matthew and Mark accounts of this same incident, along with our text from John 6:15–21, we discover that Jesus abruptly sent his disciples to a boat with orders to cross the Sea of Galilee. Then he dismissed the crowd. It was sundown, about six o'clock in the evening. Jesus retreated to the mountains to pray. The response of the people had been precipitous. He would not be a king on their terms. There was so much

still to be said and done before his hour would come—
including Calvary.

The disappointed disciples were left to row the six miles
across the sea under orders alone. I can feel what they
must have felt as they cast off from the shore. Their
feelings were a mixture of awe, wonderment, and frustration. They didn't like being ordered away. But Jesus could
not be coerced or manipulated; all they could do was
obey. And why didn't he come with them? I can imagine
that they took their tension and frustration out on the
oars, wondering to each other why Jesus had refused the
adulation of the crowd.

They were not far from shore when the experienced
fishermen among them felt and smelled a storm brewing.
When the wind began to howl, they knew what was
coming. The rowing became more difficult, and yet they
pressed on.

The Sea of Galilee is below sea level, and situated like a
bowl of water surrounded by mountains. The gorges
between the mountains perform like wind tunnels which
concentrate the blasts of wind down on the relatively
shallow sea. Sudden, violent storms rise quickly.

Peter, John, Andrew, and the others had ridden out
many a storm like that; it was part of their trade. They
were men of the sea, and had an experienced respect for
its temperamental nature. But this was no ordinary squall.
It lasted for nine hours. And they had only rowed three
or four miles by the fourth watch of the night (three to
four o'clock in the morning). They seemed to make no
progress at all. No wonder they were afraid. The turbulent sea matched the storm in their hearts.

It was when the situation looked most impossible that
Jesus came to them, walking on the water. Now the
disciples *were* frightened. Their friend, teacher, master—
walking on the water! He had not allowed the crowd to
make him a king, but here he was stepping through the
whitecaps and the restless foam of the sea.

Then he spoke. His voice thundered with authority and
power. "I am. Have no fear." It is the second *egō eimi*, "I

am," assertion of Jesus in John's account. The English translations of the Greek do not catch the commanding majesty of Jesus' words. "It is I; do not be afraid," misses the force of the Greek: *egō eimi mē phobeisthe*. To me, the literal impact is, "Yahweh, have no fear!" The God of Moses' burning bush had come to the disciples in Jesus of Nazareth. The same Word by whom all things were made, who brooded over the waters at creation, came walking on the angry sea as if it were asphalt. He was greater than the sea, more powerful than the wind. "I am" calmed the sea and brought the disciples to the shore safely.

Empathize with the disciples as they crawled out of the boat and staggered on the shore. Nine hours is a long time to be tossed about like a cork on the sea. Had it happened? Had Jesus really come to them? Yes! Mark tells us that they were amazed. Indeed. The Lord had come to them and not only stilled the sea, but calmed their hearts. Later in the day, when the multitude had learned that Jesus was at Capernaum, they got into their boats and crossed the sea to find him. "How did you get here?" they wanted to know. "We looked for you anxiously on the other side of the sea, but you were gone. You did not get into the boat with the disciples, and there is only one boat here!" Imagine how the disciples must have exchanged knowing looks at that. They knew! And so do we.

The account stands in John's Gospel as a further sign that Jesus is exactly who he says he is: God with us, conquering our fears. The reason the account is so stirring is that it describes our condition on life's turbulent sea and confronts us with one who gives us an imperative command, "Have no fear!"

What can we do with that? We have fears, and yet the Savior says, "Don't be afraid." It was his watchword all through his ministry. "Fear not!" punctuated his message. "Have no fear" was his constant assurance. He vividly articulated the antithesis of people's need. "Do not fear, only believe" (Mark 5:36). The Lord who came to heal the cause of fear promised, "Fear not, little flock, for it is your Father's good pleasure to give you the kingdom" (Luke

12:32). He died on the cross to defeat Satan's power to engender fear. He rose triumphant from the grave, and his postresurrection words to the frightened disciples were, "Do not be afraid" (Matt. 28:10). He comes to each of us right now. His imperative is really an invitation. "Here, let me help you overcome your fear!"

Here's how he does it. Years of experience with the way the Lord takes care of my own fears, and of talking with others about theirs, have taught me some basic steps for dealing with fears. They work for me; I hope for nothing less for you.

Step one: *Describe your fears.* Single them out one by one. Most of us live with the low grade fever of generalized dread. Fear is the composite of individual fears. List them. Dare to say, out loud, "My fears are the following . . ."

Some time ago, I had an uneasy feeling of fear and panic. Then the Lord said, "Okay, Lloyd, let's take a look at what's making you afraid." I wrote them down. And I found that things weren't as bad as I had thought. I could deal with the problems one by one. That leads to the next step.

Step two: *Dissect the fear.* Is it based in an actual person or situation? Is the fear we feel a justified reaction to real circumstances? Or has our floating fear latched onto facts and blown them out of proportion? Fear is most often caused by previous hurts or defeats. We can keep fighting old battles in new situations. The Lord has said to me often, "Let's deal with the real cause and not the symptom. Why are you afraid, really?"

Step three: *Disown the fear.* Once we are down to the core of the cause, we are ready to make a choice. Will we completely surrender it to our Lord? Fear can become a false source of security. The Lord asked me the question which I asked the woman mentioned earlier: "How long do you feel you need those fears?" Life is a scary business for most of us. Yet being afraid becomes a habit pattern, an inadvertent response to life. We clutch, tighten up, worry. And the Lord says, "I love you so much that you can keep that response to life as long as you feel you have to, but when you're ready, I'm waiting." That's comfort and cheer—and a disarming challenge.

In response to that, I ask myself further questions. "What's the worst that could happen? If it happened, would I be beyond the Lord's help? Is anything too big for him to handle? Can't he use all things for his glory and my growth?" When I answer these questions, I am confronted with the Person who says "I am, have no fear." The Lord of the resurrection, who vanquished death, stands behind his promise, "You shall receive power when the Holy Spirit has come upon you" (Acts 1:8).

Life for me was a constant battle with fear until I received the Holy Spirit. The same God who created the world and who came in flesh in Jesus Christ returned as the Holy Spirit to indwell us. That's the miracle of Pentecost. Frightened disciples become fearless apostles. I know it's true. It's still happening. Jesus Christ, our living Lord, comes to indwell our frightened hearts. Then we can say with Paul, "God did not give us a spirit of timidity but a spirit of power and love and self control" (2 Tim. 1:7). He could say that, because he had personally experienced the resurrected Lord, the Holy Spirit. When Paul was alone and afraid in Corinth after his defeat in Athens, the Lord came to him and said, "Do not be afraid, but speak and do not be silent; for I am with you" (Acts 18:9–10).

That leads us to step four: *Displace the fear*. The same disciple John who was on that boat on the troubled sea and heard Jesus' imperative command was also the apostle John who wrote these words of hope to the early church: "There is no fear in love, but perfect love casts out fear. For fear has to do with punishment, and he who fears is not perfected in love" (1 John 4:18).

It had taken years for John to appropriate Jesus' *egō eimi* imperative about fear. I suspect that when he looked back on that event on the Sea of Galilee, and remembered how fearful he was, he knew the cause of his fear. There had been something very wrong with his relationship with Jesus. He and the disciples had not been listening to Jesus' teaching about faith. They had seen Jesus' miracle of multiplying the loaves and fishes as a chance to glorify themselves as the Lord's disciples. There's more than meets the reader's eye in Mark's account, "Immediately he [Jesus] *made* his disciples get into the boat" (6:45). I believe he discerned a selfish lust for power in his disciples. It caused a distance between him and them. That's why, in my opinion, the disciples were so afraid on a sea where they had battled storms many times before.

When John was imprisoned on Patmos many years later, he had an experience with the living Lord which conquered his fears. It was an intimate encounter in which he felt the Lord's presence and heard him speak to his troubled, frightened heart. John felt alone and discouraged on that lonely isle. He could look across the sea and imagine what was happening to the cause of Christ among the new Christians in the churches of Roman Asia. His heart was sick with worry. Then the Lord came to him. When John saw the Lord and sensed his commanding power, he fell at his feet as if dead. "But he laid his right hand upon me," John exclaims in Revelation 1:17. The Lord's words contained his familiar imperative admonition which banishes fear and inspires adoration. "Fear not, I am the first and the last, and the living one; I died, and behold . . . I have the keys of Death and Hades" (Rev. 1:17–18).

Our fears can be conquered only by One who made us, redeemed us, defeated the fear, which is the inner cause of our dread of life, and comes to us with power to make a difference in our hearts. No one else can command us to stop being afraid and have the power to heal what motivates the fear.

At the end of his life, John gives us the dynamic of the displacement theory he had learned so well in his own life. The same emotions that channel love channel fear. *Perfect love,* that is, the kind revealed in Jesus' life, death, resurrection, return, and presence, displaces fear. The conquest of fear is accomplished by a love relationship with the Lord. His kind of love is pure, unchanging power. The word for "perfect" in Greek means that which accomplishes its purpose. Perfect love accomplishes its purpose of exorcising fear. We become perfected; we can fulfill our reason for being alive without the anguish of persistent fear.

John has given us the liberating secret: "Fear has to do with punishment." We will never be free of fear until we experience the grace of God for our guilt. Consistently fearful people have unresolved and unreconciled memories, failures, and sins which have never been confessed and forgiven. People who hide aspects of their lives end up being fearful, often in areas unrelated to what they are hiding. Clandestine living in any aspect of life will protrude as a fear in another aspect. Adam said, "I was afraid . . . and I hid myself" (Gen. 3:10). We say, "I hid myself and I was afraid." We become like the Ancient Mariner of Coleridge's poem:

> Like one, that on a lonesome road
> Doth walk in fear and dread,
> And having once turned round walks on,
> And turns no more his head;
> Because he knows, a frightful fiend
> Doth close behind him tread.

But once we know Christ as a faithful friend we can turn around and face the frightening fiend. We can look him full in the face and say, "Christ defeated you on Calvary. You have no power over me. Get off my trail!" But that kind of courage is based in an ultimate kind of fear which banishes our fears.

The only time Jesus told us to fear was when he cautioned us to fear God (Luke 12:4–5). That fear is not debilitating fear, but awe and wonder. It is the fear of missing the reason we were born. It was said of the Calvinists at one point that they feared God so much they never feared anything or anyone else. That awesome adoration of God results in a healing love which sets us free from the domination of our fears. Solomon was right: "The fear of the Lord is the beginning of knowledge" (Prov. 1:7). And, I say, the beginning of victory over our fears.

I overheard a man who was working a crossword puzzle ask, "What's a four-letter word for a strong emotional reaction to difficulty?" One man responded "fear." Another spoke up and said, "love." The latter was on target.

Step five in our conquest of fear is based on all the others: *Dare to deal daily with fear.* Emerson said, "He has not learned the lesson of life who does not every day surmount a fear."

How shall we do that? There's a sentence in John's account of Jesus' coming to the disciples at sea that gives us the answer. "Then they were glad to take him [Jesus] into the boat . . ." (John 6:21). John's record of this event says nothing of the calming of the sea. That was not the most important thing to John as he recaptured the significance of the event. All that was important was that Jesus was in the boat with them.

That's all we need to know. Jesus never promised an easy life. "In the world you [will] have tribulation, but be of good cheer, I have overcome the world," he told them elsewhere (John 16:33). "I am with you always!" was his signature on all that he said and did. There will be new fears every day. But we need not be afraid. He's in the boat with us! Are you "glad to take him into the boat"? That's the only question to answer!

How long will we need our fears? Until we allow our Lord to love us sufficiently, profoundly, expulsively! Love dislodges fear. The response to Christ's love is faith—complete trust that, as *egō eimi,* he has specific power to invade not only the situations which cause us to be afraid, but also the inner need in our hearts which motivates us to fear.

Then we can say with the apostle Paul, "I can do all things in him [Christ] who strengthens me" (Phil. 4:13). And with the Psalmist, "I fear no evil; for thou art with me" (Ps. 23:4). That's all we need to know.

Edmund Vance Cooke's stanza about trouble could be reworded about fear:

> A fear's a ton, or a fear's an ounce
>   Or a fear is what you make it,
> It isn't the fact you have fear that counts
> But only, how you take it.

And the best way to take it is to allow the Lord to take it. And in its place he gives the gift of love.

With that assurance we can say to all our fears what Rostand's Cyrano de Bergerac said with gusto about the number against him: "What! Odds of only a hundred to one?" Our odds are better. Our odds are a hundred to two—the Lord and us.

I don't need my fears anymore! What about you?

4

When Your Heart Aches

The Hungry Heart

"I am the bread of life."
John 6:35

I SAW AN OLD FRIEND of mine the other day. We'd lost contact, and I was out of touch with what had been happening in his life.

"How's it going?" I asked jovially.

His face darkened. "Well, to be honest, I've had a lot of heartaches in the past year," he responded seriously. I was alarmed that I hadn't known and had been insensitive in my jolly greeting. He told me about the problems he was facing. Most of them resisted solution, he said. After he had shared his needs he said something that I can't get off my mind: "I feel a dull, persistent ache inside. It won't go away."

Heartaches. We've all had them. Some of us are suffering from them right now. No one seems exempt from the disease. What life does to us or the people we love causes deep emotional hurt.

We feel heartache when we fail or miss an opportunity, or when our egos are wounded by our being rebuffed or relegated, misunderstood or mistreated. Broken relationships cause the inner anguish. Heartache can come from what was said or done to us, or worse, what we said or did that we wish we could expunge from our memories. Our

49

hearts throb with pain when we feel life has cornered us with seemingly impossible and unresolvable tensions. "What am I going to do?" we ask desperately.

Often we have the same feeling of helplessness when it comes to caring about loved ones, friends, or troubled people. How we long to reach out and keep someone from being hurt! If only we could do something! Be something! Say something! Most often all we are able to do is empathize and then internalize; we long to help, and all we can do is share the heartache.

Heartache is an inseparable companion to grief when we lose someone we love. It's not easy to pick up the pieces, fill the emptiness, conquer loneliness, and begin to live again. Sometimes the ache lasts for years; often it never goes away.

The more I've thought about the heartaches we all endure, the more I've been pressed to ask, "Why? Are they just a part of being human or daring to care?" And that's led to a deeper question: "Where is God when my heart aches?" Doesn't he care? If he does, why doesn't he take it away?

I want to share the answer which has come from years of thought, study, and prayer about our heartaches.

An aching heart is a hungry heart. A heartache is a spiritual hunger pang. Just as physical hunger alerts us to the need for food, so too a heartache forces us to realize the need for solid spiritual nutrition. We need to take nourishment that will pervade our thoughts and feelings, like vitamin-and-mineral-packed food satisfies our bodily hunger.

When we experience the dull persistent disturbance of a heartache we are painfully awakened to the fact that we do not have the inner resources to face the external circumstances and people-problems of life.

C. S. Lewis said physical pain is the megaphone of God. He uses it to speak loudly of our need for him. Though he does not send or cause the pain, he uses it to help us lean totally on his grace and healing.

A heartache is the same. It is caused by a loss, a

disappointment, or a feeling of impotence. We feel like a cannonball has been shot through our inner being. There is a gaping hole, emptiness, a frightening insufficiency—malnutrition of the soul. Heartache is a megaphone announcement that something, someone, is missing. And what does God have to say now that he has our attention? What he said in Jesus Christ and has said to aching, hungry hearts ever since—"I am the bread of life; he who comes to me shall not hunger, and he who believes in me shall never thirst" (John 6:35).

A bold claim! Look at the context, the feeding of the five thousand as recorded in John 6. When the multitudes did not comprehend the significance of Jesus' miracle of multiplying the loaves and fishes, he had to make it undeniably clear. The Lord drew the sharp distinction between natural food, which was necessary but impermanent in value, and spiritual food, which would satisfy their deepest needs. "Truly, truly, I say to you, you seek me, not because you saw signs, but because you ate your fill of the loaves. Do not labor for the food which perishes, but for the food which endures to eternal life, which the Son of man will give to you." The people's immediate response was, "What must we do, to be doing the works of God?" Likely question. We always think there's something we should do rather than something we desperately need to receive. The Lord did not give them a further rule of self-adjustment to a set of obligations. They needed to accept a gift for their hungry hearts. "This is the work of God," he said, "that you believe in him whom he has sent."

That pressed the crowd to make a decision about him. They demanded a further sign to authenticate Jesus' messianic intimations. But their minds were still on their temporal, transitory needs. They made historical reference to Moses and the manna which had been provided for the daily, physical hungers of the Hebrews in the wilderness during the Exodus. Jesus swept that aside with authority: "Truly, truly, I say to you, it was not Moses who gave you the bread from heaven; my Father gives you the true bread from heaven . . . and gives life to the world."

Now the spiritual hunger of the people became acute. No wonder they said to him, "Lord, give us this bread always."

It was then that Jesus proclaimed the third "I am," *egō eimi*, Yahweh self-disclosure. He had not come to provide physical bread, but to be the bread of life. "I am the bread of life!" is stated twice and then a third time with amplification. "I am the living bread which came down from heaven; if any one eats of this bread, he will live for ever; and the bread which I shall give for the life of the world is my flesh" (v. 51).

Bread was the basic staff of life in that day. The people to whom Jesus spoke knew that they could not live without its daily sustenance. He used an impelling image to teach them about their spiritual need.

What bread is for the physical body, Jesus Christ is for our hungry, aching hearts. He alone can satisfy that hunger and the dull, pervading ache it causes. But just as Jesus refused to give another sign by providing more physical bread, so too, he wants to do more than ease our heartaches with quick solutions to our present problems. He wants to go deeper to heal the real source of our emotional pain. When we consider his triumphant *egō eimi* claim in the context of the total impact of this passage we discover the three ways that Jesus feeds our profound hunger. The Bread of Life saves, satisfies, and strengthens. There's the source of healing our heartaches.

Note the emphasis on life. *Jesus came to save us from all that debilitates and cripples life.* The bread he is can set us free to live fully now and forever. Our deepest hunger is for intimate fellowship and relationship with God. Heartaches are but pain-spasms of that hunger.

Look carefully at the promise of "I am." "All that the Father gives me will come to me; and him who comes to me I will not cast out. For I have come down from heaven, not to do my own will, but the will of him who sent me" (vv. 37–38). Our hunger is a gift, the evidence that we belong to Christ. Now read on to catch the impact of why he came. "For this is the will of my Father, that every one

who sees the Son and believes in him should have eternal
life. . . ." John Henry Jowett, the great English preacher,
said, "Our religion is dead and burdensome until it
becomes a personal relation, and we have vital communion with Christ."[1]

We are called, chosen, and elected to receive the Bread.
It is because the Lord has excavated an emptiness in us
that we long to find life. Our heartaches are the indication
of how much we need him. When we see Christ in all his
fullness, we realize what we are missing. Eternal life is the
Master's description of a quality and a quantity of life now
and forever. "Truly, truly, I say to you, he who believes
has eternal life. I am the bread of life . . . if any one eats of
this bread, he will live for ever" (vv. 47–48, 51).

The word for *life* used here by Jesus, when he says he is
"the bread of life," is *zōēs*. But when he alludes to himself
as the "living bread" (v. 51) the word is *zōn,* the present
active participle of the verb *zāo,* meaning "to be alive" or
"giving life." Jesus is the bread of life who gives us life.
How he does that is in the promise, "The bread which I
shall give for . . . the world is my flesh." That means the
cross. Nothing less would do it. Jesus went to the cross to
die for the sins of the world. We have been forgiven, now
and forever.

The basic cause of our heartaches is separation from
God, who made us for himself and keeps us hungry until
we are fed by the only thing which fills our hunger and
assuages our thirst. We need to be loved, forgiven, and
accepted. Only God can do that. That's why he came,
Yahweh himself, to suffer for us and forgive us once and
for all. Sin is separation. But when we "see the Son and
believe in him," we are reconciled. Everything which can
defeat us, which robs us of life as it was created to be, has
been confronted and conquered on Calvary.

The Bread of Life saves us from fear of death, worry
over our welfare, anguish over the welfare of others,
frustration over our failures, anxiety about our status and
image, fears about the future. There is not a heartache I
know which does not stem from a failure to accept the

unchangeable fact that we belong to Christ. If your heart aches right now, the cause is one of two things: you have never accepted him as your Savior and Lord; or you believe in him, but are still running your own life.

Heartaches are really a method of self-justification. They mean that we have taken charge of our own guilts, fears, frustrations, or concern for others. We bridge the gap between what we have been and should have been, what others have done and should have done, with our own oblation of ache. It is our way of atoning or controlling—the most subtle form of arrogance!

Let's try on that theory in some practical illustrations. Take for example the man who failed miserably in his marriage. He ached over what might have been and over the eventuality of a divorce. His grief over the loss was healthy—to a point. When it went on for a prolonged period, self-doubt took the place of honest confession of his part in the fracture. Soon he began to doubt whether he could love or be loved. The ache of self-condemnation grew. Though he was a Christian, he tried to handle the whole affair on his own. At no point did he dare spread the ache out before the Lord for judgment and grace. God's salvation could have saved him from a near nervous breakdown. The Bread of Life was ready and willing.

Or take the college woman who was deeply hurt in a romantic relationship. Her heart ached over a cutting rejection. She brooded over it for months and became a very unattractive person. Her prayers were ineffective, she said. "How could God allow this to happen to me? I've believed and been faithful. The Lord let me down." At the time she needed the Lord's love and acceptance the most, she excluded herself from the flow of his affirmation. Her heartache got her a lot of sympathy, but no help from the One who could save her from despair over her disappointment.

Then reflect on the heartache of a father over his son. The lad was in serious trouble. But that trouble was nothing compared to the effects of worry on the father. He could not eat, his work was slipping, and he refused to give the love and affection his wife and other children needed because of the obsessive distraction over his failure with his son. Most tragic of all was the fact that the father could not trust the son's future to the Lord.

Or take the mother who became emotionally paralyzed by heartache because her daughter had been rejected by friends. The woman felt deeply for her lovely daughter, who looked just like her. But what she didn't realize was that all the old memories of her own teen years were stalking about in her mind. What the daughter needed was a strong center of assurance. What she got was a mother whose heartache showed and whose anguish doubled the young woman's problems. The mother had never accepted Christ as her Savior. How could she now trust her daughter's growing pains to him as Lord?

A man who professes great belief in Christ introduced himself as a widower. Since I felt that this self-identification indicated a desire to talk about his wife, I asked him when she had died. "Twenty years ago!" he replied quickly, "And my heart aches like it was yesterday." He could not (or would not!) allow the Lord to save him from his broken dreams and help him live again. When I asked him whether he believed his wife was alive with our Lord, he responded with piously intoned words about death. But heartache, not Christ's victory, dominated his emotional condition. We never know how much we believe until it's tested. Then its truth or falsehood becomes a matter of emotional survival.

On the positive side let me hasten to give you two illustrations of people who have allowed the Lord to heal their heartaches.

I met a man recently whose emotional scar tissue showed in the expression of his face. His wife had been emotionally ill for a long time before the day he had returned home to find that she had committed suicide and taken their two children with her. We can only imagine at a distance the anguish the man had felt. He had first tried to blame himself. Then he had worried over the "what might have beens." Finally, he had claimed the fact that he belonged to Christ, and that life had to go on. He said, "I believe the God who saved me can now save me from a life of remorse." What courage! I couldn't help but think of Corrie ten Boom's statement: "However deep the pit, God's love is deeper still."

Then there was a couple who were led to surrender their lives to Christ as a result of heartache over their marriage. Neither could love the other in language and actions which could be heard or accepted. So they decided to get some help, and came to church. That led to their attending a new members' class, and an opportunity to accept Christ as Lord and Savior. He moved into their hungry hearts, and the experience prompted them to realize the need for deeper healing of specific attitudes and reaction patterns. Counseling helped. Their comment to me the other day was classic. I wrote it down with their permission to include it in this chapter: "We're glad we went through the heartache; it got us to the end of ourselves. The hurt got so bad we had to do something. Now we know it was the Lord who used the heartache to help us realize how empty our lives had become."

The Bread of Life saves! But that's only the beginning. *The Bread of Life also satisfies.* Many of our heartaches are caused by stifled needs. Think of the basic needs we all have—the needs for love, affection, self-esteem, importance, sexual fulfillment, success, approval of others, recognition, significant involvement in something that counts, a sense of usefulness, financial security, and material possessions. These are common to life. We all have them.

But what happens when circumstances or the strange evolution of our destinies precludes any or all of them? Hunger for self-realization results. Our human potential is thwarted. And the gap between what we need and what we get is filled with heartache. How can the Bread of Life do anything about that? And if we get all we think we want, would we be satisfied—really?

All the lusts of life run the danger of being substitutes for a soul-satisfying relationship with the Bread of Life.

We are never truly satisfied until we are willing to allow him to feed our needs. He said, "Blessed are those who hunger and thirst for righteousness, for they shall be satisfied" (Matt. 5:6).

When we get right with the Lord at the core of our ambitious, acquisitive natures, then we can see the temporary needs in perspective. I am convinced that we should tell the Lord when we get frustrated with our unfulfilled needs. That does two things: it breaks the aching bind, and gives us a sense that we are not alone. We will never be free until we trust that he will meet our basic need for satisfaction and security in our hearts. He is able to guide us toward being fulfilled in creative ways which bring him glory and help us grow. The Psalmist was right: "For he satisfies him who is thirsty, and the hungry he fills with good things" (Ps. 107:9).

No human being can satisfy our deepest needs. No position, recognition, or financial security can fill our emptiness. Why else would people who have all these still have hungry, aching hearts? We are like Isaiah's analysis of the human condition, "As when a hungry man dreams he is eating and awakes with his hunger not satisfied, or as when a thirsty man dreams he is drinking and awakes faint, with his thirst not quenched" (Isa. 29:8). The same is true of our ambitious hungers and our lusty thirsts. The prophet goes on in a later chapter with a question which demands an answer: "Why do you spend your money for that which is not bread, and your labor for that which does not satisfy?" (Isa. 55:2).

Well, why do we? Many of us would have to respond that although the Bread of Life has saved us he has not been allowed to satisfy us.

Paul Scherer, the contemporary American theologian, was on target: "The greatest question of our time . . . is whether man can bear to live without God." He was in tune with the Psalmist, "As a hart longs for flowing streams, so longs my soul for thee, O God. My soul thirsts for God, for the living God" (Ps. 42:1–2).

A vital relationship with Christ meets our need for

security with his power to protect and guide us. He satisfies our lust for power and praise with his assurance and delight in us. He conquers our passions with a love for people engendered by his loving concern for our ultimate good. Our need for the affection of friends is satisfied by involvement with people who need our encouragement and understanding. Instead of demanding that people care for us, we join in caring for others.

The forgiving love of Christ heals our guilt. His ever-present companionship fills our loneliness. Our assurance of his intervening love for people we love frees us to relax our tenacious grip on them, to give up our overprotective manipulation. Pain and sickness will be preludes to deeper fellowship with him and an evidence of his healing power. Fear of death will be swallowed up in an expectant anticipation of the next phase of our eternal life. Jesus Christ the Bread of Life satisfies!

But that's not all. *The Bread of Life strengthens.* As food strengthens the physical body, Christ infuses strength into our total life. The strength of conviction for our intellects. The strength of love in our emotions. Volitional strength in the courage to know and do his will.

Look at Paul. Long after he had become a Christian, he knew the dull, persistent pain of heartache. He had what he described as a "thorn in the flesh"—most likely a virulent form of malaria. He was weakened by the disease and troubled that although he prayed there seemed to be no answer. Later he wrote to the Corinthians about how the Lord dealt with his problem. "Three times I besought the Lord about this, that it should leave me; but he said to me, 'My grace is sufficient for you, for my power is made perfect in weakness'" (2 Cor. 12:8–9).

That confronted the last vestiges of self-justifying perfectionism in Paul. He wanted to be strong for the Lord. And the Lord showed him that his weakness was an occasion for greater trust. If the Lord had answered the Apostle's first request, Paul would have lost more power than pain. James Denney, the great Scottish scholar of another generation, said, "A refusal is an answer if it is so given that God and the soul henceforth understand one another."

We cannot be strengthened by Christ if we want to be strong on our own for Christ. A great difference! When we admit our need for strength, he gives us sufficient measure. Sufficient for what? To do his will on his timing—where, when, and with whom he chooses. We cannot expect his strength for our schemes. We can expect abundant energy, wisdom, and power to do what he wants us to do. The closer I come to an intimate relationship with Christ, the more sure I am that ideas, insights, sensitive love and empathy, plus sheer energy, are available.

We have come full circle to where we began. Our heartaches are caused by our hungry souls. We do not have what it takes alone. That's why the Lord came and comes with the strength of his sublimely sufficient "I am" assertion, "I am the bread of life; he who comes to me shall not hunger . . ." He alone can save, satisfy, and strengthen. The source is infinite and more than adequate:

> He giveth more grace as the burdens grow greater;
> He sendeth more strength when the labors increase.
> To added affliction He addeth His mercy;
> To multiplied trials, His multiplied peace.
>
> When we have exhausted our store of endurance,
> When our strength has failed ere the day is half done,
> When we reach the end of our hoarded resources,
> Our Father's full giving is only begun.
>
> His love has no limit; His grace has no measure;
> His pow'r has no boundary known unto men.
> For out of His infinite riches in Jesus,
> He giveth, and giveth, and giveth again!
>
> Annie Johnson Flint[1]

---

1. Copyright 1941. Renewed 1969 by Lillenas Publishing Co. Used by permission.

5

Lord, What Is It You Want Me To Do?

Daily Guidance of the Light of the World

"I am the light of the world."
John 8:12

DECISIONS, DECISIONS, DECISIONS! The future looms with choices. Some are insignificant and easily made; others are momentous and soul-sized, demanding and difficult. The alternatives are equally beguiling or befuddling. It's difficult to know which bridges to burn and which to cross. A heavy fog of indecision, confusion, and uncertainty gathers around us, and it is dark.

I call this the midnight muddle of our minds. It is no respecter of persons or timing. It can happen in the brightness of day or the sleeplessness of night. Our minds are darkened. We long for vision of what's best or right. The terrifying possibility of missing the maximum for our lives engulfs us. Suddenly the icy fingers of self-doubt grip our hearts. The intimidating memories of foolish choices and wrong decisions prance about in our minds. The mistakes, misfires, and missed opportunities of years gone by haunt us. The "if onlys" of the past give illegitimate birth to the "what ifs" of imagined dangers. We talk to ourselves about what to do, and we answer ourselves with caution and concern. The midnight muddle becomes a dark night of the soul, and persists through the day.

An old ditty captures our condition.

> There was once an old sailor my grandfather knew
>   Who had so many things which he wanted to do
> That, whenever he thought it was time to begin,
>   He couldn't because of the state he was in.

We laugh, and then the laughter catches in our throats. We are not sure if we should laugh or cry. The old sailor's problem is ours!

Sound familiar? Of course. All of us are on the edge of some crucial decision. The deadline is approaching. Some of us are facing a penetrating evaluation of our next steps. Others have excruciating perplexities which demand difficult decisions. Most of us have people problems in which decisions are painful. And every one of us has daily choices about the investment of time, money, or energy. What shall we do? Career choices, marriage problems, family needs, the passages of life—all dish up more quandaries than we're capable of handling at times.

Focus your mind on a crucial decision you are facing right now. On what basis will you make it? How will you know what you are to do? When you've made the decision, how will you know you've done the right thing regardless of what happens?

It's in the midnight muddle of indecision that we are forced to think about our life agendas and the priorities they dictate. The reason many people have difficulty with decisions is that they have no game plan for their lives. They drift from crisis to crisis, problem to problem, without a satisfactory value system that works. The exclamation points of happiness become lurking question marks of indecision.

When I did the survey on the deepest needs of people that is the impetus behind this book, I received hundreds of responses with words and phrases like "decisions," "need for guidance," "difficult choices," "direction for my life," "fear of making wrong decisions," "how to know the will of God," and "what does it mean to allow God to guide your life?"

A prominent physician wrote in a letter: "In response to your inquiry about our deepest needs, I put one word above all others—*priorities*. This matter can be divided into four subelements: 1) the principles behind the selection of priorities; 2) the establishment of specific priorities in their order of importance; 3) the implementation of priorities; and 4) the maintenance and achievement of priorities." This busy surgeon, author, and administrator is besieged by opportunities and demands. He longs to find a basis of making his choices and decisions according to what's ultimately important.

There are nine words which are the answer to the needs articulated by the surgeon and others. They form life's most crucial question—a question which can turn the midnight muddle into a dawn of vision. It's based on an audacious assumption and a grand assurance—that God has a purpose and plan for every individual. If we believe that, we can dare ask, "Lord, what is it you want me to do?"

I have never asked that question without receiving a clear and unambiguous answer. Years of helping people with decisions have convinced me that it is the liberating question when we need to clarify our life agenda, our priorities, and the next steps in the Lord's strategy for us. Our extremity of need for specific guidance always gives the Lord an opportunity to help us evaluate our ultimate direction.

The answer to the nine words of our question is given in twenty-three words of one of Jesus' most dynamic "I am" promises. Here is a shaft of light for our midnight muddle of uncertainty: "I am the light of the world; he who follows me will not walk in darkness, but will have the light of life" (John 8:12). The answer to all our questions and the direction for all our decisions is a personal relationship with Jesus Christ himself. The Light of the

World pierces our darkness, penetrates our minds to show us the way, and helps us assign priorities to the opportunities and challenges which confront us. He is the source of guidance; he gives us the secret of receiving guidance; he provides serendipities of guidance.

Jesus made his dramatic promise in a startling context. I believe it was the final statement of his message on the last night of the Feast of Tabernacles in Jerusalem. People from all over Palestine had come to the Holy City to celebrate the memory of the blessings of God on the Israelites during the wilderness wanderings of the Exodus from Egypt.

God had guided the Israelites with a pillar of cloud during the day and a pillar of fire at night (Exod. 13:21–22). Moses and the people had obeyed the movement of the pillar. Where it rested they had pitched their tents, and they had moved on only when its movement beckoned them onward. The pillar of fire had been the evidence of the presence of God with them. He had been light in the darkness giving direction and courage; when the pillar had hovered over the tent of Moses, the people had known that God was speaking to them (Exod. 13:21; 33:9–10).

To commemorate this guidance of God there was a ceremony in the Feast of Tabernacles called the Illumination of the Temple. It was held each night in the Court of the Women. Great galleries were erected around the court to hold the spectators. When the sun had set and darkness settled in the sacred precincts, the people gathered to witness a remarkable spectacle. Four great candelabra stood in the center of the court. At the dramatic moment, these were set ablaze as a memorial to the light God had been to his people in the dark uncertainty of the Exodus. The people would sing and dance with joy and adoration all through the night.

For a moment, allow your gift of imagination to put you in the gallery watching the vivid and impressive ceremony. Let your emotions soar with the people as they celebrate with unfettered delight. Join in singing the psalms of praise for the light in darkness God has given his people in all ages.

Now allow an awesome chill of excitement run up and down your spine as you watch Jesus walk to the center of the court and stand in the midst of the four candelabra. All eyes turn to him. His voice pierces above the singing and the rhythm of the tambourines, trumpets, and drums. Pointing to the candelabra, he speaks, and his voice rings like thunder: "I am the light of the world! He who follows me will not walk in darkness but will have the light of life."

Nothing could have startled and shocked the people any more. It was as if he said, "God's presence was a pillar of fire for Moses and our forefathers. Now the pillar of presence is here in person. I am, *egō eimi!* Yahweh is here to be the light of life. These candelabra will go out by the time the cock crows at dawn, but I am light which lasts and can never be diminished, for I am God's light dispelling the darkness. Come, follow me, and you will be able to walk in the light forever!"

Jesus could not have made a more astonishing claim. The word *light* was directly synonymous with God himself. The Psalmist asserted, "The Lord is my light and my salvation" (Ps. 27:1). "In thy light do we see light" (Ps. 36:9). "Send out thy light and thy truth; let them lead me" (Ps. 43:3). Isaiah prophesied, "The Lord will be your everlasting light" (Isa. 60:19). Micah's confession of trust was, "When I sit in darkness, the Lord will be a light to me" (Mic. 7:8).

In claiming to be the light of the world, Jesus clearly declared himself as the Messiah. One of the names of the expected Messiah was Light. There could be no question about his self-identification after that!

Nor can there be for us. Jesus strides into our midnight muddles with the same awesome claim: "I am the Light of the world, your life. Follow me!" Discovering our direction, discerning the Lord's will, and making our decisions all begin with living and walking in his light. In his letter

to the early church, John declared the authority of the
Light and his central message: "This is the message we
have heard from him and proclaim to you, that God is
light and in him is no darkness at all. . . . If we walk in the
light, as he is in the light, we have fellowship with one
another, and the blood of Jesus his Son cleanses us from
all sin" (1 John 1:5, 7). L. Nelson Bell said it plainly: "To
be a Christian means to have a vital, personal relationship
with Jesus Christ, and until that is established all other
concerns are secondary." *Christ himself is the source of light in
our darkness.*

Jesus does for us what light does to the darkness. He
illuminates, dispels doubt, and guides. Experiencing the
Light is intellectual, emotional, and volitional.

The reason we have difficulties with our decisions and
priorities is because of profound intellectual misunderstanding. Our minds are darkened by distortions which
debilitate our desire to know and do God's will. We ask,
"How can God know and care about me with all the
billions of people in the world? What right do I have to
seek guidance knowing what I've been and done? If God
knows everything, why pray? If I do pray, how can God
answer in a way I can know and understand?" These are
the questions which keep us glued to dead center.

And that's why God came himself as the Light of the
World to penetrate our minds with truth about his nature
and his attitude toward us. Jesus told us that God's love is
not merited or negated by our goodness or badness. He
assured us that he cares about all our needs, that he
created us to be able to talk with him and tell him about
our difficult decisions. The Light of the World implores
us to ask, seek, and knock. He invites us to abide in him
and to open ourselves for him to abide in us. A divine
wisdom can pervade our minds to give us insight, sensitivity, and specific direction. The radiant truth of the
pillar of light revealed in Jesus' total message and life is
that guidance is the result of an eager mind, honed by
habitual communion and conversation with him. The
cloudy dimness of our minds must be broken through so

that we can see things as they are—Christ as he is and ourselves as we are. The illuminating revelation must be such that at the same time it shows us the truth and makes it possible for us to deal with it. Jesus, the Light of the World, does exactly that!

The Light of the World not only illuminates our intellectual understanding of truth; he exposes our feelings, attitudes, and hidden sins. Experiencing the Light is an emotional trauma if we are not free. Jesus said, "And this is the judgment, that the light has come into the world, and men loved darkness rather than light, because their deeds were evil. For everyone who does evil hates the light, and does not come to the light, lest his deeds should be exposed. But he who does what is true comes to the light, that it may be clearly seen that his deeds have been wrought in God" (John 3:19–21).

If we wish to be guided by the Light, we must open ourselves to his penetrating truth. Nothing can remain hidden from him. The darkness of our midnight muddle is often our fear of being known and exposed. We want the Lord to lead us and give us an answer to what we should do. But he resists a simple answer until our emotions have been flooded by his light. He knows we will not be able to act on any guidance he gives until we are at peace with him and ourselves.

The secret of guidance is in following the Light of the World. Guidance is volitional: it is given to those who will to do the Lord's will. He offers us the light of life. The Greek verb translated "to follow" is *akolouthein*. It implies faithfulness, obedience, discipleship, and companionship. Jesus' clarion call was "Follow me! Walk in my footsteps. Lean on me. Put me first in your life." John said, "In him was life, and the life was the light of men" (1:4).

All of our difficult decisions are rooted in clarifying our priorities on the basis of Jesus Christ's agenda for us. The only way through the darkness is to follow the light he gives us. Any confusion about a specific decision is a telltale sign that we need a closer walk with him. Our times of indecision help us to realize that we have lagged behind or taken a path away from him. We have become too busy for consistent prayer. Then suddenly we are faced with a crisis. Having to seek the Lord's will is a sure sign that we've been out of it. The Lord is more than a source of answers for our complexities. He wants us to live so close to him that we know intuitively what he would want us to do in a specific situation or relationship.

The teaching of the kingdom of God was the central theme of Jesus' teaching. The kingdom means the reign of God in our lives. Jesus came to call into being a new breed of people who would accept his complete and unreserved direction of our lives, who would let his will for us become the guiding priority.

Jesus said he came not to do his own will but the will of his Father. He taught his disciples to pray, "Thy kingdom come, Thy will be done, On earth as it is in heaven" (Matt. 6:10). In the anguish of Gethsemane he prayed, "Not my will, but thine, be done" (Luke 22:42).

Obedience is the key to receiving and knowing the will of God. We are given fresh guidance on the basis of our obedience to previous guidance. When we seek the Light for a dark time of decision making, and have consistently resisted what we know already, it will be difficult for us to accept the next steps and take them.

"Our wills are ours, we know not how;/ Our wills are ours, to make them thine." That simple prayer from Tennyson's *In Memoriam* unlocks the Lord's guidance. Jesus promised "If you continue in my word, you are truly my disciples, and you will know the truth, and the truth will make you free" (John 8:31–32).

Paul discovered *the secret of guidance*. His moment-by-moment fellowship with Christ gave him the clarity for his daily decisions. He shared the secret with the Christians at Rome. "I appeal to you therefore, brethren, by the mercies of God, to present your bodies as a living sacrifice, holy and acceptable to God, which is your spiritual worship. Do not be conformed to this world but be transformed by the renewal of your mind, that you may prove [test through experience] what is the will of God, what is good and acceptable and perfect" (Rom. 12:1–2).

Paul had learned that, when he committed his life daily in an unreserved surrender, he was given the gift of knowing what the Lord's will was in his choices. The purpose of Paul's ministry to the Gentiles was "to open their eyes, that they may turn from darkness to light" (Acts 26:18). He challenged people to "cast off the works of darkness and put on the armor of light" (Rom. 13:12).

To Paul, Jesus was the light of God's presence. "For it is the God who said, 'Let light shine out of darkness,' who has shone in our hearts to give the light of the knowledge of the glory of God in the face of Christ" (2 Cor. 4:6). Christians were "children of light" and "saints of light" for the Apostle. He believed that to be in Christ was to be filled with light. The purpose of the Christian life was to walk in the light.

In that context we can take an incisive inventory based on our ultimate priority of following the Lord. We can ask these basic questions honestly about any course of action:

1. What is my life agenda? My ultimate purpose? Is it to know and do the Lord's will?
2. Which of the alternatives before me will be congruent with this life agenda?
3. Can I do it and keep my priorities straight? Does it contradict any of my basic values?
4. Will it extend the kingdom of God in my own life, relationships, and society?
5. If I made that choice would it glorify my Lord and help me to grow as a person?
6. Would the choice bring me into a deeper relationship with the Lord?
7. Does it enable the ultimate good of all concerned? (The word *ultimate* means that in spite of pain or difficulty it would be finally creative for everyone involved.)
8. Can I maintain my self-esteem if I make this choice? Can I look back on having done it and still love and accept myself?

9. Will it cause stress, anxiety, or dis-ease of soul?
10. Can I take the Lord with me in every aspect of carrying out the decision?

When I dare to ask and answer these questions, the darkness of the midnight muddle begins to lift. There are alternatives which suddenly seem absurd and untenable. How could I have ever entertained the possibility?

But I must be honest enough to share with you the fact that there have been times when all the alternatives have passed the inventory test. What to do then?

That leads to the third aspect of how the Light of the World gives us the light of life: *the serendipity of guidance*. The Lord will use any and all means of getting through to us. If we have surrendered a decision to him, he begins to marshal all the resources that can help us be sure of what he wills.

The Bible is basic. When we return to the well of his wisdom in Scripture, he will guide us to passages which deal with people who faced similar decisions, or to verses which flash truth for our complexity.

This week I had to deal with a perplexing problem. I was confronted with the need to give strategic leadership. The people involved needed my intervention, but what should I say? Should I be tender or tough? Only the Lord knew what was best. My studies in 1 Thessalonians led me to that dynamic second chapter about how Paul had dealt with the needs of the Thessalonians. He reminded them, "We were gentle among you, like a nurse taking care of her children. So, being affectionately desirous of you, we were ready to share with you not only the gospel of God but also our own selves, because you had become very dear to us" (vv. 7–8). Then I read on, "For you know how," said Paul, "like a father with his children, we exhorted each one of you and encouraged you and charged you to lead a life worthy of God, who calls you into his own kingdom and glory" (vv. 11–12). The Lord showed me two dimensions of the leadership that I was to have—firmness, directness, toughness, and yet at the same time tenderness and compassion. As I prayed, I felt the Lord telling me to be both gentle and direct. One without the other would not do. I had my answer.

Often the Lord answers our prayers for guidance through another person. He invades our circumstances with an unexpected gift of grace that makes the next step undeniably clear. Something said, advice given, or wise counsel communicated can be used by the Lord to drive home to us what he wants us to do.

Be sure of this: the Lord can get through to us. He will use all the resources at his disposal to break through to our minds so that we can understand without any confusion what it is he wants us to do.

But of all the ways the Lord guides us, personal prayer is the ultimate confirmation of the direction. When we have inventoried our lives' agendas and checked our priorities, we must leave the last and final word to him. He can use our minds and emotions to speak to us. Daily times of prolonged prayer, plus moment-by-moment "flash prayers" prepare us to know what to do.

Solomon gave us a proverbial basis of complete openness to the Lord's guidance. "Trust in the Lord with all your heart, and do not rely on your own insight. In all your ways acknowledge him and he will make straight your paths" (Prov. 3:5–6). The *Living Bible* paraphrase makes that advice all the more impelling. "In everything you do, put God first, and he will direct you and crown your efforts with success" (Prov. 3:6, LB).

The Light of the World is with each of us right now—pillar of fire in the darkness. God himself with us. If we dare to follow him, we will have the light of life—we will know when to wait and when to move, when to be silent and when to speak.

Speak to Him, thou, for He hears, and Spirit with Spirit can meet—
Closer is He than breathing, and nearer than hands and feet.

—Alfred, Lord Tennyson

The Light of the World has ended the midnight muddle. If we ask the Lord for guidance, he will use all means possible to show us the way. We can pray with confidence:

"Lord, what is it that you want me to do? I surrender my decisions to you. I believe that if I belong to you totally, you will show me what to do. Here is my mind, think through it; here are my emotions, help me feel what is right; here is my will, give me courage to follow your priorities for my life. And Lord, now that I have given this decision over to you, help me not to take it back with worry in a midnight muddle of fear. Go before me to show me the way, above me to watch over me, beside me to be my constant companion, and within me to give me peace. Amen."

6

Love Is Not Blind

To See Ourselves and Take Responsibility

> *"That those who do not see may see . . ."*
> John 9:39

I WAS HAVING LUNCH ALONE, reading a book, and trying to mind my own business. Two secretaries who apparently worked in the same office were seated at the table next to mine. Their conversation became so animated that I couldn't help overhearing.

The two young ladies were busy devouring more than their lunch. A young bachelor executive from their office had just entered the restaurant with a woman they both agreed was unworthy of his discerning taste. Neither could understand why he was paying any attention to her!

"What does he see in her?" one asked. And the other replied in agreement, "With all of us in the office to choose from why did he fall for her?"

I looked across the restaurant at the love-struck couple, trying to discern what was wrong with the young man's romantic selectivity. His choice didn't look so bad to me! I concluded that the deeper question being asked by the two ladies next to me was why the attractive catch had not asked either of them to lunch.

When the two gossips got up from the table to pay their check, they were somewhat embarrassed to note that I had probably overheard their entire conversation. Looking over at the couple in question, one of the jealous twosome said to me, "Well, all you can say is—love is blind!" With that they pranced out of the restaurant, leaving me to finish my coffee and to ponder their catty comment.

Strange, isn't it, how a tattered old shibboleth, tossed off as a thoughtless throwaway line, suddenly sticks in the center of our thoughts, and demands reevaluation. Is love blind? Oh, I knew what she meant, and why she said it, but did she understand what she said? By the time I had finished my coffee and paid my check, I wanted to find those two women and tell them I disagreed heartily.

Love is not blind! In fact, love has eyes to see far more than the physical eye can focus. The heart has eyes to see. We can have twenty-twenty vision in our physical eyes and suffer from spiritual glaucoma in the eyes of our hearts.

It's fascinating to reflect on the dual use of the words *see* and *blind*. We say we see something or someone. We also express comprehension or understanding when we say, "I see what you mean." There are times when we say we saw a person or situation but did not really see the deeper issues or needs beneath the surface. In the same way, it's possible to be blind both physically and spiritually. Eye blindness is a tragedy, but it is nothing in comparison to heart blindness. To see and be blind to what we saw is spiritual blindness.

Someone asked Helen Keller an impertinent question: "Isn't it terrible to be blind?" Her response was a classic: "Better to be blind and see with your heart than to have two good eyes and see nothing."

Indeed! But if you had to choose between being physically or spiritually blind, which would you choose? If you had to give up either the eyes in your head or the eyes in your heart, how would you decide?

Suddenly we are forced to wonder what it would be like to be physically blind. We empathize with the anguish of no longer seeing loved ones, the beauty of the natural world, or the splendor of daily life which we so easily take for granted. I have a friend whose eyesight is diminishing and will be gone in a few months. That has made me think about how I would feel and what and whom I would look at before the light faded, never to return.

But what if I had to lose the eyes of my heart? If we think of the heart in the Hebrew sense of combined intellect, emotion, and will, we are painfully aware of the greater tragedy of heart blindness. I know people who have lost their eyesight but who see far more than I do with the eyes of their hearts; their other senses are heightened with awareness. Most of all, they can sense what people are feeling better than those of us who have physical eyes with which to see.

And yet we must not be simplistic. There are those who are physically blind whose hearts are also darkened, and many of us who see with our eyes also need the healing of the eyes of our hearts. It is with the inner eyes of the soul that what our physical eyes focus on is distilled in praise and adoration. When we have heart-eyes to see what is registered on the tissues of our brain, what we see is expressed in our emotions and implemented by our will. We all need the healing of our heart-eyes to be able to see ourselves as we are and can become, others in their need and their potential, life as we are living it, and the fullness God intended.

Jesus is God with us to heal our heart-eyes. The promise of the prophets was that the Messiah would come and would open the eyes of the blind. Wherever Jesus went, he healed the physically and spiritually blind. His response to John the Baptist's question, "Are you he who is to come, or shall we look for another?" was, "The blind receive their sight . . ." (Matt. 11:2, 5).

But many who had physical sight desperately needed the eyes of their hearts healed. The leaders of Israel saw Jesus' signs and miracles, but could not see that he was God with them, the anticipated Messiah. They had eyes, but could not see. Prejudice, jealousy, and religious traditionalism kept them from beholding "the glory of God in the face of Jesus Christ" (2 Cor. 4:6, KJV). No wonder Jesus called them "blind guides" (Matt. 23:16). It was for them, as well as for the physically blind, that Jesus repeated his "I am" assertion and self-disclosure about being the Light of the World. In his first statement about being the Light of the World (John 8:12), he affirmed his messianic authority to guide all men to the truth; in the second (John 9:5), he declared his power to heal blindness.

The significant difference between the two "I am the Light of the World," *egō eimi* proclamations is that in the second the article is missing from the Greek. The profound contrast does not show up in our English Bible. The second "I am" statement about the Light of the World should be translated, from the original Greek, "I am light to the world, whenever I am in the world." The absence of the definite article focuses on Jesus' ministry of healing the sight of the blind. But when he said, "I am light to the world," he had more than physical sight in mind. In fact, I am convinced that the timing and strategy of the healing of the physically blind man in John 9 was to alert the spiritually blind of their deeper need for the healing. Jesus' target was the blind guides among the Pharisees, to those who had eyes to see but could not see, to you and me!

Let's consider the total impact of the account which is so vividly dramatized in our scripture—the healing of the man born blind.

Jesus and his disciples were walking in Jerusalem. They saw a man who had been born blind on the side of the road begging. Note the difference in Jesus' and the disciples' response to the pitiful plight of the man. The disciples were picking up the theological argument, which must have been in fashion, about the cause of congenital illness. "Rabbi," they asked, "who sinned, this man or his parents?" An insensitive, irrelevant question! It was based on the distorted idea that any illness from birth must have been caused by sin in the parents or by sin resident in the soul of the unborn child. Jesus swept that question aside. "It was not that this man sinned, or his parents, but that the works of God might be made manifest in him. We

must work the works of him who sent me, while it is day;
night comes, when no one can work. As long as I am in
the world, I am the light of the world."

We are unsettled by that! Did Jesus mean that God had
caused the man to be born blind so that he could be the
prop for a messianic miracle? Hardly. Remember that the
original Greek had no punctuation marks. That was up to
the translator. I wonder about the commas and periods of
this sentence as we have it in our English Bible. G.
Campbell Morgan suggests the following punctuation:
"Neither did this man sin, nor his parents. But that the
words of God should be made manifest, we must work the
works of him who sent me, while it is day; the night
cometh, when no man can work."

Whether we follow Dr. Morgan's punctuation or not,
we do have to consider the words "but that," meaning
purpose or result, destiny, or opportunity. I prefer the
implication of opportunity. God did not make this man
blind for Jesus' miracle. How he got blind was not the
issue. The stark reality was that he was blind and that
Jesus could heal him. Jesus' bold declaration, "It was not
that this man sinned, or his parents," stood alone as a fact.
That he was blind also could not be denied. And the
assurance that God was present to work through the
Messiah was the only source of hope.

That's disarming for those of us who like to define the
causes of our own or others' difficulties. "What did I do to
cause or deserve this?" we ask. Or, "There must be a
deeper cause of that person's sickness or calamity. He
probably got what he had coming."

Jesus asks none of these questions. He faces the reality
of our need as an occasion for the glory of God to be
revealed. The point is that the man was blind and needed
to see. And so do we!

Don't miss the implication of how and when Jesus
healed the blind man. It was on the Sabbath. Healing was
forbidden on the holy day. There was a specific dictum
against even setting a broken bone or healing an open
wound. There was also a definite rule against the applica-

tion of spittle on a wound on the Sabbath. And yet Jesus did just that! Spittle was believed to have healing power. The Lord spat on the ground and made clay of the spittle and anointed the blind man's eyes. Then he sent him to the Pool of Siloam to wash his eyes. We can picture the man making his way to the pool. "Will it work?" he thought anxiously and hopefully. But when he washed the clay from his eyes he was able to see! Jesus had healed his eyes.

Why this elaborate healing process? In other cases of healing the blind, Jesus simply pronounced the healing and the blind saw. If he had deliberately broken the Sabbath rule, why did he dramatize it so vividly in a way that would attract the attention of everyone—especially the Pharisees? Did he purposely precipitate a disputation with officialdom?

The more I study this chapter the more convinced I am that he did. He wanted to heal more than the blind eyes of the lonely beggar. He wanted to focus attention on the deeper needs, the spiritual blindness of the leaders of Israel.

What I think he anticipated actually happened. The people who had known the blind man from his youth were astonished. "Is not this the one who used to sit and beg?" they asked with excited voices. "It is he!" some responded, amazed. Others doubted the miracle: "No, but he is like him." But listen to the man's own response: "I am the man!" he said forcefully and joyously. Then he explained what had happened to him when a man called Jesus healed his eyes.

"Where is he?" the people wanted to know, expecting that there would be a grave dispute with the Pharisees about a healing on the Sabbath.

Now the plot thickens, as Jesus knew it would. I suspect that the Master was off to the side of the crowd smiling at the predictable fickleness of the people. He knew what they would do. They took the man to the Pharisees and exposed the fact that a healing had been performed on the Sabbath. We marvel at the response of the leaders.

They showed an awesome lack of gratitude for a miraculous healing. Consternation flowed within them over an infraction of the Sabbath law. Gross legalism!

What ensued was a heated dispute over what had actually happened. The healed man tried his best to explain and claimed that Jesus must have been a prophet. His parents were brought in for questioning. They evaded being implicated by saying evasively, "He is of age, ask him." Hard to believe. Their son, blind from birth, had been healed and they did not know who had done it; nor did they claim any loyalty or gratitude. They feared being put out of the synagogue. Excommunication was the sentence for any involvement or association with the breaking of the Sabbath. "Ask him," they said in equivocating evasion, pointing to their son. "He is of age."

Further questioning of the man brought forth the best witness he could muster in defense of Jesus for healing him on the Sabbath. The Pharisees charged, "Give God the praise; we know that this man [Jesus] is a sinner." The healed man wouldn't accept that: "Whether he is a sinner, I do not know; one thing I know, that though I was blind, now I see."

The man's faith was growing. When the Pharisees asked him a third time to repeat the account of how he had been healed, he responded pointedly, "Why do you want to hear it again? Do you too want to become his disciples?" That brought a reviling retort: "You are his disciple, but we are disciples of Moses. We know that God has spoken to Moses, but as for this man, we do not know where he comes from."

The liberated beggar was then given wisdom beyond his experience to respond with great logic and power. Only one from God could do what no man had ever been able to do in giving sight to the blind: "If this man were not from God, he could do nothing," the blind man asserted with courage.

That did it. His witness for Jesus earned him the frightening fate of excommunication from the synagogue.

But Jesus knew. When he found him, the man was still

surrounded by the judgmental Pharisees. The Lord knew that the healing of his eyes was only the beginning of the healing he needed in the eyes of his heart.

Within hearing distance of the "blind guides," Jesus asked the man life's ultimate question. In a way, he was also asking the Pharisees, "Do you believe in the Son of man?" The healed beggar was ready for a deeper healing. "Who is he, sir, that I may believe in him?" he asked urgently. "You have seen him." Two stages of healing! To see him, and then to hear him as he speaks to the heart. The twice-healed man responded, seeing both with his eyes and his heart, "Lord, I believe."

Now Jesus swung about and faced the blind leaders of Israel. They needed healing of their spiritual sight most of all. "For judgment I came into this world," he thundered, "that those who do not see may see, and that those who see may become blind." Piercingly direct. Those who admit their blindness of eye and heart can be healed; those who refuse remain blind. No wonder they exclaimed, "Are we also blind?" Exactly the conclusion Jesus was pressing toward in the whole drama of confrontation. "If you were blind," he said forcefully, "you would have no guilt; but now that you say, 'We see,' your guilt remains."

The remarkable thing is that none of the leaders admitted his blindness and asked to be healed. The terrible plight of the spiritually blind is that they cannot admit it. Humility is lacking. Arrogance pervades. Pride dominates all responses.

The dynamic account ends dramatically. The blind man who could not see with the eyes of either his head or heart had received sight for both; the Pharisees who could see physically but not spiritually refused the heart healing which would have enabled them to see themselves, Jesus as the Messiah, and the abundant life he offered them.

"What does all this mean to me?" you ask. Just this. Magnificently this! Jesus comes to each of us. If we can admit that we are blind, he can give us eyes to see. The blind beggar could admit the blindness of both his eyes and heart and received his sight. In response, the Lord gave him physical vision to see the world around him, and spiritual vision to see Jesus as Savior, hope, and the source of eternal life.

The alarming truth for us is that what we see with our eyes is dependent on what we see with our hearts. Our perception of reality is clouded until our heart-eyes are healed. We look at life negatively and defensively; our view of ourselves and our potential is limited. We see people in fuzzy images of fear or competition, out of sync with the wonder each person is to be.

An oculist can give us a test to discern the capacity of our physical eyes. What he or she cannot do is test the capacity of the eyes of the heart. New glasses sometimes sharpen things more clearly than our heart-eyes are ready to focus. There was a man who went to his ophthalmologist, sat down in the examination room, and declared, "I'd like to see a little more poorly, please." Sometimes we see more than we want to see.

There is a great story about Joan Rivers, the humorist. She had been fitted for contact lenses. The first night she used them while performing, she saw the audience for the first time in years. It was so frightening to her that she excused herself and took off her contacts and returned onstage to entertain a more familiar, faceless blur. That's not unlike many of us spiritually. Our image of ourselves and others, as well as the magnificent beauty around us, is a dull blur, and often we would rather keep it that way. But if we want to see, really see with new vision, Jesus can heal us.

How he dealt with the man born blind and the blind Pharisees gives us the progression of how healing of the eyes of our hearts can take place. First must come the recognition that we are blind, or that the vision of our hearts is badly impaired. How can we know that and admit it? Here's a spiritual heart-eye test.

1. Are you excited about living?

2. Are you moved daily by the wonder of life around you?

3. How good is your perception and your discernment of what's happening around you? After a difficulty or crisis do you ever say, "I didn't see what was happening. How could I have missed the real issue?"

4. Do you see beneath the surface of people? Are you aware of the unexpressed needs? Are you the first to affirm the potential greatness inside of people that is longing to be expressed? Can you say about people what Michelangelo said about great blocks of marble, "I see an angel in each block of marble waiting to be set free"?

5. Are you delighted to be you? Can you see yourself in all your failures and shortcomings and honestly admit your need? Are you able to picture the person God intends you to be and to boldly claim that what he has focused in the tissues of your imagination will be true if you give him control of your life?

6. Do you believe that your best days are still ahead? A sure test of twenty-twenty heart-sight is the indomitable hope in the future because, whatever has been, the best is still to be.

7. Have you ever seen yourself through the eyes of Jesus Christ? Can you picture yourself as he sees you—loved and forgiven, free and unbound, empowered and enabled?

8. Are you able to see life's problems as the raw material of the fresh miracles of the Lord in your life? Do you look for, expect, and anticipate him to break through any moment with the answer which, in all your planning, you could never have expected on your own strength?

9. Do you see yourself as the container and transmitter of immense spiritual power that enables you to live a daring and adventuresome life?

10. Do you look forward to your own physical death as
a triumphant transition in your experience of
eternal life? Are you sure that you will live forever
because you belong to Christ and that death has no
power over you? Has heaven begun for you?

Unless you can say yes to all ten of these questions, the
eyes of your heart badly need healing.

That leads to the second phase of healing. If we realize
our need for heart-vision, we can ask the Lord for
healing. That healing takes place when we accept him as
our Lord and Savior, turn the control of our lives over to
him, and ask him to live his life in us.

The Lord's healing of our inner eyes comes through the
gift of faith, the greatest of all the gifts of the Spirit, the
one which makes all others possible. Remember what
Jesus said to Peter when he was able to finally say, "You
are the Christ?" "Blessed are you, Simon Bar-Jona! For
flesh and blood has not revealed this to you, but my
Father who is in heaven" (Matt. 16:16–17). The Spirit of
the Living God gives us the greatest gift for the healing of
our spiritual sight. It is the ultimate miracle. When we
have doubted or resisted, we are given the gift to say with
assurance, "I believe! Christ is my Lord!" Seeing him we
are ready to see with eyes of faith all of the unlimited
possibilities of what he's ready to do in our lives.

That's what happened to Paul. After a grotesque career
of persecuting the Church, he saw in a blinding vision the
resurrected Lord of the Christians he was harassing and
murdering. The eyes of his heart had been dark and
inhabited by the dragons of hate, fear, anger, and self-justifying religiosity. Then the vision of Christ blinded his
physical eyes. The imperious Paul was led like a helpless
child into Damascus. There he sat in a stupor, the
blindness of his heart now matched by the blindness of his
eyes. It took physical blindness to force him to see how
blind he was in his heart.

The Lord sent Ananias to heal Paul. And Paul received

sight in both his eyes and his heart. The rest of his life was spent opening the heart-eyes of people.

What Paul later wrote to the Ephesians gives us the delineation of the third step of the healing of our heart-eyes. Listen to the promise the Apostle offers: "I do not cease to give thanks for you, remembering you in my prayers, that the God of our Lord Jesus Christ, the Father of glory, may give you a spirit of wisdom and of revelation in the knowledge of him, having the eyes of your hearts enlightened, that you may know what is the hope to which he has called you, what are the riches of his glorious inheritance in the saints, and what is the immeasurable greatness of his power in us who believe, according to the working of his great might which he accomplished in Christ when he raised him from the dead . . ." (Eph. 1:16–20).

That is what's available when the eyes of our hearts are healed. Note the progression: we are given the spirit of wisdom and revelation. That means that we can see things from God's point of view. We will be able to pierce the darkness of life with penetrating vision. We can see what he is doing and wants to happen. Wisdom is deeper than human analysis of the fact. It gives us divine discernment. Wisdom is another description of the indwelling of the Holy Spirit. From within, we will be able to see our lives, other people, circumstances, problems, and the future vividly. In each aspect of reality God will give us a revelation of himself and what we are to do and say. That enlightens the eyes of our hearts.

Through our healed eyes we will see the hope to which we were called, the legacy of unlimited grace available to us because we are the adopted sons and daughters in the eternal family, and the power which will be given to us for each challenge. Hope, inheritance, power. All things are ours.

Do you sense, as I do, what a difference that could make in our daily lives? We don't have to live in the darkness of uncertainty any longer. When others cannot see what's ahead, we will be able to see vividly what the Lord is ready to accomplish. Our hope will be built on the assurance that he will enable whatever he infuses into our imaginations to envision. Our inheritance, which our enlightened heart-eyes enable us to see, is the kind of life revealed in Christ—a life that is ours now! The Son of God has made us heirs along with him. As the Father said, "This is my beloved Son, with whom I am well pleased," he says the same to us. The identical love which was revealed in Christ is put into our hearts. Most of all, the power which raised him from the dead can make our lives a resurrection miracle. We can be raised out of the graves of doubt, discouragement, and despair. Can you see that? Is that your vision for yourself?

The fourth aspect of our healing is the test of all the rest. We will know that we have experienced healing of the eyes of our hearts if we feel a new love for people. We are still partially blind if we are not filled with a passion to share what we have experienced. Who has had his or her eyes of the heart enlightened because of you? The blind are all around us. Who has the Lord appointed for you to heal? We cannot give what we do not have. Spiritual sight is transmitted by those who can see.

The healing of our heart-eyes is only a prayer away. It can happen right now, to you and me. Love is not blind! When our hearts are filled with the Lord's love we will see indeed. The old hymn says what I want to say to the Lord.

> Open my eyes, that I may see
> Glimpses of truth Thou hast for me;
> Place in my hands the wonderful key
> That shall unclasp, and set me free.
>
> Silently now I wait for Thee,
> Ready, my God, Thy will to see;
> Open my eyes, illumine me,
> Spirit divine!

7

How Do You Take The Pressure?

Learning from Christ to Live with Pressure

"I am the witness concerning myself."
John 8:18

ONE SUNDAY AFTERNOON recently, the pressures of life got to me. It had been a busy, demanding morning for me, with two services to lead and an endless stream of people to talk to after the second service. It seemed like everyone needed a piece of me, and by one o'clock there wasn't much left. In the afternoon I had a deadline to meet that demanded intellectual and emotional energy. Tension mounted in the pressure cooker. The members of my family did all they could to help ease the schedule by paving the way and picking up after me. Then, in an unguarded moment, I was unnecessarily sharp and critical of one of my family. My behavior was totally uncalled for. I went off to my speaking engagement to preach about the love of God, knowing I had blown it with someone I love very much.

I think of myself as a person who can live with an immense amount of pressure. My image of composure was shattered. As I traveled to speak, I said to myself, "How can you preach tonight? You need God's love more than the people to whom you are about to preach!" Then the Lord reassured me that often the best preparation to preach is to have a fresh experience of grace for my own needs. He told me to do two things: "Before you speak, make a phone call and say you're sorry for venting your pressure on a person who was only trying to help. Then, tell your audience that what you're going to preach is real to you, and share your fresh discovery of my love in this specific experience!"

I followed orders in both instructions. My apology was accepted graciously. And the most remarkable thing happened with the audience. My vulnerability engendered a warmth of communication. After the message, a businessman came up to me and said, "Thanks for sharing your experience of this afternoon. That happens to me all the time. I would not have imagined it ever happened to you. Your honesty opened me up to hear what you had to say in the rest of your message."

Pressure—we all feel it at times. Pressure comes from having too much to do, poor planning, demands from other people, guilt over things undone. Conflicting schedules for family, job, church, or community put us under time pressure. We are challenged to measure up to our own or others' images, and we feel the disparity between what we want from life and what life extracts from us. Unsatisfied needs, ambition, competition, deadlines—all add to the pressure we feel.

Pressure can be defined as the burden of physical or mental distress. It's oppression, stress, the urgency of matters demanding attention. Pressure is as catching as a virus. The contagion attacks and sucks us into the whirling frenzy of the escalating pace of life. We are either under pressure, the cause of pressure, or conduits of pressure—sometimes all three at the same time.

The other day I had to fill out an application for a club I wanted to join. The questions asked determined my qualifications to belong. It made me think about another kind of club for which most of us qualify eminently—The Order of Pressured Americans. A membership application for that club would probably include some of the following qualifying questions.

1. Do you usually plan more for a day than is humanly possible to accomplish?
2. Are you disappointed with yourself and self-condemnatory when you don't accomplish all you've planned?
3. Are you ever driven by ego needs to take on more than you can handle? Do you feel guilty when you're not under pressure to meet some deadline?
4. Do you ever take worries over unfinished tasks to bed with you?
5. Do you ever feel tired just thinking about all you have to do?
6. Does a feeling of panic ever engulf you over all you want to do and the things others are demanding of you?
7. Have you ever felt your life was out of your control?
8. Do the expectations of life, other people, or your employer ever contradict your own life agenda—what you want from life?
9. Do you feel at times that you are meeting everyone's needs except your own?
10. Do you often feel impatient with people?
11. In the past year, have you felt physically ill with no apparent cause?
12. Have you ever felt you would like to resign from the human race and just do what you wanted for a solid week?
13. Are you ever tied up in knots emotionally? Does your pulse quicken under pressure? Are you ever so churned up you feel short of breath or speak excitedly?
14. Do you lose your temper with little cause? Ever fly off the handle at people?
15. Do you feel anguish over past mistakes? Do they rob the present of enjoyment?

Well, how did you do? Qualify? Some of us should be awarded life memberships. The "order of stress-mess" is not exclusive. What can we do to disqualify ourselves from the questionable distinction? The crucial question of this chapter is, "How do you take the pressure?" I want to ask and answer that question. And I need to accept what I have to say as much as any of you who read it!

Pressure is a life or death question for most of us. A lot of illness comes from a chemical imbalance in the body caused by constant stress and strain. The balance of our chemistry is maintained by three small glands—the two adrenals and the pituitary. The hormones secreted by these little glands affect the body balance. When we are under pressure, anxious, and agitated, the glands have to work overtime to keep balance. Sometimes they can't keep up. We know what happens then: high blood pressure, heart disorder, colds, even the flu. The physical machinery breaks down.

Also, under pressure, we sometimes use physical illness as an escape valve to stop the world and get off for awhile. As one woman said last winter, "Just had my yearly bout with the flu. It was so good to crawl in bed, pull up the covers, and turn the world off for a week!" Years ago, I used to have a bad cold and flu symptoms the first week in January on a regular yearly basis. I was really sick; my internist prescribed the usual remedies, but the cause was more than the midwest winter or an epidemic of flu. When I realized my regular illness always followed a demanding holiday season of special services and responsibilities and learned to pace myself, I was less susceptible physically and emotionally. We dare not be simplistic about real germ disease, but we do need to consider that illness is often a response to pressure.

Anyone who knows me knows that I'm no mechanic. Whenever I have to assemble a piece of equipment that comes with all the parts prepackaged in a crate, I have a difficult time. I dump all the parts out on the floor. There's always a moment of decision: to plunge into the task or read the instructions. Recently I saw a crate which had a bold warning written on the side: "Be sure to read the manufacturer's instructions before assembling this equipment." Then, in smaller letters—"You will not be able to assemble this product unless you follow the instructions step by step." Why is it I always want to try it without the instructions? I usually end up with a pile of extra bolts and screws.

The manufacturer's instructions! You are probably ahead of me in the parable I got out of that. I usually come to the end of my efforts with a poorly constructed article, extra parts, and lots of frustration. Then I have to go back, take it all apart, and start over following the instructions faithfully step by step.

The same is true for our lives. Our manufacturer, creator, and Lord revealed the way he wanted his people to live. When we had messed it all up, he had to come and show us how to live in Jesus Christ. The Word of God, who created us, came to be the blueprint for how we were meant to live the years of our lives, here and forever in eternity. We'll not learn how to live with pressure until we go back to the manufacturer's instructions. When pressure gets to us, it's time to find out what's wrong. We've tried to run our own lives and it hasn't worked. When the pressure builds, and we holler "Help!" he's there to show us where we have overloaded the circuits and shorted out him, other people, and the joy of living. When we consider how Jesus lived with pressure, we discover the secret of how he can help us today.

The Lord knew painfully acute pressure. His family misunderstood him and tried to manipulate him. The disciples resisted at every turn the implications of his ultimate purpose. Impetuous Peter tried to dissuade him from the cross, and the others had their wish dreams for him. The scribes and Pharisees, trying to unsettle him, were a constant source of pressure. The Zealots were bloodthirsty for revolution and wanted to press him into political conflict. The priests in Jerusalem twisted his words and finally engineered his death because he would not conform.

Jesus Christ was determined to be a very different kind of Messiah than Israel expected or demanded. His life was saturated in prophetic scripture and bathed in constant prayer. As Immanuel, "God with us," he modeled life as it can be lived in spite of the demands of people, problems, and perplexities. He contradicted religious provincialism; became a friend of the lost, lonely, and loveless; challenged the values of his time; and went to Calvary to be the sacrifice for the sins of the world.

There were times the crowd almost crushed him in their needs. They pressed in upon him demanding signs, miracles, and physical healing. The immensity of human need was insatiable. Some were magnetically drawn to his healing power; others felt the warmth of his love; all wanted something from him. But few heard or heeded his call to the exciting adventure of the kingdom of God or the cost of discipleship. He frequently retreated to the mountains to pray in order to be replenished for the pressure. He went through the pressures of human existence and daily life to battle the powers of darkness which beset us so that we could cope with pressure triumphantly.

It was during one of the pressure-filled debates with the Pharisees that Jesus gave us the clue to how he lived with pressure. When he claimed to be the Light of the World the leaders said, "You are bearing witness to yourself." What they were implying was that, according to Mosaic regulation, any claim or fact had to be attested by two persons to be accepted as true or validated in a court. Jesus' response is one of his least understood and least appreciated "I am" statements. It contains the secret for pressure. Many of the English translations miss the impact. In the Greek it stands bold and clear. When attacked about his claims, the Lord said, "I am the witness concerning myself" (John 8:18). The Revised Standard Version loses the force of that: "I bear witness to myself." The New American Standard Bible is closer to the Greek: "I am He who bears witness of Myself."

Jesus' "I am" self-disclosure was very incisive. As the Messiah he could bear witness to himself. His life was a self-authenticating witness as Immanuel, God with us. But to satisfy the Mosaic two-witness code, he added, "And the Father who sent me bears witness to me." He could take the disturbing pressure of the leaders because of his sure conviction that he knew his roots and destiny. "Even if I do bear witness to myself, my testimony is true, for I know whence I have come and whither I am going" (v. 14). His assured self-identification within enabled him to withstand the pressure from people. The creative inner pressure offset the external pressure. Intimate union with God was the key.

That gives us five basic aspects of the Lord's answer for how to live with pressure.

The first is: _know who you are_. As long as we are in search of ourselves and our true identity, we will be under pressure. The whims and wishes of people and groups will push us around. We will be pressed in all directions. Until we are clear about our own essential personhood, we will thrash about seeking a clear self-image. We will blame others for pressuring us into molds of their own making, but our vacillation will be a constant invitation to that invasion. Our self-identification must be more than the classification of our sex, status, or profession. We must know who we are by knowing whose we are!

That's what Jesus meant when he said he was the witness concerning himself. It was as if he had said, "I know who I am!" More than being Mary's son, Galilean, Rabbi, Master, or Healer, he knew with certainty and assurance that he was the Son of God, Son of man, Messiah, Savior of the world, the Lamb of God for the sins of all people in all time. He had no doubt. In action and word he proclaimed, "Hold off! I know who I am. Don't try to confuse or distort me. I am who I say I am!" The Lord was faithful to be who he was so that by his power we could realize who we are.

Allow your mind to relish who we are because of Christ. Beneath all the layers of personality or the wrappings of contemporary classifications, we are the children of God, the called and chosen, the beloved, the saints, the cherished treasures, the loved and forgiven, the children of light, the coinheritors with Christ, the new creation. Our minds soar with praise when we consider what Christ called us. We are followers, disciples, friends, beloved, his sheep, pearls and treasures beyond price, salt of the earth, the light of the world. What more do we need to know? That should be enough, but there's more.

Jesus' self-identity was expressed in the words "I and the Father are one" (John 10:30). But he also prayed that we may be one with him and the Father. "That they may all be one; even as thou, Father, art in me, and I in thee, that they also may be in us" (John 17:21). That's the basis of an unswerving security in the midst of pressure. To know what we have been called to be is wonderful, but to have the indwelling power of assurance is even greater.

The first step to combating pressure is to accept the sublime status we have been offered. The Apostle John knew this: "See what love the Father has given us, that we should be called children of God; and so we are. . . . We are God's children now; it does not yet appear what we shall be . . ." (1 John 3:1–2). That's like saying, "We know all we need to know about who we are now—all it can get is better!"

Pressure from outside will be countered by an inner center of security. We can say, "I am God's person. He guides my life; whatever else I am is an expression of my essential calling. I can no more deny who I am than stop eating or breathing." That's the source of courage in pressure.

We are sure targets for pressure until we have that inner creative power to fulfill the reason we were born. There must be a center of calm in us, or we will never be free of external pressure. There are often many selves in us vying for control. We put ourselves under more pressure than people could ever exert. There are drives and needs in us that pull and push. Until these needs are satisfied we will pressure ourselves for achievement, advancement, recognition, and approbation.

We are our own worst enemies when it comes to pressure. We blame other people or our schedules. But usually when we do too much, overload our lives, become frantic, and end up with nervous exhaustion, we ourselves have been the hard, driving taskmasters. Our lives get out of control because we refuse to take charge of the person inside us.

Over the years I have come to a basic theory about pressure in my own life and the lives of others I try to help: no one is a victim! We victimize ourselves long before we allow ourselves to be victims of other people's pressure. No one can use pressure to demean us without — our permission.

If we will not take charge of our destiny, someone else will. Human relationships abhor a vacuum as much as the natural world does. People have an irresistible urge to control other people who seem to be without a clear inner direction. We may complain when this happens to us, but in most cases we have given others the opportunity by not taking charge ourselves.

The only person ultimately reliable to determine our direction is Jesus Christ. He alone knows what's maximum for us. When we yield our nerve centers to him, a unity of purpose begins to emerge. We must take charge, give him charge, or someone in our lives will grasp the reins and drive us in directions we don't want to go.

In that light, consider the <u>second</u> thing we learn from Jesus about how to live with pressure. <u>We must think, *Who* — *are we trying to please—people, ourselves, or God?*</u>

There was no question about that for Jesus. He said he was an adequate witness to himself; then he added that his Father was witness to him. He lived his whole life for the Father, who had provided the solid center of security in the affirming words, "This is my beloved Son, with whom I am well pleased" (Matt. 3:17). Living in total dependence on the direction of God freed him to confront the pressures of people who tried to make him into something very different than what he felt called to be. He called a group of followers who would seek first the kingdom of God, although he knew that eventually the disciples would face debilitating pressure to change and adjust. But he was insistent upon the same single-mindedness from his disciples that he himself displayed. We are invited to join the magnificent procession of people who put God first in their lives. It's the secret of freedom in pressure. But that's dependent on pleasing him first, because he is pleased with us in spite of all we have been or done. I once had a secretary who worked for me because she felt led by the Lord to take the job. Alice Sellers was indefatigable in her work. One day I thanked her profoundly for all she had done for me. "My dear friend," she replied, "I'm not doing it for you! I am here on orders from the Lord."

Alice felt no need to please me. She was working for the Lord and was playing her part on the stage of life for him. Paul would have affirmed that. He said, "And whatever you do, in word or deed, do everything in the name of the Lord Jesus, giving thanks to God the Father through him" (Col. 3:17).

Until Christ is securely in charge of our lives, our insecurity will make us vulnerable, hungry for other people's approval. Our need to be loved, accepted, and approved will drive us to comply with what people want us to be and do. We can blame others, but the blame lies with ourselves. People climb on our backs because we have provided them the saddle and the stirrups and the sharp spurs.

We all admire people who know who they are and where they are going, whose inner nerve center gives them a clear eye and a firm jaw. They are selective of what they do on the basis of a clear agenda. There is no vacillation or equivocation. If what we need from them is in keeping with what they know is best for them, they will do it; if not, they can refuse without self-incrimination or fear of our rejection.

Christ enables that healthy kind of self-love. As we are loved by him, we can love ourselves. This creative self-preservation comes from knowing our value to him and therefore to ourselves. Self-interest is not sin! It's caring deeply for one of God's precious persons—ourselves. If we don't believe we are worthy of care and preservation, we need a profound experience of Christ's love for us.

The third thing we learn from our Lord about how to live with pressure follows naturally. After we know who we are and whom we want to please, *we can know what we are to do*. Because Jesus knew who he was, he knew what he had come to do. That's always the result of knowing the true person inside us.

Listen to the Lord's bold assertion: "I know whence I have come and whither I am going" (John 8:14). Everything he said and did was consistent with his purpose on Calvary. We are told that he set his face to Jerusalem near the end of his ministry; his heart had been set there from the beginning. He was determined because of an inner direction. Note John's analysis of why Jesus took the role of a servant and washed the disciples' feet on the night before he was crucified. "Jesus, knowing that the Father had given all things into his hands, and that he had come from God and was going to God, rose from supper, laid aside his garments, and girded himself with a towel. Then he poured water into a basin, and began to wash the disciples' feet" (John 13:3–5). Note the progression: Jesus did what he did because he knew where he came from and where he was going.

That means everything for us and our pressures. Knowing that we came from God and will return to him puts our pressures into perspective. If our destiny and destination are settled, we can relax and enjoy life. There is no panic in heaven. Our overpressured lives are sure signs that we have taken on more than God intended and that we are fulfilling needs other than the need to please our Lord. Our assurance of belonging to God because we have accepted his love and given him control provides several necessary antidotes to pressure. We can be daring to do what he wants. There will be an incisiveness about our choices. And we will feel a liberating release from the demands of people and life in general.

The fourth aspect of Jesus' secret of living with pressure is *to be what we want to be*. Much of the pressure of life is the result of stifling our freedom to do and be what we want. The key is discovering what our Lord wants and daring to do it with abandonment and joy. If we are forced to do things we don't want to do, it may be that we were never intended to do them. We may need to find out what the Lord intended. We can be sure of this: he will give us new heart for the things we don't happen to like to do, if it is part of his strategy for us to do them. Many of us live with a love/hate feeling about responsibilities and relationships—a push/pull that results in pressure.

But wait, you say. Not all of life is in keeping with the law of creative self-interest. We live in families in which others may not share our agendas; we work where our self-fulfillment is not the primary concern of our superiors. Now we're getting to the raw nerve of conflicting needs and desires. Many people live with hidden agendas. Because we do not expose who we are and where we are going, we often communicate an outer compliance with the direction or plans of others.

It's a perplexing problem for marriage. Often the need for security or the flight from loneliness prompts people to get married to someone who has a very different set of goals. Fear of rejection often causes them to hedge their bets, hide their real desires, and end up in marriages that are filled with pressure to comply to a mate's idea of what's important or should be done with the resources of time, energy, and money—all because they either didn't know or were too afraid to state their vision of what they need and want. That more than anything else accounts for the fact that in California there are as many divorces as marriages in any one year—in some years, more!

A man came to see me recently who said that he had discovered he and his wife were pulling in different directions. "She puts me under tremendous pressure!" he said frantically. "I'm just not the man she thought I was. And I want to tell you she sure kept her real self and desires hidden all through courtship and the early years of marriage! I don't believe in divorce. So what am I going to do—give in or give up?"

Give in or give up! Those are the two obvious alternatives to pressures that face us. But there's a third: find out who you are and dare to be that authentically. The only hope for this man's marriage—or any marriage—is for two people to find a common agenda for life. Only Christ can provide one that's adequate. When two people love him more than they love each other, they will be able to love each other more than they ever imagined. We are all self-willed and want to control relationships. But when our wills are committed to Christ we begin to want what he wants. It's the beginning of joy and bliss when a husband and wife both want the Lord's will for their individual and married lives. That's when "one plus one plus one equals one!" as one of my beloved predecessors, Louis H. Evans, Sr., used to put it.

The same is true for our work. My experience of searching for and hiring professional clergy has shown that when what God has guided me to want to accomplish in an area of our church's life is the same thing as what he has guided a person to want to do in life, the working relationship is sheer joy! If not, friction, unhappiness, and multiplied pressure result for all involved.

Life is too short to spend working for a company or person with values and goals irreconcilably opposed to ours. Here again we need to be clear about what we want. If we can state that clearly and enumerate our goals, an employer can make a decision about whether what we want to do is what he wants done. Problems come when we try to reorganize a place of work around our own goals, when we did not make those clear from the beginning.

A choice to take a job which is not what we ultimately want is okay only if we know what we are doing. If it puts bread on the table or provides needed income for other aspects of our agenda for life, that's fine. But we should not blame our employer because he or she has pressured us to do something we don't want or like to do.

It is our own responsibility to meet and know the person inside us, to give that person over to the lordship

of Christ, to allow the Lord to reshape the hopes and
dreams of our lives and then get those hopes out in the
open for others to see. We owe it to ourselves and others
to clarify what is no longer negotiable for us because of
our commitment to Christ. Dishonesty about that, or the
debilitating duality of being one thing outside and hiding
another inside, will cause more pressure on us than all our
friends, employers, or loved ones in life's intimate relationships could ever produce.

I am convinced that many of us become depressed
because we do not have the raw courage to discover and
declare who we are and then to demand the respect of
others for our direction.

I have a friend who is habitually under financial
pressure. He compulsively enters into large investments
and "get rich" schemes which consistently fail or make less
than what he anticipated. I've tried to help him realize
that he has some kind of self-destructive wish to be in
financial crisis. He says he can't say no; he's like an
alcoholic who has never learned that he cannot drink. The
anguish of pressure has become a familiar security. He's
not happy unless he is on the brink of disaster.

We laugh at that, but then wonder what it is that we
habitually say yes to that contributes to a pressure-filled
life for us. Christ can toughen us up to that kind of self-
gratification. He says, "Get tough with yourself so you can
be firm with people and their demands!"

All through the Lord's confrontation with the Pharisees
we feel a kind of holy toughness about his response to
their pressure to change and mold him. He exemplified
his own admonition that our yes be yes, and our no, no
(Matt. 5:37). It's a great sign of maturity to be able to say
either decisively. It takes courage to say no to some of
life's opportunities because, good as they may be, they
may not be maximum for us.

This sanctified selectivity is our escape valve for the
build-up of pressure. But it requires prayer and listening
to what the Lord says to us. If we ask him to help us deal

with pressure we can be sure of his toughness when we need it. Our Lord will help us want what he wants for us. We can trust our thoughts and feelings if we have surrendered them to him. He will use them to help us know and feel what's best and will not create pressure.

If we are in the flow of the Spirit we will have a feeling of rightness or wrongness about certain alternatives. This capacity should not be misused to insinuate the Lord's blessing on everything we want to do. He never denies the Ten Commandments, his own message, or the fundamental law of love. Anything we want to do that we could not do with an inner assurance of his approval is not creative for us and will add pressure. If it cannot be done in the open with no fear of exposure, we can be sure it will create inner tension. But if those basic tests are satisfied, we can live with courageous confidence, saying yes to some things and no to others.

The final aspect of Jesus' prescription for pressure is the one that makes all the others possible. If we know who we are, know whom we want to please, know the purpose and plan of our lives, honestly state what we want because we know what the Lord wants, *then we can receive the equalizing power of his indwelling Spirit to combat pressure.* We will receive the gift of serenity and peace in the midst of life's pressure.

That means several liberating things for our daily lives. Life can be put into day-tight compartments. We can do each day what the Lord wills according to his agenda for us. Mark Twain said, "Never put off to tomorrow what you can do the day after tomorrow." Bad advice! I say, do today what needs to be done today in a relaxed way. Dare to be maximum in each task, working with excellence. Then allow God to work while you sleep. We become harried when we take to bed the unfinished tasks or worries of the day and the unsolved problems of tomorrow.

Receiving the power of the Spirit to combat pressure also means we can follow the Lord's timing. He was never in a hurry. Someone said that the shortest duration of time is between the moment a traffic light changes from red to green and the guy behind you blows his horn. So many of us are racing towards uncertain destinations at breakneck speed. The Lord's warning is: slow down or break down. Some people pride themselves in saying, "I may wear out but I will never rust out." Neither is a good alternative. There's always enough time to do what the Lord wants us to do.

Also, Christ's indwelling presence produces a profound peace. Isaiah was right: "Thou dost keep him in perfect peace, whose mind is stayed on thee, because he trusts in thee" (Isa. 26:3).

Paul encouraged us to have the mind of Christ. The word *mind* can also mean disposition or attitude. We can have more than the Lord's guidance; we can have his disposition when he lives in us as the equalizer of pressure. Viktor Frankl wisely said, "Everything can be taken from a man but one thing: the last of the human freedoms—to choose one's attitude in any given circumstance." How true! And yet acquiring the Lord's attitude requires listening to his inner voice. We need a quiet time each day and then frequently during the day to see things from the Lord's perspective. Then we can ask him to take charge of things and show us how to act and react.

All of this is sound biblical advice. If we follow it, we will be on the way to peace in pressure. But there will also be times when we will fall back into an old pressure pattern, as I did that Sunday afternoon. But we can know it and realize that we were never intended to live that way, confess what caused the pressure, and amend what we did to others and ourselves. The moment we admit that we are under pressure, the Lord is there ready to help us. Our struggle will become a stepping stone!

8

I've Decided to Live!

The Creative Will
to Live

*"If you do not believe that I am,
you shall die in your sins."*
John 8:24

I OPENED THE LETTER cautiously. The familiar stationery and return address told me it was from an old friend. I knew he had been going through a difficult time, and I was very concerned about what I might find in the letter.

The last time I had seen my friend, we had talked at length about his life. He had seemed tired, out of steam, completely lacking his usual enthusiasm for living. I was alarmed over his negativism about himself and the future. Though he was at the prime of his life, the problems he was facing had stirred up self-doubt inside him. Life had become a hassle. Challenges he had tackled easily before now seemed insurmountable.

Most disturbing of all was his lack of verve and vitality. The civil war inside him had drained off his creative energy. He was at war with himself. Physical ailments were blown out of proportion, even though his doctor had assured him he was in good health. He feared a heart attack, and talked about the possibility in a way that made me wonder whether the danger he feared was not an eventuality he desired.

Though he was a member of a church, his rather traditional faith had not given him the hope he needed. At our last meeting, we had talked about God's love for him and the transforming power of faith. After hours of conversation about how to surrender our wills to the Lord and trust him with our future, I had said, "Sooner or later, you've got to decide whether or not you want to live the rest of your life!" He had promised he would write and tell me his decision.

Now you can understand why I opened my friend's letter with such anxious anticipation. The body of the letter contained only four words and an exclamation point, but it was all that I needed to know.

> Dear Lloyd:
> I've decided to live!
> Dick

I was overjoyed and filled with gratitude. But then I began to think about all the people I know who are like my friend Dick. The world is filled with them—people who have never made the basic decision to live the rest of their lives.

What about you? Have you ever decided to live? "Decided to what?!" you exclaim. "So who's got a choice?" We all have. And some never make it.

That's the problem Jesus confronted all through his ministry. Have you ever wondered, as I have, why people resisted his message and rejected his life-affirming ministry? They had never made a basic decision to live. This fact prompted one of Jesus' most awesome and dynamic "I am" self-disclosures: "You will die in your sins unless you believe that I am . . ." (John 8:24).

Note the context. That startling statement was made to the Pharisees who challenged the authority of his ministry. They were the religious purists of the time; their lives were morally impeccable. A sinner in their eyes was a non-Hebrew, or one whose behavior had prompted excommunication from the synagogue. Tax collectors in collusion with Rome and those who broke the moral code were put in the same condemned category. And yet Jesus called the Pharisees sinners, and warned them about dying in their sins. What did he mean?

Sin for Jesus meant more than wrong behavior. It meant an unwillingness to live—now and forever. The Greek word *hamartia* means to miss the mark. It comes from an archer's word for sending an arrow which misses the target. The Lord's use of this word for the Pharisees implies that, although they fulfilled the law and followed their endless multiplicity of rules and regulations, they had totally missed the reason they were born. Jesus was God with them and they rejected his offer of eternal life. They were spiritually dead because of their resistance to life, and they would die physically in that condition.

Essentially, sin is separation from God. An intimate relationship with him enables us to live life abundantly. Death cannot destroy that relationship. Our inner self—mind, emotion, and will—lives on after death. We all live forever—with or without God. Death is only a transition in living. If we reject his overtures and rebel against him in this life, we will spend eternity separated from him.

In that light we can understand what Jesus meant in his "I am" statement. "I am God with you. If you do not accept who I am, you cannot receive the gift of life I offer you right now. If you persist, the condition of your lives will extend into eternity."

We can only imagine the shock treatment that was. He said that not only were they sinners, but that they had no hope of life after death unless they accepted Jesus as the Messiah. The staggering blow was that rejection of Christ would spell their rejection at the time of physical death.

We gain a deeper understanding of what Jesus wanted for these Pharisees from his conversation with Nicodemus (John 3:1–21). Jesus did not recommend that the Hebrew leader needed to live a more moral life, or try to do better, or be more religious. When the revered religious leader came to Christ one night, the Lord told him that the deepest need in his life was to be born anew. The words

mean born from above, implying the birth of a relationship with God.

Nicodemus was alarmed. "How can a man be born
when he is old? Can he enter a second time into his
mother's womb and be born?" (v. 4). Jesus' response was
to tell him that there is a physical and a spiritual birth.
"That which is born of the flesh is flesh, and that which is
born of the Spirit is spirit. Do not marvel that I said to
you, 'You must be born anew'" (vv. 6–7).

Nicodemus' problem was that he did not know God
personally. "How can this be?" he asked with agitated
consternation. Jesus' answer was a crystallized statement
of hope: "For God so loved the world that he gave his only
Son, that whoever believes in him should not perish but
have eternal life. For God sent the Son into the world, not
to condemn the world, but that the world might be saved
through him. He who believes in him is not condemned;
he who does not believe is condemned already, because he
has not believed in the name of the only Son of God" (vv.
9, 16–18).

Jesus came that we might have eternal life—a life of joy,
peace, and power in a union with God which death has
absolutely no power to end. Scriptural and historical
evidence indicates that Nicodemus accepted the gift. He
made a decision to live and experienced a spiritual
rebirth. Subsequently he became a follower of Jesus,
spoke in his defense during his ministry, helped in his
burial, and became a leader in the early church after the
resurrection. Unlike the other Pharisees, he did not die in
the separation of sin.

We wonder what made the difference between Nicodemus and the Pharisees to whom Jesus gave his "I am"
warning. That presses us to question why some of us
refuse and others of us accept the wondrous offer of the
abundant life in fellowship with our Lord, now and for
eternity. The reason is that many of us have either lost or
stifled the will to live. And Jesus says, "Unless you believe
that I am you will die in your sins." What does that mean
for you and me today?

First of all, it tells us of the *plight of our human nature.*
The more I come to know and understand about our
inner selves, the more aware I am that there are two basic
instincts in all of us: the instinct of creativity and the
instinct of destruction. The capacity to affirm life and to
negate it. Within us is the power to preserve life and to
prevent life. We can each be our own best friend or our
worst enemy. To love or to hate. There is in our psyche
the will to live and the will to die.

This is not how God created us or intended us to be. He
made us with the instinct of creativity and the will to live.
But mankind rebelled and fractured the purpose God
had for us. Jesus clearly identified the instinct of destruction with the power of evil. Paul called Satan the "De-
stroyer." Our minds and hearts become the battleground
of the warfare between God and evil. And Jesus came to
defeat the power of evil and to set us free. But until we are
born again, start life all over through a total commitment
of our lives to our Lord, the instinct of destruction can
dominate us. We are part of the dead and dying, fallen
creation. The will to live is debilitated.

When the instinctive scale is tipped by training, conditioning, or circumstances, we can turn against ourselves.
Pogo was right. "We have met the enemy and they are
us!" You and me. We negate our potential, resist the
enjoyment of life, hold ourselves in check by self-criticism.
The destructive tendency gains dominance over the creative will to live fully. We become pitted against ourselves
and against a joyous affirmation of life. We commit
spiritual suicide, inch by inch.

That explains the Pharisees, and the Pharisee in each of
us. They were controlled by the spirit of destruction.
That's why they were so hostile to Jesus. It's the same
reason so many people refuse to take Jesus' offer of life
seriously. If our will to live is crippled, his insistence that
we be born again must be resisted.

But this also explains why so many church people,
traditional Christians, do not live the adventure of positive faith. Many of us have drifted into the church or were

conditioned in childhood that religion is a basic necessity to a proper life. But our will to live has never been converted. That's why some people who are Christians do not model the affirmation and encouragement Christ came to make possible.

One of the greatest needs in the organized church is the rebirth of its members. We believe in Christ but have not allowed him to transform our instinctive nature, which is a part of our human heritage but untouched by the new creation in Christ. When we speak of the transformation of personality and character, we mean the reorientation of unconscious behavior tendencies that are rooted in the core of our nature.

There's a moving story of Forian, the great French painter. He was seriously ill and consulted a team of highly trained specialists. They all found little to explain his illness. A cardiovascular specialist said his heart was in excellent shape; the lung authority declared his lungs to be fine; the kidney internist judged his kidneys were working properly, and so on until Forian broke in: "Then gentlemen, it seems that I am dying in perfect health!"

What a grim self-prognosis. Dying in perfect health. Or put it another way—dying while we are alive. Forian was ill because he had lost his will to live. He had never decided to live the rest of his life. He was being controlled by the instinctive power of destruction: he was part of the living dead.

The more we learn of the holistic approach to health, the more we discover and are convinced that the will to live has profound impact in healing and health. It explains why some people are immune to some diseases, and why some recover from illness so quickly and effectively. Below the level of conscious thought, there is a dynamic desire to live. Some people are ill because sickness is still the most acceptable expression of the urge to destroy. Some who could not abide the thought of suicide are intent on the destruction of their own lives because they have lost any real reason for staying alive. This is the reason that sickness so often follows a personal tragedy or shock to the ego. The instinct of destruction has risen to dominant power.

A few years ago, I was part of a professional team battling for a woman's life. The internist, psychiatrist, and a score of specialists worked together to try to find out why this woman was chronically troubled by one sickness after another. The more we penetrated into the cause, the more we were aware that the woman had made an inner, instinctive decision that her life was all over. She had raised her children, had been widowed a few years before, and had been rejected in a love affair she had hoped would bring new joy to her lonely life. Until she discovered a reason to live, she got progressively worse. A decisive encounter with Jesus Christ finally reversed the process. She experienced his unqualified love for her. That gave her the courage to accept the future as a friend.

The same is true of the emotional realm. We all know grim, loveless, cold people. They resist the healing, satisfying power of love. The terrible twist of our natures is that we can negate our feelings and starve the people around us as a result of emotional self-destructiveness. We become judgmental, critical, and reserved. We live as if joy had gone out of style.

Ever wondered why some people are so negative about life? The instinct of destruction has engendered a self-hate which will not permit an enjoyment of life and its delights. The will to live with abandonment has been smothered by a pervasive self-negation.

The people around this kind of person become the targets of niggardly selfishness. Selfishness is not putting ourselves first, but last. It's refusing to allow ourselves, and subsequently others, the pleasure of self-satisfaction. We willfully do those things which deny our needs and the needs of the people around us.

But there is no more tragic manifestation of the lack of the will to live than in the spiritual realm. We often think that the reason some people resist the Christian faith is that they have theological or philosophical problems. We think that some are too self-centered or proud to accept the love and forgiveness of Christ as the Lord of their lives. Not at all! Anyone who hears the gospel offer of grace, acceptance, power to live fully, and freedom from death, and refuses to accept it, is a person who is dominated by an instinctive death wish. Why be troubled with an offer to live now and forever, if your nature is bent on self-destruction? That's why the people who responded to Christ during his ministry were people who basically yearned to live. The infection of self-hate had not gained control of them.

But again we must ask, "Why is it that there are so many Christians who do not have a lively excitement in life?" Why are the most critical, hostile, and frustrated people among those who call themselves Christians? It is because to them Christianity has become merely a religion, and not an invitation to life. If religion becomes little more than a composite of "oughts" and incriminations for failure, it refortifies the instinct of destruction.

Jesus did not come to fashion one more religion, but to set people free to live in love with God, themselves, other people, and life itself. But many of us are like the caterpillar who observed a butterfly and said, "You'd never get me up in a thing like that!" Resistance to the possibility of new life, rooted in our instinctive will to destroy, keeps us bound in death throes while we are alive.

That leads us to the second thing Jesus' "I am" declaration means to us: *the permanence of death.* Death is the dramatic demarcation which determines the permanence of the spiritual condition in which we are living. Jesus' warning, "If you do not believe that I am you will die in your sins," simply means that sin causes death now, and that if we die in a state of sin we will spend eternity in that condition. We must hear Jesus' admonition with two ears—one for now and one for beyond the grave. It requires bifocal vision to see the immediate results of sin and the ultimate result after our physical demise.

Sin is the blatant refusal to live. If we have refused to know God now, why should we want to know him after death? The ditty on a gravestone sums it up, "Don't bother me now; don't bother me never; I want to be dead forever and ever."

Jesus' "I am" statement is that many will have that wish fulfilled, unless they believe that he is who he says he is. George MacDonald knew the assurance that contradicts that gravestone; he said, "I came from God, and I am going back to God, and I won't have any gap in the middle of my life."

Finally, Jesus' "I am" proclamation offers a *promise:* "Unless you believe." Unless! That's not just a warning; it's a promise of life—the magnificent possibility. "Unless" offers the positive side of a terrible warning; it implies, *"If you believe, you shall all live!"* But that requires radical liberation of our instinct and will to live. Jesus meets us eye to eye. Do you want to live? Would you like to be free of the negative resistance to life? You can!

But how does belief in him assure us of life? Believing in Christ means more than conceptual cognition. It implies relationship, wholeness, assurance. When we believe in Christ, we experience a personal relationship with him. He comes to live in our conscious and our subconscious lives. His work begins in the transformation of our instincts. The will to live is set free and nurtured; it becomes the controlling factor in our conscious thoughts. Conversion is nothing less than that: we are transformed from having the will to destroy to having the will to live.

Belief enables union with Christ. We become recipients of his deathless life. The assurance is that physical death will have no more power over us than it did over him. The sin of separation is past. Eternity is open wide!

One of the best illustrations of how this worked is in the life of another Pharisee, the Apostle Paul. Here is an example of a religious man with a rampant instinct of destruction. His own self-hate and angry pride made him the ambitious persecutor of the Christians. Then his encounter with the resurrected Lord himself resulted in an invasion of love in his deepest nature. The will to live was revived and released. A profound fellowship with

Christ grew. His death passion was replaced with Christ passion. All through his new life he said, "For me to live is Christ!"

Later in his Christian life, Paul sat down to put into words the secret nature of his rebirth experience. He explained it in his recapitulation theory. When we receive Christ as Savior, we die to ourselves. That means that our will to destroy or limit our control of our life is surrendered to Christ. He then takes up residence in us. We become partners with the Lord in resurrection living. Every day is Easter. We die and are raised up. Physical death is no more to be feared than going to sleep; our essential self is now inextricably united with Christ. At death, we are raised out of our bodies into complete and unfettered fellowship with the Lord in heaven.

Look at the triumphant good news of Romans 6. "Do you not know that all of us who have been baptized into Christ Jesus were baptized into his death?" (v. 3). That means that accepting Christ as our Lord enables the death of both our self-dominance and the pervasive influence of death's destructive instinct. Paul goes on: "We were buried therefore with him by baptism into death, so that as Christ was raised from the dead by the glory of the Father, we too might walk in newness of life" (v. 4). The will to live is liberated! "For if we have been united with him in a death like his, we shall certainly be united with him in a resurrection like his. We know that our old self [the instinct of death] was crucified with him so that the sinful body [our human nature bound by the urge to debilitate and limit] might be destroyed, and we might no longer be enslaved to sin [the negation of life]. . . . But if we have died with Christ, we believe that we shall also live with him [but if not now, never!]. . . . The death he died he died to sin, once for all, but the life he lives he lives to God. So you also must consider yourselves dead to sin and alive to God in Christ Jesus" (vv. 5–6, 8, 10–11).

But don't stop there! All of this is available right now. Paul soars in excitement, and now gives specific implications: "Let not sin therefore reign in your mortal bodies, to make you obey their passions. Do not yield your members to sin as instruments of wickedness, but yield yourselves to God as men who have been brought from death to life" (vv. 12–13).

The secret of new birth is further revealed by Paul in his letter to the Ephesians. This passage reveals the same insight into the healing of our instinctive nature. "And you he made alive, when you were dead through the trespasses and sins in which you once walked, following the course of this world, following the prince of the power of the air, the spirit that is now at work in the sons of disobedience. . . . But God, who is rich in mercy, out of the great love with which he loved us, even when we were dead through our trespasses, made us alive together with Christ (by grace you have been saved), and raised us up with him, and made us sit with him in the heavenly places in Christ Jesus. . . . For by grace you have been saved through faith; and this is not your own doing, it is the gift of God" (2:1–2, 4–6, 8).

There it is! Becoming and growing as a Christian means passing from death to life.

How can we be sure it's happened to us? Here's a series of tests. Do you have a freedom to live without resistance and reserve? If you were to die physically today, are you sure that your death would be nothing more than a transition in living? Have you ever made a complete and unreserved surrender of your negative instinct of destruction? Do you have a positive excitement about living? Do you see the potential and not the problems of people and perplexities? Is joy the vibrant emotion of your heart? Can you love yourself and others deeply, warmly? Are you free of death?

To be sure of all this, I want to invite you to your own funeral. Picture your old self in the coffin—the old person intent on self-limitation and negative resistance to life. This is the moment of the death of death for you. Let go of your death grip on life, of all the debilitating patterns. Then picture the lowering of that old self into the grave.

Gone from sight and feeling forever. Now invite Christ to live his resurrection life in you. Picture your new person motivated by the will to live. How will you act? What will you do? How will you express Christ's love? Hold the picture. You have been born anew! D. T. Miles once said, "The resurrection that awaits us beyond physical death will be the glorious consummation of the risen life we already have in Christ!"

Someone once said, "Don't take life so seriously; you will never make it out alive." Not true! We will live forever. But how we live now determines where, how, and with whom. If we have come alive in Christ now, then we need not take life too seriously. We will live each day with gusto and joy.

I leave you with the same challenge I gave my friend Dick. "Sooner or later, you're going to have to decide whether you want to live the rest of your life!" Before and after death. What keeps you from living fully? Now's the moment to decide to live. Can you say those four victorious words, "I've decided to live!"? Why not?!

9

Freedom from Guilt

The Cross and Our Feelings of Guilt

"When you have lifted up the Son of man,
then you will know that I am . . ."
John 8:28

A VERY HUMOROUS THING happened to me on the way to work one Monday morning. I stopped at an intersection and waited for a green light. While I sat there, for what seemed to be an interminably long time, my thoughts were enveloped in the busy week ahead of me. I was caught up in the Monday morning muddle, feeling an uneasy frustration over things not completed from the week before. There were letters to write, calls to make, people to see, tasks to be tackled. This week was going to be different, I promised myself.

Then suddenly I was aware of the woman in the car next to mine. She was very agitated and animated as she talked, shaking her head and finger vigorously for emphasis. Someone was getting a stern "what for." The ludicrous thing about it was that she was alone in her car. She was talking to herself!

When she caught my eye, she was very embarrassed. Her face got red and she seemed terribly flustered. She motioned for me to roll down my car window. Just as the light turned green and our cars moved into the intersection, she shouted across the empty seat that contained the imaginary person getting her tongue-lashing. "Sorry!" she chagrined, "I was giving myself a good talking to. It's Monday morning and I was just whipping myself into shape!"

With that she stepped on the gas and sped down the street ahead of me. I was left to wonder whether whipping herself into shape made a difference in her week. Then I realized that in a less animated way I had been doing the same thing in my inner conversation with myself about the week ahead. Monday mornings sometimes require that, often the other days of the week as well. And for some people, it's a twenty-four-hour-a-day, seven-day-a-week assignment. We become demanding taskmasters over ourselves.

The other day, I was standing in a long line waiting to get a basket full of groceries checked out in the grocery store. A couple in front of me was having a heated argument. The man fussed at his wife continuously, hassling her about possibly forgetting something and about the cost of the groceries in their basket. Why had she done this, and why hadn't she done that?—his cranky tone communicated a fussy, negative attitude toward his wife that I suspected involved more than the groceries. Finally the woman had had enough. In a loud voice which echoed around the store and attracted everyone's attention, she retorted, "Nag, nag, nag! Albert, all you do is nag!"

Nobody likes a nag. Such a person's frustration with life causes terrible friction; he or she is difficult to live with, work with, or work for. But what if the worst nags in our lives live in our own skins? Can anything be worse than being the target of a relentless self-renovation program which we never quite pull off to our own satisfaction?

Our dissatisfaction with ourselves usually involves more than the "Monday muddle" or the grocery bill. What we do or fail to do, what we remember about past failures, unmet goals, and unfulfilled expectations—all add to our self-depreciating attitudes. We live our lives self-sentenced in what I call the guilted cage, and the sweet bird of life is imprisoned. Our creative, life-affirming, fun-loving, productive selves are negated by our feelings of guilt.

Are you ever troubled, disquieted, or haunted by guilt feelings? We all are at times. For some, it becomes a constant way of relating to ourselves, a learned response to reality. The purpose of this chapter is to examine what guilt is, what causes it, and what God can do about it.

Guilt is a feeling of self-judgment. It's conditional approval of ourselves, the God-given capacity of self evaluation gone sour. It may be rooted in a specific wrong act or failure, but more often it's a floating dis-ease caused by dis-grace—uneasiness fostered in a lack of gracious acceptance of ourselves. It's the restless disapproval of self which thrashes about in us looking for tangible evidence of our shortcomings. That kind of guilt is our particular focus in this chapter. What causes this feeling?

There are three people living inside all of us—the ideal self, the performing self, and the punitive self. We all have some image of the person we "ought" to be or long to be. That person is a composite of our values and vision, goals and hopes, training and conditioning. The conscience has assimilated the beliefs, customs, and patterns of parents, family, and society; its task is to get us to live up to our ideal self.

But often our ideal, though laudable, is difficult to maintain. Our performing self is an ever present contradiction; very few of us measure up to our own expectations. It's then that the punitive self swings into action; we assume the responsibility of punishing ourselves for being less than we think we are capable of being. Our punitive self nags the performing self, trying to whip it into shape. The result is a feeling of guilt.

There's an inner child of the past in all of us. The same fears we had as children influence our adult lives. If we sensed as children that love and approval were dependent on our performances, we place similar conditions on ourselves in adulthood. The fears of our growing years become the settled condition of our souls. We fear punishment, rejection, and alienation, and this anguishing trinity of incrimination remains in us long after we have grown to maturity and left home.

The other day I talked to a woman who is a new Christian, but who complained that she did not feel the joy others talked about as a result of their faith. The more we talked, the more aware I was of the fact that her punitive self controlled her feelings. She felt she had never quite satisfied her mother's expectations. In an unguarded moment of self-criticism, she suddenly stopped and began to laugh. "You know, I sounded just like my mother when I said that!" Her mother had been dead for fifteen years.

A successful businessman confided in me that he was never free of his father's constant question, "Are you movin' up, boy?" He realized that his lust for wealth and power came from a need to prove to his dad that he was of worth because of his accomplishments.

A college student said that his deepest longing was to please his parents with good grades. "So far, I pulled it off. But what do I do if I get a 'B'?" That's the nerve-racking pressure. The problem will not go away even after a summa cum laude graduation.

But before we are too hard on parents, we need to empathize with the performance plight. It is easy for parents to get their own need to succeed entangled with their relationship with their children. Often a parent's approval of himself or herself is inseparably related to the extent that the children meet the parent's standards. And it's not easy to develop creative motivation in a child without engendering guilt feelings.

Furthermore, the habit pattern of guilt and self-recrimination does not come from parents alone. Our performance-oriented culture is always ready to refortify our lowered self-evaluations. The message which is communicated subtly, but which shouts in our hearts, is "You are of value only if you produce." Soon we are saying it to ourselves.

Organized religion and the institutional church often

do little to help. Rules and regulations, intended to develop character and guide conduct, can instead promote feelings of guilt and failure. Robert Louis Stevenson once said, "I've been to church and I'm not depressed!" Why should that have been an unusual delight? He was pleased with a one-time contradiction; the "ought oriented" religion of his church usually depressed him.

Sometimes organized religion not only fosters but perpetuates guilt; the ideal self is extolled and the punitive self refortified. I once overheard a woman's comment about a sermon: "It was a great message. I feel so guilty." Her standard of great preaching was a sermon that made her feel bad about herself. The church can often be more of an institutional parent than the center of creative, guilt-free motivation.

The result is that many good church people are riddled with feelings of guilt. They are filled with guilt if they work too hard or don't work hard enough. Life's responsibilities become goads of guilt. There's always something to be said, done, or accomplished. And when these tasks are neglected, restless feelings of guilt come home to roost. As one man said, "When I'm at work, I feel guilty about not being home more; when I'm at home, I'm haunted by unfinished tasks at the office."

Guilt is the virulent poison which pollutes the joy of life. Parents feel guilty over their kids; kids feel guilty over disappointing their parents. Unanswered letters or phone calls distress most of us. Life piles up. Our material wealth haunts us when we think about the less fortunate. Some of us feel guilty about having too much money; others about unpaid bills.

What is it for you? What has the capacity of stirring your feelings of guilt? The other afternoon there was a religious fanatic walking up and down Gower Street here in Hollywood. His prophetic message, repeated ad nauseam, was, "You are guilty. Repent!" I overheard one man laugh and say, "Who told him about me?"

Get beneath the surface of most anyone and you will find turbulent feelings of guilt. True guilt for unconfessed failures and sins. False guilt over the "oughts" of our own and others' compulsive judgments. All guilt nonetheless. What can be done to heal our guilt and set us free to live?

The cross of Jesus Christ is our only hope. The Lord's incisive "I am" statement about his death gives us the healing hope: "When you have lifted up the Son of man, then you will know that I am" (John 8:28). That is Christ's prediction of the cross and the power it would release for the healing of guilt. Jesus knew why he had come. He was to die for the sins of the world. His whole life was leading to the cross. In this "I am" disclosure he affirmed the purpose and plan of God for the redemption of the world. In substance he was saying, "When you do your worst, God will give his best. When I am crucified, then you will know that I am God."

The Lord's understanding of his messianic task was based on the writings of the Old Testament prophets. The charter of his ministry and mission was clearly given in Isaiah 53:4–6.

> Surely he has borne our griefs
>   and carried our sorrows;
> yet we esteemed him stricken,
>   smitten by God, and afflicted.
> But he was wounded for our transgressions,
>   he was bruised for our iniquities;
> upon him was the chastisement that made us whole,
>   and with his stripes we are healed.
> All we like sheep have gone astray;
>   we have turned every one to his own way;
> and the Lord has laid on him
>   the iniquity of us all.

Isaiah's prophecy was fulfilled in every detail. Christ went to the cross, not as a helpless victim, but as a sacrifice for the sin of the world. The Lord's death was expressed perfectly in every aspect of the sacrificial system of ancient Israel. Just as the sacrificial lamb was slain each year on the high altar of the temple, so too Jesus, the Lamb of God, was slain for our sins:

> He was oppressed, and he was afflicted,
>   yet he opened not his mouth;
> like a lamb that is led to the slaughter,
>   and like a sheep that before its shearers is dumb,
> so he opened not his mouth (v. 7).

John the Baptist was awesomely prophetic when he beheld Jesus and said, "Behold, the Lamb of God, who takes away the sin of the world!" (John 1:29).

The only way to experience the depth meaning of the cross is to look at it through the loving eyes of God. He had created mankind for fellowship with himself, to receive his love, and to love him in return. History is the pitiful tale of what happened instead. God did not change. His loving plan and purpose were always the same. But we rebelled against his love; we wanted to be our own gods, determine our own destinies, and run our own lives.

Separation from fellowship with God has consistently resulted in the feeling of guilt—specific guilt for definite sins; generalized guilt for the root sin of separation. The feeling of guilt is a sure sign of an uneasy state of grace. Guilt is the absence of love—the refusal to receive love and love God in return, the failure to love ourselves as we are loved by him and to love others graciously as he has loved us. The question remains: if we feel distant from God, who moved? We did!

That's why he himself came to us, in his Son. He came to his people who could no longer come to him. And his purpose was to expose his loving heart. There was a cross in the heart of God before there was a cross on Calvary; the eternal grace of God was revealed on that treacherous Friday afternoon outside of Jerusalem.

How else could he do it? What else could he say that would penetrate the guilt-ridden hearts of men and women? The cross was love to the uttermost, grace's ultimate entreaty. And as the Lamb of God was nailed on the cruel cross, his words echoed from the heart of God, "Father, forgive them; for they know not what they do" (Luke 23:34). Indeed, they didn't know what they were doing. The people who crucified Jesus did not realize that the ultimate sacrifice for man's sin was being enacted once and for all, then and for all time.

It was only afterward that Jesus' "I am" prediction was understood. After the Resurrection, when his disciples and followers looked back on the cross, they could exclaim with awe and wonder, "That's how much God loves us!" The cross became the center of their gospel message. It invaded the guilt-infested hearts of people and became the power that transformed their lives.

This "I am" statement must be understood and appreciated in the context of a statement made just before the Lord's crucifixion. "And I, when I am lifted up from the earth, will draw all men to myself" (John 12:32). (John's editorial comment was, "He said this to show by what death he was to die," v. 33.) Jesus' death on the cross has the magnetic power to draw people out of self-negation into the positive power of God's love. The old gospel hymn said it: "Love lifted me! Love lifted me! When nothing else could help, Love lifted me." Our greatest need is to be drawn out of the sinking sand of guilt feelings. And only the love of the cross can do that.

But we ask, How can the death of a man two thousand years ago help us in our feelings of guilt?" That question exposes our misunderstanding of time. The love revealed in Christ's death for our sins existed before Christ died and is the essential attitude of God toward us now. God knew that we would need a tangible, historical exposure of his love for us.

Now Jesus' "I am" declaration becomes most personal. "When you have lifted up the Son of man, then you will know that I am," means several crucial things to us today.

First, it means that, when you confront and contemplate the cross, by the gift of faith you will know that it was God himself through his Son who loved you. The wonder of the cross is that the more we lift it up as the exposure of the eternal heart of God, the more we are assured of his individual love for us. We can say, "Behold the Lamb of God, who not only takes away the sins of the world, but *my* sins."

The great classical words of the Christian faith thunder in our souls. The cross is our *atonement.* Our at-one-ment with God. The chasm of separation caused by our sin is bridged by unlimited love from the heart of God. We are *justified* before God, made right with God. By faith in what God did for us, we become *righteous.* Not that we are perfect on our own merits—we are declared right in spite of everything! Christ is the *expiation* for our sins. The cross has expunged our failures. Because of Calvary, God relates to us as if we had never done or said the things which expressed our loveless separation from him, which can be identified with the turbulent reaction of guilt.

The cross heals our feelings of guilt because it takes us seriously. Beneath our guilt feelings are the things we have done against God, ourselves, and others. It does no good to say that they do not exist. We miss the message of the cross if we think it simply says, "Not guilty!" That's not true. We *are* guilty and need forgiveness. The dynamic message of the cross is the loving assurance, "No longer guilty!" Christ took our sin, which is the root of our guilt feelings, upon himself. He suffered for us, once and for all.

The second thing Jesus' "I am" statement means to us today is that it cuts out by the roots the causes of our guilt feelings. Fear of punishment is gone. Anxiety over rejection is past. Doubt of our self-worth is healed. The cross tells us that we are of ultimate worth to God. There were no limits to what he was willing to do to have us be sure of his unchanging love. When we accept the cross, God does not punish us for our sins. He forgives and gives us the power to begin a new life. The punishment we attribute to God is self-inflicted. He wants our redemption, not our damnation. When we look back on the cross, fear of rejection is over. There is nothing we can do which will make God stop loving us!

The final thing Jesus' "I am" statement means is hope for the future. The triumphant disclosure is in the future subjunctive. The actual meaning of the Greek is, "Whenever you lift up the Son of man, then you will know that I am."

That means that each time we crucify Christ anew by our actions and attitudes, our refusal to live, we will know in a fresh way that he is the expression of God's forgiving love for us. It's a powerful way of saying, "When the worst happens, the best will be given to heal and help you!" The impact of that saying is that when we fail, and a spasm of guilt grabs our emotions, we can return to the cross and receive a new assurance of hope. Then we can say with the psalmist, "Oh the bliss of him whose guilt is pardoned, and his sin forgiven! Oh the bliss of him whom the Eternal has absolved, whose spirit has made full confession!" (Ps. 32:1–2, Moffatt).

Jesus' "I am" disclosure is that God is greater than anything which can be done to us or by us. James Stewart, the great Scottish theologian, said that we all have two basic needs in life's perplexities: the need for intervention and the need for interpretation. The cross is both. God intervened at history's darkest hour. The cross is an interpretation of our guilt and his grace.

That takes care of worry over our tomorrows. The fear of future failure is over. It's one thing to know that there is nothing in our past that can keep us from God's love. And it's a far greater thing to know that we will never be able to do anything that God can't use to bring us closer to him. We cannot live fully until we know that. When Christ is lifted up in the future, once again we will know that he is Lord, our Lord.

When Luther was ready to leave for Augsburg, his friends warned him not to go. "At Augsburg are the powers of hell." To which Luther replied, "At Augsburg,

Jesus reigns!" And he will reign in our lives whatever happens.

Jesus, our crucified Lord, the Lamb of God, has covered the contingencies of past, present, and future. The cross heals our feelings of guilt over the past and all its failures. The daily experience of the cross exorcises guilt feelings, as the inner causes of fear of punishment, rejection, and loss of esteem are satisfied in the wonder of God's love for each of us. The future is now opened wide with expectation. There is nothing we can ever do or be which will reverse God's loving attitude toward us.

Now we are ready to receive the gift of the uplifted Lord—the awesome, satisfying, comforting gift of unconditional, unrestrained acceptance. We don't need to nag ourselves any more. The motive of love replaces whipping ourselves with feelings of guilt. Behold the Lamb of God who has taken, is taking, and will take away your guilt!

Now we can sing with gusto,

> What wondrous love is this, O my soul, O my soul,
> What wondrous love is this, O my soul!
> What wondrous love is this that caused the Lord of bliss
> To bear the dreadful curse for my soul, for my soul,
> To bear the dreadful curse for my soul.
>
> To God and to the Lamb I will sing, I will sing;
> To God and to the Lamb I will sing;
> To God and to the Lamb, who is the great "I Am,"
> While millions join the theme, I will sing, I will sing,
> While millions join the theme, I will sing.

10

How to Deal with Anxiety

Christ and Our
Anxiety

"I am the door of the sheep . . ."
John 10:7

EARLY ONE EVENING when I was traveling in the Holy
Land, I took a long walk in the hills outside the village
where I was staying. As the shadows of evening length-
ened, I sat on a hillside and watched a large flock of sheep
in the valley below. Several shepherds were tending the
flock, and the restless sounds of bleating wafted up from
the canyon, echoing around the hills.

Then, as the sun began to set, I watched a remarkable
thing take place. Suddenly, as if by some prearranged
signal, the shepherds began to call out to the sheep. Each
walked in a different direction. To my utter amazement,
the sheep, after some millng around, divided, and a
separate group followed each shepherd. What a lovely
sight—the shepherd out in front, the sheep following
faithfully behind. They knew their shepherd and he knew
his sheep. Each shepherd led his sheep to a different
sheepfold. Each sheepfold had four walls, with a man-
sized opening on one side. The shepherds stood inside the
sheepfolds and called their sheep inside. Then they built
fires just ouside the door and began preparing their
evening meal.

It was almost dark when I started back to the village. I turned for one last look at the magnificent scene below. The picture is still etched in my mind. The sheperds seated in the doors of the folds, fires blazing, the sheep secure inside. Before long, the fires would be banked, and the shepherds would curl up in their blankets for a long night of watchfulness in protection of the sheep. They actually would be the door of the sheepfold. No sheep could go out, and no invading danger could come in.

The same customs and practices of sheepherding have been followed for centuries. In that evening I felt that I had been ushered back two thousand years.

It was dark when I reached the main road. As I walked through the night, I pondered what I had seen. Then the words of Jesus' dynamic "I am" proclamation thundered in my mind. 'I am the door of the sheep. . . . if any one enters by me, he will be saved, and will go in and out and find the pasture" (John 10:7,9). I thought of the sheep in the fold. With the shepherd as the protecting door, the sheep need not be anxious.

Just then, a jet fighter screeched across the sky, and a truck filled with armed soldiers whizzed by me on the road. I was jerked back into twentieth-century reality. The peaceful scene back in the hills made a vivid contrast to the modern world of technology and alertness for war.

That set me thinking about the implications of Jesus' "I am" promise. What does the pastoral imagery have to do with life today?

I thought of the exasperated exclamation of a little boy who came home from Sunday school and was asked what had been talked about. "Ah, same ol' stuff. Shepherds and sheep—sheep and shepherds!"

I smiled to myself with empathy. The closest most people get to a shepherd is in a Christmas pageant. About all we know of sheep is the price of lamb in the meat department of a supermarket. And yet, the impact of Jesus' "I am" assertion contains an answer for one of the greatest struggles we all face. It offers us an antidote for anxiety.

My inventory of the deepest needs of the American people revealed that the struggle with anxiety outnumbered all the other needs expressed. In response to my question, "What do you feel is the deepest need with which you struggle?", the answer of the greatest number was written in one word—anxiety.

One man expressed his response in the form of a question: "How do you deal with anxiety?" This chapter on the "I am the door" text is my response to that question. It is written with the empathy of a shared need. I, too, battle with the dragons of anxiety. The secret I want to share about how to deal with anxiety is one of the most exciting personal discoveries I have been given. It's rooted in the essential message of this "I am" statement. I have kept this top-of-the-list struggle with anxiety for this particular "I am" self-disclosure of the Lord, because I know from my own experience that it contains the ingredients to heal anxiety. In declaring "I am the door of the sheep," Jesus offered us the safety, security, and serenity which can turn our struggle with anxiety into a stepping stone.

Follow the progression of my thought. I want to explain briefly what I think Jesus meant and spell out what that means for the healing of anxiety.

The Lord spoke in the images of his time. The most familiar figure in Palestine was, and still is today, the shepherd. The picture of the shepherd is woven into the language and imagery of the Scriptures. God is frequently referred to as the Shepherd and the people of Israel as the flock of God. The Psalms sing the praises of the Good Shepherd of Israel. "The Lord is my shepherd, I shall not want" (Ps. 23:1). "Thou didst lead thy people like a flock" (Ps. 77:20). "We thy people, the flock of thy pasture, will give thanks to thee for ever" (Ps. 79:13). "He is our God, and we are the people of his pasture, and the sheep of his hand" (Ps. 95:7). "We are his people and the sheep of his pasture" (Ps.100:3).

Often Jesus spoke of himself as the shepherd and the disciples as his flock (Luke 12:32); he told of his longing, loving concern for his sheep. And when Jesus said he was the Good Shepherd, he clearly identified himself with God. It was as if he said, "I am Yahweh, God with you, the Good Shepherd!" Further, he personified himself as the long-anticipated Messiah. The annointed one of God is pictured by Isaiah in his prophetic promise, "He will feed his flock like a shepherd; he will gather the lambs in his arms, he will carry them in his bosom, and gently lead those that are with young" (Isa. 40:11).

Basic for our study of how Jesus deals with anxiety is his claim to be God with us. It is with divine authority that he confronts and offers to heal our soul-sickness. *Egō eimi* is the door. He calls his sheep into the sheepfold of an eternal relationship with God. Those who enter by him "will be saved, and will go in and out and find pasture." A lovely, picturesque description of our salvation: the word *saved* in Greek here is *sōthēsetai,* the future passive of the verb *sōzō,* to save, preserve, rescue, from the root *sōs,* meaning safe and sound.

Jesus is the only way. He came to save us. The word *salvation* meant deliverance in that day. A savior was a deliverer from danger and captivity. Christ is the Savior of the world. Through his life, death, and resurrection, we are delivered from separation from God, the bondage to our human nature, and the power of fear and death. He saves us from sin and heals our hostility toward ourselves, others, and life itself. We become new creatures when we accept his love, surrender our lives to him, and experience the transformation of our personalities.

Salvation means wholeness, healing, and health. The Lord's promise that we shall "go in and out and find pasture" is our assurance that all our psychological and physical needs will be met in companionship with him as our Good Shepherd. The adventure of the Christian life is not only the assurance of eternal security but the experience of daily security now.

When Jesus calls us by name to belong to him, fear of death is past. We are reconciled forever. Nothing can change our elected status. But that's only the beginning.

He couples reconciliation with regeneration. The process of growing in his love means that he will penetrate our conscious and subconscious natures. Anything which could debilitate us will be exposed and exorcised. Mental health is the Lord's gift to his loved ones. He loves us just as we are, but he never leaves us that way. And that has everything to do with our struggle with anxiety. Christ can heal this turbulent, troublesome disturbance, which distresses so many of us who believe in him but need his healing power. He wants to help us understand both the cause of and the cure for anxiety.

Essentially, anxiety is a feeling of helplessness in the face of impending threat to our safety, security, and serenity. We become anxious whenever our lives, personalities, or the people we love are in danger. Anxiety engulfs us when we feel inadequate to meet a lurking possibility or eventuality. We feel an alarming sense of impotence.

It's crucial to distinguish between objective and neurotic anxiety. The first is a response to a real danger, problem, or difficulty. The second is an intense and pervading dread which persists even when there is no apparent cause. The Good Shepherd can heal both. He begins with the first and then cuts to the core of the second.

In the Sermon on the Mount, Jesus deals with many of the causes of objective anxiety:

> Therefore I tell you, do not be anxious about your life, what you shall eat or what you shall drink, not about your body or what you shall put on. Is not life more than food, and the body more than clothing? Look at the birds of the air: they neither sow nor reap nor gather into barns, and yet your heavenly Father feeds them. Are you not of more value than they? And which of you by being anxious can add one cubit to his span of life? And why are you anxious about clothing? Consider the lilies of the field, how they grow; they neither toil nor spin; yet I tell you, even Solomon in all his glory was not arrayed like one of these. But if God so clothes the grass of the field, which today is alive and tomorrow is thrown into the oven, will he not much more clothe you, O men of little

faith? Therefore do not be anxious, saying, 'What shall we eat?' or 'What shall we drink?' or 'What shall we wear?' For the Gentiles seek all these things; and your heavenly Father knows that you need them all.

Matt. 6:25–32

Our Lord really knows us. He understands how anxious we become over having adequate resources for our daily lives. He knows about unpaid bills and low bank balances. He is aware of how we worry about appearance, success, and security. He empathizes with our concern about deadlines and pressure. He sees into our hearts and knows all about our distress over people we love. Life is not easy. Often it is an endless succession of impossible challenges that press us from one crisis to another. We become insecure, wondering if we have what it takes to pull it off.

The only cure for this kind of objective anxiety, focused in real troubles in a very real world, is found in the Lord's admonition which concludes this section of the Sermon on the Mount: "But seek first his kingdom and his righteousness, and all these things shall be yours as well. Therefore do not be anxious about tomorrow, for tomorrow will be anxious for itself. Let the day's own trouble be sufficient for the day" (Matt. 6:33–34).

This gives us several basis steps for dealing with surface anxiety:

1. *Put God first.* We will be anxious whenever anything or anyone is given his place in our lives. Anxiety is a danger signal which tells us that inordinate importance has been placed on people, places, positions, or things.
2. *Seek his kingdom.* That means his rule in our hearts, between us in our relationhips, and around us in our responsibilities. To seek first the kingdom is to consistently, day by day, ask for his will for everything we do and say. We all need an inner center of guidance to help us establish our priorities. Often we

are anxious over the things God did not guide in the first place; we become overextended, overinvolved, overexhausted. But there's enough time in every day, and in our lifetime, to do what God wants us to do.

3. *Remember, what God guides, he provides!* That has become a motto of my life. It works. The creator, sustainer, redeemer, and Lord of the universe has more than adequate resources to see us through the crises and needs of life.

4. *Expect a surprise!* Expectaton is God's special gift for anxious people. His interventions in the lives of people who believe in him and trust him completely are amazing—always perfectly timed and suited to our needs and to his strategy for us. The Holy Spirit is always at work arranging, preparing. Then, when we least expect it, he breaks through. When the anxiety signal rings, expect a miracle!

5. *Exchange your impotence for the Spirit's immanence.* Anxiety is a sure sign that we are depending on our own strength and cleverness. It is caused by alarm at the fact that we are inadequate or will not have sufficient resources to meet life's demands. But we were never meant to be sufficient! Our Lord calls us to live a life that is impossible without the gifts of his indwelling Spirit. The promise that breaks the bind of agitating anxiety is for us: "You shall receive power when the Holy Spirit has come upon you" (Acts 1:8).

Now we need to go deeper. Neurotic anxiety is much more complex than objective anxiety. Simplistic admonitions from other people to simply stop worrying don't help. Nor are we set free simply by turning our anxiety over to God. I know good Christians who have prayed about their feelings of anxiety for years with no relief. Changes in surroundings or relationships do not change the pervasiveness of the inner ache. We take our anxious selves with us wherever we go.

If neurotic anxiety persists, it is probably caused by

responses to life that have become conditioned and habitual. We need to dig these out and look at them.

A woman expressed it this way. "I have this aching feeling inside. It seldom goes away. I go from one problem to another, but even when the problems are resolved, I continue to feel uneasy. I try to think positive thoughts about God, but they don't help the churning inside."

A Ph.D. candidate was unable to study for his oral examinations. He had an excellent academic record, but he was sure he was going to fail. No amount of rehearsal of past successes alleviated the dread. None of the thought conditioning he tried seemed to help. He became increasingly self-condemnatory and unable to memorize the facts he would be expected to know. The doctoral exam was not the cause of his anxiety. It had simply provided a temporary mooring for his floating anxiety. Unless he got to the inner causes of his anxiety, he would suffer the rest of his life.

A clergyman at a conference confided his anxiety to me. I was shocked. He was a leader in his denomination, sure to be a bishop before long, and a very popular preacher. All his study in the Scriptures and his faithful prayer life had not set him free of an anxiety which haunted his waking moments and distressed his sleep. It had driven him to immense ambition and rewarded him with great advancement, but no amount of success had eased the dull emotional pain inside.

The examples of people who suffer from neurotic anxiety could go on and on. Many of these people are Christians. Our pious response is: how can anyone who believes in Christ be troubled with deep anxiety? The answer is really quite simple. Most of them have sought Christ's help for the manifestation of the feeling of anxiety, but have not experienced healing for the deeper motivations of the malady.

All of the people mentioned above had one thing in common with most sufferers of neurotic anxiety. They all experienced apprehension triggered by imagined threats to their welfare. But that apprehension was caused by the repression of impulses deep within which they could not express. The deeper I plumbed with each of them, the more aware I became that they had never learned how to express their needs and have them fulfilled in a creative way. Anger resulted, and that anger they turned in on themselves.

The woman had been raised in a conservative Christian home in which anger was considered the cardinal sin. She had never been allowed to express her true feelings; they had been bottled up and pressed down into her subconscious. Repression of feelings became a habitual reaction to life. At the same time, she had committed her life to Christ and dedicated herself to look and act like a joyous Christian. Victorious radiance was applauded as the sign of being a Spirit-filled Christian by her church. She quickly learned the right phrases and facial expressions to please her parents and fellow Christians. Meanwhile, the inner anxiety grew.

The young scholar's story is similar. He had not learned to handle his feelings about his father, who made great demands but gave little affirming love. He admired his father's success, and felt he had to match and exceed his accomplishments. But his normal feelings of aggression in the growing years had not been expressed, or even acknowledged. Defensiveness festered in him. His hostility to his father was channeled into his studies. But he developed a pattern of dealing with people in authority as he had dealt with his father—being pleasant, affable, but dishonest. When he felt hurt or distressed by people, he could not explain how he felt or impress on them what he wanted. His solicitousness masked a very anxious inner person.

The successful clergyman preached about more peace of mind than he had experienced. His overemphasis exposed his inner weakness. He was "Mr. Nice Guy," but his inability to be confrontive in personal and professional relationships was having its toll. His conciliatory attitude had won him success at an exorbitantly high price. As people steam-rollered over his true desires and convictions, his suppressed anger was compacted into a hard inner core of anxiety. The more anxious he felt, the harder he worked. And the results of the human effort elevated him to higher and greater responsibilities and recognition.

What this man needed that week at the clergy conference was the opportunity to tell someone what was happening inside him and have it understood with unqualified love. As we talked, he was astounded to discover how angry he was, and that he had developed his uncreative way of dealing with hostility early in childhood. Since then, it's been a long, hard road to emotional honesty and the development of a healthy self-love, but the Lord is healing the inner cause of his anxiety and liberating him to be an authentic person.

The other day, I talked to a woman who had been attacked on a street in a lovely Los Angeles suburb. Fortunately, someone had come along and frightened the rapist away. But for months afterward, the woman was seized with spasms of anxiety. When we talked about her problem, she told me she felt guilty about what had happened. She had done nothing to provoke the attack; properly dressed, minding her own business, and giving no signals of availability, she had been suddenly victimized. Yet she felt it had been her fault. The more we discussed her feelings, the more aware I was that self-incrimination was a habitual pattern with her. If anything went wrong, she was to blame. When she had an argument, she must have caused it. Messed-up schedules, family problems, her children's hang-ups were surely all her doing. Her anxiety feelings had dominated her daily life for years.

The break in the bind came when this woman realized that her self-blame was a way of escaping the real world. This is a sick world in which there are disturbed people. People around us are often the cause of what happens. Selfishness in people we love causes pain and distress. When we are the cause of a problem, it's healthy to be able to admit it. But if we make ourselves responsible for everyone else's slights and oversights, we will become anxious about life. Our hostility against ourselves will develop into a habitual, conditioned pattern of response. Only Christ can help us own our real failures, disown them in his forgiveness, and press on. Then we can acknowledge the failures of others and forgive them as we've been forgiven.

Now we are getting closer to the cause of neurotic anxiety. Healthy self-love is expressed in creative self-assertion. When we feel good about ourselves, we are able to communicate our needs and expect the people around us to meet them. We are able to express our feelings without attacking people or blaming them; thus we free them to respond without being defensive. But a feeling of not being loved for the unique miracle each of us is results in diminished self-esteem. This in turn can lead us to suppress our emotions. And unexpressed emotions can fester into hostility and anxiety.

Now let's go one step further. Neurotic anxiety is at core the manifestation of being cut off from God at the deepest recesses of our psyches. It's the result of playing God. Anxiety is eccentricity—being ex-centric or away from the center. When we suppress our negative emotions, we are in effect taking punishment into our own hands. Since we have not learned to vent our anger creatively, we invert it on ourselves. There's a great difference between being sacrificial lovers of people and sacrificing ourselves for our own and others' failures. The one is self-abandonment, to which we are called as Christians; the other is merely self-blame.

The Holy Spirit wants to take us back over the years for the healing of those debilitating memories which depleted our self-images and developed the syndrome of self-condemnation. He exposes them to us if we are willing. Then he heals them with assuring love. The basic question we must ask ourselves is: "How did I become habitually anxious? When did I start condemning myself? Anxiety is spelled a-n-g-e-r. What are my unhealthy ways of suppressing my hostility? What ex-centric impulses need to be brought out into the open for the remedial correction and loving forgiveness of the Lord?"

I have a national television program called "Let God Love You!" which is also the title of one of my earlier books. A day seldom goes by that I don't receive several letters from viewers expressing the fact that they had never thought about letting God love them. They had always felt that they had a duty to love God. But only a deeply loved person can love back! Anxiety at the most profound levels of our lives can be healed when we allow God to love us. Only he knows all about us, and therefore only he can turn the tide of emotional self-judgment and incrimination into self affirmation and delight.

The Greek word for "to be anxious" is *merimnaō,* from the root *meris,* meaning a part or share and *merizō,* meaning to divide or share. A compulsively anxious person is a divided person, one who works against himself. Dr. Karen Horney calls this division "the dynamic center of neurosis." It distracts us from the immensity of God's love, our true potential, and any hope for the future. It leaves us with the belief that if anything can go wrong, it will—and we will probably be to blame.

Only the Good Shepherd can save us from that. Now we can see how the reconciliation and regeneration he offers us in the "I am" statement we are considering in this chapter is so crucial. Reconciliation to God is a gift which also reconciles us to that inner person we've been so hard on for so long. Regeneration is the reformation of our minds and emotions. This happens when we have the mind of Christ toward ourselves as well as others.

Paul exposes the difference between objective and neurotic anxiety in Philippians 4:6–7: "Have no anxiety about anything, but in everything by prayer and supplication with thanksgiving let your requests be made known to God. And the peace of God, which passes all understanding, will keep your hearts and your minds in Christ Jesus." The Apostle had found the secret! In the profound inner relationship with God, we can express our feelings and needs. He will help us sort out what's happening to us. What needs forgiveness will be healed by grace; what must be expressed to others will be guided by the Spirit. Prayer will be the nerve center which releases genuine self-love rooted in God's love. His control will be communicated in the healthy expression of our personalities as loved and accepted people.

The word *keep* in Paul's promise is crucial. It is the future active indicative of *phroureō*, meaning to be a sentinel, to guard or hold in custody. The peace of God does that. Peace is the result of an integrated heart, as opposed to a divided heart, which causes anxiety.

When our lives are centered on Christ, he develops a protective grid in our minds. The "I am" is the door, indeed! The things which could make us anxious are filtered through his perspective. We can see people and circumstances as they are and not be threatened. Christ gives us the power to discern what we are to do and say, and to leave the results to him. What a difference it makes when frightening challenges or difficulties are not permitted to go from our eyes or ears to our stomachs! Christ in us sorts and sifts, filters and refines, as he stands watch as sentinel of our minds and emotions.

Recently, I became anxious in a time of tremendous pressure. There was no way I could meet all the demands which had hit with hurricane force on my life. I added hours to my schedule, trying to catch up. Sleep and exercise were put off because of lack of time. The old feelings of inadequacy stalked around in my emotions. My mind became focused on the need to press harder.

When I realized what was happening, I dropped everything for a prolonged walk on the beach and a time of prayer. As I walked and talked with the Lord, he helped me analyze what had happened to me. The work had piled up. A period of insecurity a few months before had prompted me to take on responsibilities which, I realized now, had not been guided by the Lord and were not a maximum part of his strategy for me. In the flood of work, time for myself, my wife, my family, and friends was being denied me. Feelings of anger about my life being temporarily out of control and unsatisfying were focused with a fierce blast on myself.

"Lord, what's wrong?" I asked. "Where did I get off the track?" Then I listened intently. After a time of silence, corrective and clarifying thoughts came flooding into my mind. Forgiveness for running my own life was given and received. I experienced new love for myself as loved by the Lord. Creative energy began to surge.

Decisiveness followed. First things were put first. A plan and the power to work the plan were given. I was set free from being my worst enemy to be my own best friend. Then I returned to do what portion of the work the Lord had given priority. I was free of the anxiety which had been draining off all the energy. Kierkegaard was right: "Dealing with anxiety means having the courage to leap forward by faith into the confusion."

Charles Finney, the nineteenth-century clergyman and educator, had what he called an "anxious bench," where people could come and kneel after he had preached the gospel. Jesus' "I am" promise of safety, security, and serenity is an anxious bench for us as we finish this chapter. He is our Shepherd, the *egō eimi,* who has the power to make things happen, beginning in us. He knows us by name and calls us out of the milling flock to follow him to his sheepfold of intimate fellowship. He stands at the door, calling us to come home. And when we have entered into that union once again, we feel his love surging into our fears, frustrations, angers, and hostilities. We begin to feel delight in being who we are—his sheep. Now we can rest and expect that he can handle our tomorrows. And while we are relaxing in safety and security, he stands by the door.

11

What Are You Worried About?

Christ Will Not Fail nor Forsake Us

"I am the Good Shepherd."
John 10:11

ONE OF MY FAVORITE stories concerns Thomas Carlyle, who built a soundproof chamber in his home in Chelsea in London about a century ago. He wanted to shut out all the noises of the street so that he could work in uninterrupted silence. It worked, except for one piercing sound which penetrated through the vaulted walls. His neighbor had a cock that was given to vigorous expression several times at night and once at dawn. Carlyle would sit, pen in hand, distracted from thought and expression, waiting for that disturbing sound. Finally he protested to the owner of the cock, and was assured that it crowed only three times at night and once at dawn. "But," said Carlyle, "if you only knew all the worry I suffer waiting for that cock to crow!"

We laugh. But how very much like our lives today. And there's no soundproof, peopleproof, dangerproof chamber into which we can escape. But even if we could, we would take private enemy number one with us—worry. There's no place to hide from the universal sickness of worry. We carry it around inside ourselves. Like Carlyle, we anticipate, expect, and wait for the invasion of distracting difficulty.

Worry is thinking turned toxic, the imagination used to picture the worst. The word *worry* comes from a root meaning to choke or strangle. What an incisive insight! Worry does choke and strangle our creative capacity to think, hope, and dream. It twists the joy out of life. We get dressed up like mountain climbers and climb over molehills.

Worry changes nothing except the worrier. The distressing habit of worry is impotent to change tomorrow or undo the past. All it does is sap today of strength. William Inge, Dean of St. Paul's cathedral from 1911 to 1934, was right: "Worry is the interest paid on trouble before it comes due."

What are you worried about right now? Focus on those people, situations, or apprehensions that concern you most. Now consider a provoking question. Have you ever had a trouble or a problem that was solved or improved by worry? My experience is that 50 percent of the things I worry about never happen. Twenty-five percent of my worries cannot be changed by my worry. And 25 percent are worthy of creative concern, but my worry over the other 75 percent debilitates any productive action. Henry Ward Beecher said it well: "Worry is rust upon the blade." It renders us incapable of cutting our way through life's real problems.

There are many available lists of what makes us worry, with appropriate percentages allotted to each. A. J. Cronin, the distinguished author-physician, sorted it out this way·

Things which never happen	40%
Things in the past that can't be changed by all the worry in the world	30%
Health worries	12%

Petty miscellaneous worries   10%

Real legitimate worries   8%

When you list your worries, what percentages would you allocate? What can we do about our worries?

It does absolutely no good to admonish ourselves and others with the oft-repeated advice, "Stop worrying!" We are so conditioned to worry that the admonition makes us worried about being worried! Worry takes charge of our minds before we know it. It dominates our thought patterns uncontrollably and inadvertently. We cannot will ourselves to stop worrying. The compulsive response to life is ingrained in our brains.

At core, worry is a low-grade form of agnosticism. Shocking? Perhaps. But look at it this way. Worry is a lurking form of doubt. At base it's rooted in a question about the adequacy of God to meet our own and others' needs. And it is nourished by a fear that there may be problems and perplexities in which we will be left alone; out on a limb without him! Worry is a form of loneliness. It entails facing life's eventualities all by ourselves, on our meager strength. We feel victimized and bereft and helpless to change the course of events. A sense of helplessness begins the cycle of worry. Finally we get so used to the feeling of worry that we get worried when there is little to worry about! We thrash about looking for something or someone we can worry over.

But let's not be simplistic. Worry is very real. I experience it, and so do you. The mental anguish causes emotional distress and physical discomfort. It's no joke when people say, "I'm worried sick!" Many people do become physically ill as a result of worry. Often it leaves permanent damage: breakdown of the nervous system, stomach disorders, tension headaches, back trouble. It's not what we eat that makes us ill—but what's eating us!

Worry is really a distortion of our capacity to care. If we were thoughtless, irresponsible, impervious people, we would not worry. We want what's best for ourselves and for the people we love. This protective nature is not bad; being concerned about the problems of life is not a sign of weakness. But the thing that is wrong about worry is that it has absolutely no power to change anything except us. It makes us incapable of doing anything which would affect the problems we face.

Is it possible to be healed of the sickness of worry? Can we find a solution to the disturbing disquiet? Yes! Jesus Christ can heal the causes of worry.

If worry is caused by the loneliness of facing imagined or real problems alone, by a feeling of having to determine our destiny in life's difficulties without help, then the Lord is the only lasting hope for our battle with worry. He can use our worries as a prelude to power; they can be an occasion to discover his adequacy for whatever is causing us to worry right now.

The secret is in the "I am" himself. He said "I am the good shepherd. The good shepherd lays down his life for the sheep. He who is a hireling and not a shepherd, whose own the sheep are not, sees the wolf coming and leaves the sheep and flees . . ." (John 10:11–12).

The contrast is impelling. A hired hand will help a shepherd. But when danger lurks or a ravaging animal of prey attacks, the hired hand will run for safety, leaving the sheep alone. A good shepherd counts no cost too high to protect his sheep. At no time, regardless of what happens, will he leave the flock. He even will lay down his own life to protect them. He stands immovably between the sheep and the ravaging wolves.

Catch the impact of that. Picture it in your mind. Jesus stands between us and whatever causes us worry—physical danger, people who would use or misuse us, a hostile fate which would disturb or destroy us, powers of evil. When the going is tough, Jesus will be there! Imagine each of your worries as separate wolves lurking about, ready to attack. Are they too much for the Good Shepherd to handle? Remember he said, " I am the good shepherd." There is the liberating assurance again— Yahweh. Jesus is God with us. He has all power. His providence is our peace. We will never be alone or bereft again.

In that context I want to give you a prescription for worry. Like some prescriptions given us by physicians it has two parts: something we are to take, and something we are to do. It is a companion scripture to Jesus' "I am" promise about being the Good Shepherd. If I could give you a gift, it would be the freedom to receive and respond to Hebrews 13:5–6: "He has said, 'I will never fail you nor forsake you.' Hence we can confidently say, 'The Lord is my helper, I will not be afraid; what can man do to me?'"

Every time we are caught in the bind of worry is a new occasion for an exchange with our Lord. We accept his promise to be with us and give him our wearing worry. Consider the immensity of his promise: "I will never fail you nor forsake you." Think about both aspects of that. How could the Lord ever fail us? It would be by leaving us friendless and alone in a dangerous situation. And he claims he never will!

But we know that believing in him does not ensure us a long, smooth existence with no problems. Exactly. The Lord does one of three things: remove the danger, strengthen us to stand strongly in it, or use the situation to help us grow in grace.

We've all been through difficulties in which we have had a miraculous intervention which completely alleviated the problem we feared. Then there are times he chooses not to change the circumstances, but changes us so that we are able to take them. Also, we've all known tragic eventualities which have been the sources of our greatest growth in character and maturity. But in all these, he does not fail. True love never fails. It's because it does not forsake.

That's the second part of the Lord's promise. The word *forsake* means to disown, leave completely, abandon, desert, and reject. That's the one thing our Lord will never do. We belong to him, now and for eternity. It is this assurance which enables us to offer our worry to him and say, "The Lord is my helper, I will not be afraid. What can man or fate do to me?"

The exchange is like breathing in and out. Do that now as you focus on your worries. As you inhale, say the words, "I will never fail you nor forsake you." Feel the oxygen of hope in your soul. Now breathe out your relinquishment of the worry. As you exhale, say, "The Lord is my helper, I will not be afraid."

Now we are ready to be very specific about our worries. I find it helpful to categorize mine in five groups: worries about the past, worries about the future, worries about people, worries about my health, and worries about finances. The past is filled with worries of what we did or failed to do—things said that should never have been said, silences when we should have spoken.

Jesus Christ can heal our worry over the past. Healing comes in the assurance that there is nothing we have done or been that would cause him to forsake us. He lays down his life for the sheep. Between you and me and our worries over the past stands the cross. Worry over the past is evidence that we have determined to atone for our own failures instead of accepting the gift of forgiveness.

Many worry about having the past catch up with them; they fear some exposure of past sin or deliberate rebellion which will be open for all to see. I have been amazed at the way Jesus Christ covers our tracks after we seek his forgiveness. By his loving intervention, he keeps our secrets when the exposure would not help us or his cause. If we are still worried about the past, our worry is a sure sign that we need to take our hurting memories to the never-failing, never-forsaking Lord. If we load our minds with past failures and missed opportunities, we will not be able to live fully in the present or the future.

The uncertainties of the future cause a large portion of the worries which cause us anguish. Emerson caught the pain of worry over what may be:

> Some of your hurts you have cured
> And the sharpest you still have survived

> But what torment of grief you've endured
> From evils that never arrived.

We misuse our imaginations over future dangers. Our God-given capacity to form, hold, and anticipate images can be bane as well as blessing. We imagine the worst and even let our minds work to achieve the foreboding possibility. Once again, our problem is that we envision what might happen *without* the intervention and blessing of our Lord. If we picture the dangers of what could occur without the Lord in the picture, we will be worried. The only cure for worry about the future is to habitually practice the presence of Christ, envisioning him commanding, controlling, and conditioning every situation.

The Resurrection is our tangible source of hope. Jesus went to the cross in complete trust that God would bring good out of evil. The empty tomb is our symbol of a sublime confidence. There is nothing, absolutely nothing, including death, which can ultimately separate us from our Lord. He always holds the trump card!

There's a famous painting in which the artist depicts the great interview between Faust and Satan. Faust gambled for his soul. The painting pictures the two sitting at a chessboard, the Devil on one side and Faust on the other. The Devil leers with delight over the checkmate of Faust's lonely king and knight.

Contemplation of the painting leaves one with the conclusion that Faust is completely beaten and at the mercy of Satan. Faust's expression is one of hopeless worry. The Devil gloats with superiority. But one day a world famous master of chess went to the gallery in London to view the picture. He spent hours meditating over the seemingly impossible situation it depicted. He paced back and forth. Then, to the utter amazement and surprise of the other art viewers in the gallery, he shouted a discovery which echoed around the marble corridors. "It's a lie!" he blurted out. "It's a lie! The king and the knight have another move!"

And so with our worries about the future. There's

always one more move we never anticipated. Whenever we are tempted to say, "There's no solution. I'm finished. There's no hope. I'm beaten," we discover that God has a move we could not have imagined.

The other day a friend came to see me with the grim, gray look of worry written all over his face. His countenance communicated defeat and discouragement. When he related the impossible situation, I had to agree that the future possibilities were bleak. We spread the whole complexity out before the Lord in prayer. There seemed to be no solution, but the man accepted the fact that in whatever happened the Lord would be with him.

That's all he needed to know. A few weeks later he returned. His face was brightened. There had been a breakthrough he could never have dreamed possible. The Lord had another move. He did not fail or forsake my friend.

I have come to know this assurance about our Lord. *The unanticipated always happens.* It's like being lost in the wilds and suddenly finding the way out. That's happened to me while fishing in Canada. What a triumphant feeling it is to finally find a marker that shows the way! The same has been true all my life and ministry. There have been times when I felt cornered and without alternatives. Then the Lord opened up a possibility which no amount of crafty planning or ingenuity could have developed. With Christ, there is always a way out! He will not flee us in the moment of trial. He is Lord of all our tomorrows.

He's an experienced enabler of hope for future worries. On the cross he repeated the twenty-second Psalm. The first line has been engraved on our memories as one of the Seven Last Words. "My God, my God, why hast thou forsaken me?" But surely Jesus repeated the whole Psalm. Surely he prayed on in the words of the Psalmist:

> Yet thou art holy
>> enthroned on the praises of Israel.
> In thee our fathers trusted;
>> they trusted, and thou didst deliver them.

To thee they cried, and were saved;
  in thee they trusted, and were not disappointed (vv. 3–5).

The Psalmist ends in triumph extolling the intervening power of God. The word from the cross gives only the worrisome reality of our bereft complexity, but what the Psalm promises after that actually happened on Easter. When we claim Christ's power over our future worries, we know he understands. He's been through it. And God had the final word. The Good Shepherd laid down his life for the sheep—you and me. And God raised him up.

That takes care of the past and the future. Robert Burdette said, "There are two days in the week about which I never worry. Two carefree days, kept sacredly free from fear and apprehension. One of these days is yesterday—and the other is tomorrow."

That leaves today. And into today floods our worries about other people, our health, our finances.

Our worries over people are manifold. We worry what people might do to us. We feel helpless to control what they will do. We know our own mixed motives and self-centered designs. So often the evil or destructive actions we anticipate from others lurk in our own private, inner hearts. Our fear of others is sometimes a projection of our own attitudes. Our hidden impulses cause us distress. We think everyone is the same. And we have just enough disappointment with people to fortify our worries.

Added to worry about what people might do to harm us is the protective worry we have for people we long to be safe and secure—members of our families, friends, significant others. We wish we could form a dangerproof wall around them to keep trouble, heartache, and tragedy from them. Our worry usually immobilizes us from creative action. Our distraught emotions are transferred to them. They then have to deal with both the difficulties and our fears.

The question we asked ourselves about Christ's power to intervene in our needs must also be asked about our concerns over people. Is Christ Lord over their lives or not? Will he be able to use what they are going through to bring them to his love and care? What's the worst that they could do to themselves or have done to them? Would any indiscretion, failure, or rebellious act cause the Good Shepherd to desert them? If Christ will not fail or forsake us, why would he do less for others?

Worry over people finally brings us to the need of surrender. Have you ever completely relinquished your frustration over people? Have you confessed that you break the first commandment and play God over other people's lives? Let go! Worry never changed anyone or anything about whom we worried. We have the choice of trust or worry. And trust is the hinge on which the door of new possibilities turns for people we love. The Lord honors our prayers. He longs to help if we will ask him and leave the results to him.

The late Robert LeTourneau, a Christian businessman and philanthropist, who gave away 90 percent of his yearly income, lived what he said about worry: "Worry and trust cannot live in the same house. When worry is allowed to come in the door, trust walks out the other door; and worry stays until trust is invited in again, whereupon worry walks out." That leaves us with the question: what have we made our honored guest—worry or trust?

Another aspect of our worry about people is our concern over what they think about us. We all long for affirmation and approval. We want to be liked. We are like Mark, a character in one of C. S. Lewis's novels, of whom Lewis said, "Mark liked to be liked. There was a good deal of spaniel in him." What an image! And it's too often true of all of us—panting, solicitous, anxious to please, needing to be petted with strokes of approbation. And we'll never have enough! Christ wants to heal that tail-wagging need for approval. When we experience his love for us regardless of what we do or are, the need for others' acceptance will be filled. Then we can be affirmers of people without that unquenchable need for affirmation.

Worry over what people think is a form of pride. We imagine that people have nothing to do but ruminate over their evaluation of us. Ethel Barrett, popular children's story writer and inspirational speaker, exposes the arrogance of that assumption: "We would worry less about what others think of us if we realized that they seldom do!"

Worry over our health is equally defeating. In fact, it makes us vulnerable to sickness. Most of our worries about our health are shadows of the looming fear of death. Each pain, each illness, each physical disability is a little death, a confrontation with our finitude. Many of our illnesses are caused by fear, and only faith can heal that. But others are caused by actual disease. When that happens, we can ask the Lord to heal us.

"But not everyone who prays gets healed," you say. That's true. And yet, the Lord never fails or forsakes a sick person who has asked for his blessing. Some are healed; and others either die or live on with handicaps. But never do they drift beyond the Lord's loving care. The healing of the bind of worry over our health comes when we can say, "Whether we live or whether we die, we are the Lord's" (Rom. 14:8).

What about worry over finances? It's fascinating to note that the Hebrews' promise, "I will never fail you nor forsake you," is preceded by an admonition about money. "Keep your life free from love of money, and be content with what you have; for he has said, 'I will never fail you nor forsake you" (Heb. 13:5). There's the key—love of money. The term *money* represents all material possessions, all that money can buy or control with its power.

The solution to money worries is clearly delineated in Scripture. Jesus dealt with the problem often. Nothing is as competitive with our Lord for the control of our souls than money. Our worries over money usually come from getting enough and keeping what we have. Often our spending exceeds our income. The commitment of our finances to the Lord usually means an honest, searching review of why we spend what we do not have or cannot reasonably expect. My own experience and that of thousands of others over the years have shown that if we commit the supervision of our finances to the Lord, and ask for his guidance for how we should spend, he will help us when we are caught in unpredictable binds. He delights to surprise us in financial crises, but only so that we can get squared away and begin a new way of life.

The surrender of our worries over our finances begins with the tithe. When the first tenth of what we earn is given to the Lord, we acknowledge that all that we have and are is his. That breaks the syndrome of, "What's mine is mine!" I have yet to meet a tither who has suffered financial tragedy. Of course, business ventures come and go; some are profitable and others fail; and there are times of tightening our belts or foregoing luxuries. But the Lord provides what he guides. Most of our worries come as a result of ventures or expenditures which were not saturated in prayer for guidance.

I have found that a time of worry over money is often dispelled by a courageous, daring faith gift. I have found that when I get into a bind, either personally or professionally in some venture of the church's program, that is the crisis moment to take a significant portion of what I have and give it to the Lord. That faith gift breaks the cycle of worry. It also says to the Lord that I am seriously committed and involved in what I am asking him to bless.

This happened recently when I was concerned about the financial backing of our church's television ministry. When we didn't know whether there would be adequate funds to begin, I made a faith promise of money I did not have. It was then that the Lord began to release financial resources from others. And he has provided extra funds I could not have anticipated for me to pay my own faith pledge. Now since the long-range plans for the program are dependent on contributions of the viewers, the Lord constantly brings me back to a promise he gave to Paul in Corinth: "Do not be afraid, but speak and do not be silent; for I am with you . . . for I have many people in this city" (Acts 18:9–10). The Lord will provide!

If you are in financial need right now, make a daring faith gift of whatever you have to the Lord's work somewhere. It's the antidote to worry over money.

Oswald Chambers has a way of sending straight arrows of truth into my heart. He usually presses me on in the adventure beyond where I ever thought I would dare to go. I hope his penetrating word about worry gives you the jab it gave me: "Are you looking unto Jesus now, in the immediate matter that is pressing, and receiving from his peace? If so, he will be a gracious benediction of peace in and through you. But if you try to worry it out, you obliterate him, and deserve all you get." Ouch!

We come back to the Good Shepherd. He owns, protects, sacrifices for the sheep. We can have a carefree contentment rather than the soul-twisting, nerve-stretching rack of worry.

The question with which we began is now ready for our answer. What are you worrying about? Is it worthy of the anguish it causes? Most crucial of all, is it beyond the control and transforming providence of the Good Shepherd? Why not surrender that worry to our Lord right now? What have you got to lose? Nothing! What will you gain? Someone! The Lord himself. We can have a worriless week if each morning we repeat our portion of the prescription: "The Lord is my helper. I will not worry. What can life do to me that the Lord will not be able to handle for my good and his glory?"

Will you join me in a specific commitment not to worry for three days this next week? Yesterday, tomorrow, and today? That makes a worry-free, three-day week!

12

How to Overcome Insecurity

Insecurity and the Assurance of Christ

*"I am the Good Shepherd; I know my own
and my own know me."*
John 10:14

"I GUESS I NEED A BRAIN TRANSPLANT!" my friend
exclaimed. "You need a what?" I responded with surprise.
The man went on to explain. Though he was a very
successful businessman, he had battled the problem of
insecurity for years. He thought it would go away with
each new advancement in his spectacular career. Now he
had to stop in his fast-moving life to face the fact that
nothing seemed able to heal his growing feeling of self-
doubt. He was suddenly aware of the gross inefficiency of
his brain to interpret his past feelings of inadequacy in the
light of his present accomplishments.

"Whose brain do you want?" I asked, playfully but
emphatically. "Do you know anyone who has one that's
done any better with the problem of insecurity?" He
smiled. "It's hard to tell," he said, "the people I know who
seem most secure have the same problem when I get
underneath their polished projections of adequacy."

We laughed as I shared with him my own occasional
feelings of insecurity which should have been contradicted by evidences of accomplishments over the years.

"Not you, too!" he said with surprise. The competitive tension the man felt with me was broken, and we were able to grapple together with the universal dis-ease of insecurity.

Insecurity is the hidden scar. The chief cause of it is the ineffectiveness of the brain to interpret the past so we can function creatively in the present with self-esteem and self-appreciation.

We often hear people extol the marvel of the human brain. We hear so much about its wondrous complexity, about the capacity of its billions of cells, each intimately connected to the others, to serve the function of rational thought, memory, emotion, perception, coordination and so on. Yet, the realities of life contradict our admiration of the brain. Actually, it is very inept in sorting out and integrating the data fed to it. If the brain controls our actions, why is there so much human misery, broken relationships, and distortion of personality?

We all know that our brains often lead us into inaccurate conclusions about life and our part in it. Our memories are faulty; we remember things we need to forget, and forget what is too painful to remember. Our perception of the past is faulty, and controls what we feel about ourselves or are willing to attempt today. We must face it: the brain is deficient when it comes to self-understanding, self-analysis, and self-appreciation. It is a painfully slow process to break the nerve patterns in our brains which form our misconceptions and maintain fallacious ideas about ourselves based on previous failures, hurts, and blows to our egos. The brain seems to be incapable of integrating our emotions, self-images, perceptions of our capabilities, and plans for satisfying todays or tomorrows.

Years of caring for people have convinced me that we all feel the raw nerve of insecurity because we are unable to integrate past and present realities into a healthy self-acceptance which frees us to feel good about ourselves. We compulsively repeat past mistakes, inadvertently perpetuate distortions of our worth, and repeat the never-ending cycle of frustration over our insecure feelings.

A woman came to see me about her insecurity. She could not remember a time of feeling really good about herself. Though she was a beautiful woman, she could not believe that she was attractive. She constantly faced fears of inadequacy because of painful adolescent problems with not being accepted. Her parents had never given her a feeling of worth. A cold father had failed to give her the sense of her value as a woman, and her mother's battle with her own insecurity had caused her to be over-protective and perfectionistic toward her daughter.

A college student expressed immense insecurity over his studies. His high grades were a ledger of contradiction to his worry over his abilities. Why should he feel insecure? A bit of probing led me to unravel the fact that his academic proficiency had been rather recent. The problem of grade-school failures haunted him. A sensitive teacher in his sophomore year of high school had confided with him that he actually had a high I.Q. and was capable of doing much better in schoolwork; she had helped him learn how to study and take examinations. But his memory could not shake the impression of those formative years when he had not measured up to teachers' or parents' expectations. His brain had failed him in sorting out his real capacities, expunging the dreadful memories of childhood, and getting on with responsible, worry-free scholarship.

A man asked me to lunch to talk over a problem. During the meal, I leaned over the table and asked, "What can I do to help?" His quick retort was, "What did you have in mind?" I laughed, and the tension drained from the man's face. He talked about a growing sense of insecurity. The middle-age crisis had hit him full force. He had little chance of advancing in his job; his marriage had lost its excitement; his kids were away at college. Life had settled into routine. He had accomplished all the items on his life-agenda. "With all the good that's happened, why do I feel insecure?" he said. "I keep comparing myself with others. Most painful of all is the uneasiness I feel with people."

"Can you remember ever feeling like that before?" I asked. The man was silent for a minute, then said, "Yes, when I was in college. As a matter of fact, it's always been gnawing at my insides. I guess this is the first time in years that my life has slowed down enough to allow me to get in touch with my feelings."

All of these people I have mentioned believed in God. And yet faith had not given any of them the security of enjoying the special miracle of being one of God's children. Twenty-five years of ministry with people have convinced me that one of the most magnificent accomplishments of life is to become a truly secure person. Our deepest need is not for a brain transplant, but for a brain transformation. Only the "I am" who created us and came to give us a new image of ourselves can do that!

In the previous chapters we focused on the Good Shepherd's power to heal anxiety. The next "I am" in John's account is closely related to it, but with a special emphasis: "I am the good shepherd; I know my own and my own know me, as the Father knows me and I know the Father; and I lay down my life for the sheep" (John 10:14).

There's an assurance that can begin the transformation of our brains. Christ's "I am" statement is the assurance of belonging. And all insecurity is rooted in an inadequate sense of belonging to God. He made us for himself, to live in deep, intimate companionship with him. There is no lasting security until we are sure we belong to him. Canon Bryan Green said, "There is no emotion so necessary to a true religion, nor any so fundamental to it, as the sense of belonging to God."

Jesus' "I am" assurance astounds us. First he tells us that he knows us. Then he tells us that we can know him. And then he tells us that our relationship with him can be like the one he knows with the Father. Later in John's Gospel, in Jesus' prayer the night before he was crucified, we learn the nature of that relationship: "The glory which thou hast given me I have given to them, that they may be one even as we are one, I in them and thou in me, that they may become perfectly one, so that the world may know that thou hast sent me and hast loved them even as thou hast loved me" (John 17: 22–23).

The intimate relationship between Christ and his Father is the model of how we are to be related to him and he to us. Remember God's words at Jesus' baptism: "Thou art my beloved Son; with thee I am well pleased" (Luke 3:22). In and through Christ, we are beloved sons and daughters of God. God is pleased with us; he wants to know and love us as he did his Son.

Because of the sacrifice of Calvary, God sees us through the focused lens of the cross. We are loved and forgiven because the Good Shepherd laid "down [his] life for the sheep." We are deeply moved by how highly God values us. There was nothing he would not do; no price was too high. And all so that we might know that we are cherished. He took on himself the burden of our sin, separation, and self-negation. And here he is, in Christ, saying, "I know you and want you to know me."

Insecurity is caused by anything which fractures that relationship. No one is ultimately secure until he is secure in the grace of God. In the context of this intimate relationship, our brain transformation begins.

The Lord sees us with trifocal lenses. He sees with magnified clarity all that has happened to us to twist our self-images. Then he sees what we are going through now that tears the scabs off old wounds to our self-esteem. But then he focuses on the persons we can be in his image. In intimate communion he can take us back into those experiences which distorted our self-acceptance. Feeling his love, we can dare to see the negative influences of childhood and adolescence which gave us the wrong picture of our potential. Then he asks, "Will you dare to forgive as I have forgiven you? Will you let go of the hurts?"

He wants to reform our thinking about ourselves. He can confront our debilitating comparisons. "Don't take your measurements from what others do or accomplish. There's no one else in the world exactly like you. You have a unique destiny to fulfill. Trust me to show you your special place to stand." How shall we respond? Are we willing to give up the security of self-negation and replace it with the Lord's affirmation?

But he is not finished. We can feel the touch of his presence on our bodies. So much of our insecurity is caused by negative feelings about our physical selves. We are all uniquely wrapped. We can change proportions, but basically we must all live with what we have been given. Our dislike of ourselves is manifested in the way we mistreat our bodies. The Lord speaks tenderly: "This is my temple. I love you as you are. I have used the tall and the short, the fat and the thin, the handsome and the ugly to do my work through the ages. My Spirit living in you can make you the radiant person you long to be. Get in touch with your body. Rediscover the joy of breathing, touching, tasting, seeing, hearing. What a wonder you are!"

Next, the Lord can give us eyes to see the other people in our lives. We need their love. But most of them are so insecure themselves that there is little energy left to refortify us. "Don't build your life on what people ought to do to make you secure," the Lord says. "You will always feel insecure until you are engaged in being to others what I have been to you. Find out what you can do and say to communicate esteem to them, and leave your security up to me. When you are a channel of my love and encouragement, you will know such joy that your lust for security will be displaced by the delight of cooperating with me in building up others." When we begin to see people through the Lord's eyes, we are moved more by compassion than competition. We suddenly realize that we have discovered a liberating secret. We have been blessed by being a blessing. Security grows as we feel important to the welfare of others.

The Lord is not finished with us. He knows that insecurity is also caused by a feeling of inadequate resources to meet life's challenges. In the quiet of our oneness with him, he reminds us of the power available through his indwelling Spirit. We *are* inadequate; we were created that way so that we would depend on him for what we need to do his work. He can show us the kind of persons we could be if filled with his Spirit. The gifts and fruit of the Holy Spirit are given one after the other; we can see ourselves filled with wisdom, knowledge, faith, discernment, healing power, and praise. Love, joy, peace, patience, kindness, goodness, faithfulness, gentleness, self-control are manifested in the amazing picture he can give us of our new selves. "Why did you live in spiritual poverty when all of this was available to you? No wonder you felt insecure!" he says with incisive challenge.

Lastly, we are given the opportunity to dream. The future is going to be more exciting than anything in the past, he tells us. "What would you do and be if you did not worry about your self-imposed limitations? If you dared discard your reservations, what would you dare to attempt?" The moment is electric. Now we must ask him for guidance before we answer. "Lord, I want your dreams for me to be the focus of my vision. What do you have planned for me?" We are surprised and amazed by his response: "Don't fall back into that imagined separation between you and me. We are one. I prayed for that and went to the cross to make it possible. You belong to me now. I possess the tissues of your brain. Your imagination is my gift to you. Dare to believe that your dreams are my inspirations!"

Now excitement surges through us. Reservations and worries are gone. We now know that as long as we are competely surrendered to our Lord, we can trust and dare to plan adventuresomely. We suddenly realize that our minds have been grasped by the original innovator and visionary.

Paul explained what we've just been through: "Now we have received not the spirit of the world, but the Spirit which is from God, that we might understand the gifts bestowed on us by God. . . . But we have the mind of Christ" (1 Cor. 2:12, 16). Surely this was the basis of the Apostle's conviction that, "If any one is in Christ, he is a new creation; the old has passed away, behold, the new has come" (2 Cor. 5:17).

Indeed! A new mind with a healed memory, a Christ-oriented self-image, and a liberated imagination to form, hold, and achieve the unlimited possibilities of the future.

All because we belong to the "I am." Once again he has made things happen. And he will never let us go. Each time we feel insecure, we will be recalled to our oneness with him. With tender love he will speak, and security will return: "I know you. You have been chosen for intimacy with me. You belong to me!"

13

The Way Out of Loneliness

Loneliness Is More Than the Absence of People

> *"I am the way."*
> John 14:6

WHAT COMES TO YOUR MIND when I say the word *lonely?* What's your image of loneliness? A derelict on a park bench? A friendless person away from home in a strange city? Someone separated from loved ones over the holidays? A person with very few or no significant, satisfying relationships? A social misfit unable to relate creatively to others?

Careful. Loneliness is a much more universal emotional condition than that. We all feel it at times. Some people we'd least expect to feel lonely are seldom free from the gnawing pain. It lurks under many a jolly mask, and pulses in the hearts of the most gregarious and outgoing. It's there beneath the busy adequacy or pretended assurance of the popular, the famous, and the attractive people we admire.

One of the most crucial discoveries I have made over the years, working with and listening to people, is that loneliness has little to do with the absence of people. We can feel lonely in a crowd, among friends, in a marriage, in the family, at a sorority or fraternity house, and in a church.

Loneliness is the anxiety of unrelatedness, the disturbing realization of our separateness. It is an aloneness in which we feel an acute, chronic, nondirected sense of alienation. It's when we realize that we are unique, distinct persons with centers of individuality which we long to share, and yet fear exposing, all at the same time. Thomas Wolfe was right: "Loneliness, far from being a rare and curious phenomenon peculiar to myself and a few other solitary men, is the central fact of human existence."

Our profound misunderstanding of loneliness is expressed in the way we admonish ourselves and others when we feel its disquieting pangs. Get with people, we say. Make friends. Get married, change spouses. Join a sensitivity group. Travel. Live a little. Let yourself go. Get rid of your inhibitions. State your needs and demand that they be satisfied. Expand your horizons.

Our flight from loneliness has plunged us into a frantic togetherness. We have clubs for every imaginable purpose and some with no purpose at all. Our time is overloaded with endless activities because we fear having to be alone. We long to have friends; then, when we have them, we are alarmed because the feeling of loneliness persists. Singles want to get married to heal their loneliness, only to find out that lack of communication is the nemesis of most marriages.

Celia in T. S. Eliot's *The Cocktail Party* expressed it clearly: "No . . . it isn't that I want to be alone. But that everyone's alone—or so it seems to me. They make noises, and think they are talking to each other; they make faces, and think they understand each other. And I'm sure they don't."

Loneliness is not isolation; it's insulation. It's the fear of knowing and being known. A Hollywood star confided to me, "I have agents and bodyguards, a driver to whisk me away after a performance. Then I get home and wonder if I was a success. And my wife and kids don't seem to be impressed that they are living with a star. I have everything I've ever wanted except a truly deep relationship."

A wife shared the pain of not being able to communicate her deepest feelings with her husband. "I wish he really knew me!" she said wistfully. "I feel very lonely." The amazing thing is that, as a leading lady in the Los Angeles social whirl, she receives a lot of recognition.

A teenager said that he found it difficult to talk out his feelings with his parents without criticism or overalarm. "They seem so put together, like they never had problems or worries like I have. Sometimes I would just like to talk until I know what I want to say."

A young woman complained that she had developed the conversational habit of saying "Know what I mean?" She feels a need for some response, and now says the pleading words without thinking about it. We all long to register on someone's mind and heart what we're feeling and thinking. Know what I mean?

We can empathize with all these people I've described. I could cite hundreds of others from any one year of pastoral counseling and care. I am constantly amazed at the loneliness I hear expressed in otherwise adjusted and competent people. It comes out in an unguarded comment, a look in the eye, or undeniable body language. Each of us feels the estrangement and separateness of life. We are individual citadels, walled castles with the moat bridge up most of the time. Who really knows us? Whom do we know deeply? Wistfully we sing: "I've got to walk this lonesome valley. Nobody here can walk it for me. I've got to walk it for myself."

Not so! We do not need to walk it alone. The God who created us has come to walk it with us. In Jesus Christ he has come to heal the essential cause of loneliness. If we define loneliness as the anxiety of unrelatedness, then we can affirm a basic purpose of the incarnation as God's reestablishment of our relationship with him and one another. He came into a lonely world where people were estranged from him and one another, and revealed the way of intimacy with him and others as the cure for loneliness. From Bethlehem to Calvary, God offered love as the antidote for our loneliness.

Loneliness is none other than homesickness for God.

It's inbred in us. We cannot escape it. Nothing or no one in this world can fill it. There is in every human being a sublime nostalgia. The Greek root of this word is made up of two parts: *nostos* for "return home" and *algos* for "severe pain." There is a pain of loneliness in all of us to return home. No group, friend, or loved one can fill the longing. They were never meant to. God has placed a longing for him that no person can satisfy.

> Lord, Thou art life, though I be dead;
>   Love's fire Thou art, however cold I be:
> No heaven have I, nor place to lay my head,
>   Nor home, but Thee.
>
> Christina Rosetti

Our loneliness is a "homing instinct." Just as animals, birds, and fish have a homing instinct capable of leading them back to their original habitats, so we have a loneliness to be at home with God. We've all heard of dogs or cats that have found their way home after being lost at great distances. Pigeons are distinguished for their ability to fly hundreds of miles back to their homes; swallows make an aerial journey of thousands of miles each year and return to the exact nesting place they left. Salmon return to spawn in the very part of the river where they were hatched. The examples from the natural world are many.

God has placed the same instinct in us. And intimate communion with him is our home. God came himself to show us the way. That's the impact of Jesus' "I am" declaration: "I am the way . . . no one comes to the Father, but by me" (John 14:6). Yahweh himself came to heal our loneliness.

It was on the night before Jesus was crucified that he gave the secret for overcoming loneliness. His disciples were feeling the loneliness of impending separation from him. They feared what was about to happen. Jesus' somber predictions about his death were about to come true. What he said to give the courage is our hope in loneliness.

"Let not your hearts be troubled; believe in God, believe also in me. In my Father's house are many rooms; if it were not so, would I have told you that I go to prepare a place for you? And when I go and prepare a place for you, I will come again and will take you to myself, that where I am you may be also. And you know the way" (John 14:1–4).

What has that to do with loneliness? Everything. Jesus came from the heart of God to show us the way to the heart of God. That's the secret of healing loneliness, the homesickness for God.

We do not need to be troubled any more. The Greek word translated "be troubled," is *tarassesthō,* which means to be tossed to and fro—like restless waves under the impact of a blast of wind. Jesus' assuring word is ultimately reliable: "Believe in God, believe also in me."

Jesus and the Father are one. Jesus is God's word about himself—to us. The Father's house is the Father's heart. It's expansive and inclusive. When Jesus said it has many rooms or mansions, he meant that it is our true abiding place. Here the Greek word is *monai,* meaning abiding places. This does not mean that the Father's heart has different abiding places, but an abiding place that is grand and glorious, big enough to include all who come home through him. It is waiting for all the homesick souls who will believe and accept the love and forgiveness offered by God's invitation through his Son.

Now press on in Jesus' promise. He tells us that the house of God's heart is open not only at our physical deaths, but *now,* as a quality of eternal life to replace our loneliness during our days on earth. Heaven is a condition of relationship which begins now and is absolutely undiminishable by death.

Then Jesus asked, "If it were not so, would I have told you that I go to prepare a place for you?" Where was he going to prepare that place? We usually think of his return to heaven. Not so. I believe he was talking about Calvary. That's where he was going to prepare a place of reconciliation, forgiveness, and acceptance. The verb translated "to prepare" is *hetoimazō*, meaning to make ready. Where else could that be done but on Golgotha?

It would be after that was completed that the Lord would return in the power of the Holy Spirit. "I will come again, and take you to myself, that where I am you may be also." According to A. T. Robertson, the literal meaning of the Greek is, "And I shall take you along to my own home."[1] When would that be—when he came again? I believe he meant not only at the Second Coming, but also after the Resurrection and at the present time, when he comes to each of us. Right now!

In that light we can understand how Jesus' "I am" promise of being the Way is the answer to loneliness. He is the way to the heart of God, paved through the sacrifice of Calvary. He takes us by the hand and shows us the way to go home. Until we are "at home" with the Lord now in the days of our lives, we will be lonely. It's inevitable; we were created to dwell in him, to abide in his heart, and our hearts will be lonely until we come home. And when we do, we are welcomed home as if we never left. An intimate communion of love and forgiveness awaits us. There's only one way to God's heart, the way he ordained— through Jesus Christ, the Way. When we know that, we can sing in our loneliness,

> I've found a Friend; O such a Friend!
>   He loved me ere I knew Him;
> He drew me with the cords of love,
>   And thus He bound me to Him.
>
> And round my heart still closely twine
>   Those ties which nought can sever,
> For I am His, and He is mine,
>   For ever and for ever.
>   James Grindley Small

---

1. *Word Pictures in The New Testament, Vol. 5*, (Nashville: Broadman Press, 1943), p. 249.

The healing of loneliness begins with Christ's leading us home. But it does not end there. Christ is not only the way to God, but the way to our true selves. Loneliness is rooted in a complex of factors within us which must be transformed. Christ leads us home to ourselves. Oh, to be at home in our own persons! We cannot develop deep, fulfilling relationships with others until we can live with ourselves. Axel Munthe, the Swedish physician and writer, said, "A man can stand a lot as long as he can stand himself."

This requires solitude. There is no healing of loneliness without solitude. At the center of our separateness and uniqueness we must dare to see ourselves, to face ourselves, and dare to be ourselves. Jesus taught us the importance of solitude. He retreated periodically to be alone with God and taught his disciples to "come away by yourselves" (Mark 6:31). The Greek means, "come away for yourselves." Come away to allow God to heal, refresh and renew the true person he's created us to be. We must draw into the inner center to allow God to do battle with self-negation and distortion of our self-images. The Lord must show us the way to ourselves before he can be the way to new, satisfying relationships with others.

Solitude is not easy at first. For some it is terrifying. Privacy is not a priority in our present age. Often we escape the need for solitude by flinging ourselves back into conversation with people, into some activity, or into some television program. One man I know stays up late each night just to hear the closing devotion on the television, so he can hear a human voice say a benediction and a warm "good night."

But those who dare to persist in a habitual daily time of quiet solitude find resources for living nothing else can provide. Jeremiah said, "I sat alone, because thy hand was upon me" (15:17). God lays his hand of blessing and power on us when we are quiet. Then we can ask life's deepest questions and have the Lord raise questions with us about what we are doing with the gift of life.

Here again Jesus has prepared a place—the place of

forgiveness, assurance, and hope through the cross. In solitude we can stop running; we can allow God to love us. He breaks through the layers of defensiveness and lays us open so that we can see ourselves. His forgiving love reconciles those things in us which cause self-hate and destructiveness. We meet the person in us whom frantic activity and overinvolvement has produced—the depleted self, spent in exhausting human relationships.

Solitude is not for evasive talking to God, but for incisive listening. "Be still, and know that I am God" (Ps. 46:10). "In quietness . . . shall be your strength" (Isa. 30:15). In solitude, all our ways of preventing God from getting at us melt away. Be sure of this: if we will not choose solitude, God will allow an occasion for it we may not like. Sickness, a break in our meteor flash of success, a forced removal from the pressures of people. There is no creative thinking, no important decision-making, no change of personality or life style without solitude. As Paul Tillich said, "In the moments of solitude something is done to us. The center of our being, the inner self which is the ground of our aloneness, is elevated to the divine center and taken into it. Therein we can rest without losing ourselves." It's in isolation that the insulation that keeps us from other people is torn away.

What Artur Rubenstein said of practice, I say of solitude: "If I fail to practice one day, I know it; if I miss practicing two days, my agent knows it; if I refuse to practice three days, my public knows it." And so with us in our relationships. If we have no solitude, we have nothing to give to people when we are with them.

Now Jesus is ready to lead us out of solitude to other people. He is the way of a new humanity. "The Way" became a synonym for Christianity in the first century. The quality of relationships in the early church earned Christians the distinction of being called "followers of the Way." This became the ethics and ethos of the church.

So many of the reasons we are lonely stem from the fact that we do not know how to follow Jesus' way of communication. Here are seven aspects of his way of living with other people which will banish loneliness:

First, Jesus' way is nondefensive. It is easy to project onto other people our negative attitudes toward ourselves. Such transference takes place in a subtle way. Because we do not really like and love ourselves, we expect the same attitude from others. We see other people as our enemies, and constantly set ourselves up for the disappointment we expected all along. Then an inadvertent, subconscious thing takes place. People feel our insecurity and read back to us in their attitudes what we are feeling about ourselves. And so we continue to be shut up in the prison of loneliness.

A second aspect of Jesus' way is acceptance. People long to be with a person who accepts them as they are. Our attitudes toward people are often so filled with our agendas for them that they feel we are trying to control them. We end up feeling lonely because in such a situation people cannot be themselves or open themselves to us, nor we to them.

Third, Jesus' way is nonjudgmental. He made it painfully clear that judgmentalism always boomerangs: "Judge not, that you be not judged. For with the judgment you pronounce you will be judged, and the measure you give will be the measure you get" (Matt. 7:1–2). Judgmental people are lonely people. Not only do others avoid a self-appointed critic, but they are also motivated to return judgment for judgment. Charles Kingsley, the nineteenth-century English clergyman and writer, said, "If you wish to be miserable, you must think about yourself; about what you want, what you like, what respect people ought to pay you, and then to you nothing will be pure. You will spoil everything you touch; you will make sin and misery out of everything God sends you. You can be as wretched as you choose."

As wretched as I choose? Yes! Judgmentalism is the sure path to wretchedness, the loneliness of the self-appointed efficiency expert who tries to check everyone's productivity according to his own standards. If we keep that up, we will always be lonely.

Fourth, Jesus' way is the way of forgiveness. His promise of our forgiveness has a burr on the end of the hook: "For if you forgive men their trespasses, your heavenly Father also will forgive you; but if you do not forgive men their trespasses, neither will your Father forgive your trespasses" (Matt. 6:14–15). People already know how bad they are; they need to know how great they can become. A warm, sensitive, forgiving person will have more friends than he or she knows how to handle. When we follow the way of forgiveness, our prisons of loneliness will be invaded by hundreds of people who want to be with us because of the gracious attitude which we radiate. The world waits for someone who will understand, forgive before they ask to be forgiven, and offer comfort for life's failures.

The fifth aspect of Jesus' way is vulnerability. This dynamic ingredient means openness about ourselves and a willingness to share both the difficulties and joys of our lives. Ever notice how quickly a friendship grows with a person who shares his inner life with us? We feel trusted, affirmed, of value, and free to share ourselves in turn. Honesty with people does not mean telling them what they should do or be, but sharing our struggles and delights.

Two people come to mind. One has become one of my closest friends. One night while we were having dinner, I shared a very personal hurt in my own life. That moment galvanized our relationship. He has referred to that time repeatedly and has opened his life to me. I could never be lonely with a friend like that.

Another person had real needs and wanted my help. But each time we were together he had to first straighten me out about how I was leading my church; then he would dump his needs on me, hoping I would respond tenderly and empathically. A love-hate, impulsion-repulsion syndrome was constantly at work beneath the surface. He had never discovered the dynamics of vulnerability—that it was his first to share his needs and ask for help, then to let me share my needs and allow him the privilege of giving advice. He was a very lonely man because he treated his friends, wife, and associates the way he did me.

Sixth, Jesus' way is the way of initiative love. Most people are so insecure that they will wait to be loved before they are free to love. But when our solitude in the Father's house has given us the liberating assurance of God's love, we can become primary, first-move lovers of people.

My friend Lloyd Umbarger lived in the home of Henrietta Mears, the great Christian educator. One day, while he was watering the grass, he noticed a beautiful young woman coming to see Dr. Mears. After spending several hours with that powerful person-liberator, the young woman came out radiant. Lloyd asked her how she was doing. The young woman confided that she had gone to see Dr. Mears about her feelings of loneliness, and had confessed that she had few friends. "What did Dr. Mears say?" Lloyd asked. "Well," the young woman responded, "she asked me to name the qualities I would like in a friend. So I told her I needed people who accepted me, would not misuse me, on whom I could count in spite of everything, and who could share my hopes and dreams. Then Dr. Mears said an amazing thing. 'Go be that kind of friend to other people, and you will find that is what they will be to you.'" Powerful advice about being an initiative lover of people. It's sin to be lonely alone in a lonely world!

Finally, Jesus' way out of loneliness involves being part of a movement that is following him in changing the world. He wants to give us the gift of solitude in which he can transform those things in us which keep us from satisfying relationships with people, and he longs to enable us to be people who conquer loneliness by being wound-healers in others.

We don't have to be part of the lonely crowd any longer. Jesus walked the lonesome valley for us so we no longer need to walk it alone. Listen to his promise: "Lo, I am with you always." Our response? Well, here's mine.

> I cannot do without Thee
>   I cannot stand alone,
> I have no strength or goodness
>   No wisdom of my own.
> But Thou, beloved Saviour
>   Art all in all to me,
> And perfect strength in weakness
>   Is theirs who lean on Thee.

14

Freedom from Inhibitions

The Truth Sets
Us Free

"I am . . . the truth."
John 14:6

A FRIEND OF MINE ended a letter recently with the words, "My prayer for you is that the Lord will continue to set you free to live an uninhibited life!" The word *uninhibited* gave me pause. My friend is a careful scholar, and always chooses his words thoughtfully. I checked the definition and derivation of the word. An inhibition is a self-imposed prohibition or restraint, an inner check on free activity or expression. In the positive sense, an uninhibited life would be one that was guided by an essential truth which liberated a person from confused thinking and restrained feeling. Jesus Christ came to set us free from distorted thinking about God and the meaning of life, so that we could be unbound from our inhibitions and made able to love God, ourselves, and others. My friend's prayer was on target. What he wanted for me, I want for myself.

And so do millions of others. We all long to become free people—able to be ourselves, love deeply, live joyfully. I should not have been surprised that a large number of people who responded to my inventory of needs expressed a longing for personal freedom. Many said they wanted to be free of inhibitions which kept them from enjoying the freedom of Christ. They were aware of the fact that true freedom is not lawlessness and irresponsibility, but a much more profound kind of liberation. Christ's freedom liberates us to love, care, and be responsible in a creative way. The Lord releases us from the reserve and reservations which keep us bound up, inverted on ourselves, stingy in our affirmations, and cautious in our acceptance of others. We all want that kind of release! We gladly join those who said that their deepest need is to become a free person.

The world into which Jesus came was bound up in gross contradictions, distortions, and misunderstandings both of God and the purpose of life. He came to set things right and to call a new people who would be distinguished by their freedom.

To Jesus, truth and freedom were inseparable. He said, "I am . . . the truth" (John 14:6). Don't miss the definite article *the*. The word is *hē* in Greek. The meaning is undeniable in any language. This powerful "I am" statement means, "I am Yahweh, God with you. I am the truth about God, you, and life itself." Jesus Christ is not one savior among many. He is the ultimate truth. The Greek word used here for truth implies undistorted reality. Jesus was the absolute truth, contradicting all of the false ideas about God and life which people had developed through the ages.

This "I am" declaration must be closely tied to the Lord's promise, "If you continue in my word, you are truly my disciples, and you will know the truth, and the truth will make you free. . . . If the Son makes you free, you will be free indeed" (John 8:31–32, 36). The only way to freedom is intimate union with the Truth.

Let's inventory all the things from which Jesus Christ, the truth, has set us free. We are free of guilt, condemning consciences, haunting memories, the insecurity of inadequacy, the frustration of self-negation, the dread of the future. Worry over death is past. We are assured of abundant life now and eternal life forever. There is nothing which can happen to or around us that Christ cannot handle. He towers over history. He is the ultimate point of reference about reality.

This is magnificently focused in one of my favorite verses from Ephesians: "For he has made known to us in all wisdom and insight the mystery of his will, according to his purpose which he set forth in Christ as a plan for the fulness of time, to unite all things in him, things in heaven and things on earth" (Eph. 1:9–10). Christ is the image and illumination of eternal truth. He is God's word about himself, the liberating word of truth which sets us free.

Christ's truth is intellectual, emotional, and relational: it reorients our thinking, becomes the basis of sorting out our feelings, and gives us a new way of relating to people with forgiveness and unqualified love. That can only happen if we come to *egō eimi* as the ultimate truth. The white light of the truth exposes our need of him and all that we do and say to contradict him. When Jesus says, "I am the truth," he indicates, as Paul Tillich put it, "that in him the true, the genuine, the ultimate reality is present, or, in other words, that God is present, unveiled, undistorted in his infinite depth, in his magnificent mystery."

For something to be called the truth, it must be consistent with reality in every way. It must cover all contingencies and be universally applicable. Jesus Christ is the truth because he *is* reality; his revelation of God is consistent with God's essential nature, and his message is God's way for man to live with him and with one another. There is nothing left out, no question unanswered, no eventuality not covered by what he was, said, and did.

But knowing that Jesus is truth is very different from experiencing him as truth. William Temple, the former archbishop of York and of Canterbury, said, "The ultimate truth is not a system of propositions grasped by perfect intelligence but a Personal Being apprehended by love."

We are not set free from our inhibitions only by knowing Jesus as a conceptual truth, but by giving our lives to him and following him in absolute obedience. The secret of becoming a free person is to be taken captive. We will constantly be inhibited in some area until we accept liberating bondage to Christ. Just as a violin string is not free to accomplish its purpose until it is stretched on a violin, we are not free until we are captivated by Christ.

We have been given the awesome power of free will. We each have the capacity to choose our direction in life, to determine our destiny. It is with our free will that we choose our master. Everyone must have one—the person or goal that demands our unreserved commitment.

Now we must ask: Has our free choice given us freedom or inhibition? If we are committed to legalism, then we will be inhibited from loving those who do not meet the test of our rules and regulations. If our goal is money, then we will be inhibited by anything which threatens our material wealth; we will spend our days sorting, counting, and keeping. If we are committed to self, our inhibitions will be legion. We must protect, expand, and defend our status at all costs.

On the other hand, true freedom means to give up, give in, and then give out. Our inhibitions are conquered when we give up our lives to Christ, give in to his absolute lordship, and then give out his love to others. The only free people I know are those who have been liberated from their inhibitions by an absolute, unreserved surrender to Christ. Paul Scherer was right: "We find freedom when we find God; we lose it when we lose him." George Matheson expressed it clearly:

> Make me a captive, Lord,
>   And then I shall be free;
> Force me to render up my sword,
>   And I shall conqueror be.
> I sink in life's alarms
>   When by myself I stand;
> Imprison me within Thine arms,
>   And strong shall be my hand.
>
> My heart is weak and poor
>   Until it master find;
> It has no spring of action sure,

It varies with the wind;
It cannot freely move,
   Till Thou has wrought its chain;
Enslave it with Thy matchless love,
   And deathless it shall reign.

My will is not my own
   Till Thou hast made it Thine;
If it could reach a monarch's throne
   It must its crown resign;
It only stands unbent,
   Amid the clashing strife,
When on Thy bosom it has leant
   And found in Thee its life.

The "I am" comes as liberator, emancipator, and enabler of freedom. Think for a moment about your own set of inhibitions. What keeps you bound up, uptight, restricted? Now picture yourself as a free person liberated by the Truth. Determine today to live and love, give and forgive as a free person. It will not be easy at first; old habits of holding back will get in the way. But *Egō eimi* is with you. Each time you are tempted to pull back, tell him you need his help. You will develop new ways of reacting. And you are on the way to freedom!

The other day, I received a lovely gift in the mail. It had a special tag attached that could be returned through the mails to assure the sender that the gift had been received. All I had to do was sign and seal it, and put it in the mail. It said, "Thank you for your gift. It arrived safely today and I plan to enjoy it."

That makes me wonder how I could tell the Lord I had received his gift of freedom rooted in truth. I decided to live it and share it. He'll know. And so will the people in my life!

15

Our Battle with Boredom

Experiencing a Thrilling Life

> *"I am . . . the life."*
> John 14:6

A TRAVEL AGENCY displayed an attractive, but beguiling advertisement in its window: "Escape the ordinary, the usual, the predictable, the boring. Take a fun-filled trip with us!"

I overheard two young women who were looking wistfully at a poster displaying the adventure of travel to faraway places. One said, "Doesn't that sound exciting?" The other replied negatively, "Sure, if I didn't have to take the ordinary, the usual, the predictable, the boring with me." "Who's that?" her friend responded with surprise. "Me!" she said dolefully.

As I walked on down the street, I looked into the faces of people who were hurrying back to work after lunch. I wondered how many of them find life a thrilling experience. Were there others who were taking the ordinary, the usual, the predictable, the boring back to work with them? And how many would find their work anything more than that? What about when they got home that night?

Someone once said that the most terrifying thing in life is to do anything for the last time. Allow me to suggest something much worse. It is to do the same things over and over again, with the same people, in the same places, in the same old ways. Sameness results in the blandness of boredom.

When I did my inventory of deepest needs, I was alarmed and amazed to discover how many people said they were bored. Often they did not use the word, but it was there beneath the expressions of their need.

One man wrote, "I'm in a rut and need out—I need something new!" A woman said, "All the excitement is gone. My greatest fear is that everything will stay the same." Another person said, "What's wrong with me? I have everything, but I've lost all zest for my marriage, my job, my future." Still another said, "I used to be a very optimistic person. Now I realize that I no longer believe that a change of scenery, job, or mate is going to make things better for me. I feel like I'm imprisoned in a cell of sameness." A teenager, bogged down in studies, put it this way, "I seem to have lost the reason I'm working so hard for grades. I'm really bored and need a fresh jab of enthusiasm."

Boredom is tedious dullness. When boredom strikes, life loses its sparkle, people their wonder, and daily life its luster. And it can happen to any of us. For some it's a constant condition.

What about you? Are you ever bored? Be careful how you answer; your immediate response may be no, but the inner condition may be expressing itself in subtle ways. Let me ask you—do you ever live with the hope that someone, something, some new experience will invade your life and give it new excitement or purpose? Do you ever long for some adventure to sweep you off your feet with an impelling challenge, opportunity, or change of scenery which would put some gusto into your life? Does the thought of life remaining as it is depress or discourage you? Is there something in you that has sort of given up and feels that life has passed you by?

Most of all, could you say that your life is thrilling? If you cannot say that you are thrilled about your daily life now, not in some far-off future, then you are bored! I talk with people every day who do not find life a thrilling experience. The telltale signs of the blight of boredom are evident in their voices, their expressions. The opposite of boredom is not activity; it's excitement!

Kierkegaard said, "What is anxiety? The next day!" And I say, what is boredom? It's the fear that the next day will be the same as today! We long to escape into some new experience which will cure our boredom. For many, life is lived in anticipation that some hoped-for change, event, person, or rearrangement of circumstances will suddenly release them from the prison of boredom. When the anticipated future turns out to have been oversold, there's nothing left but the ruts of routine.

It's startling to realize how few people are finding life today an exciting adventure. Boredom, more than being the condition of a few unadjusted people, is the spiritual sickness of millions of Americans—young and old, single and married, people in strategic jobs and people in unrewarding jobs that do little more than provide bread on the table, the famous people and people who are seldom noticed.

What would it take to make your life thrilling? The definition of *thrilling* is not limited to a roller coaster or a new sports car. The word refers to having a feeling of excitement. Often it's sharp and sudden, but the kind of thrill I mean is that which persists in the midst of the mundane, the usual, the ordinary. We will never win the battle with boredom until we discover how to live in the present, rather than in some imagined future, with the people life has given us and in the circumstances in which we find ourselves and still keep a sense of excitement. A delightful change or unexpected surprise may come when we least expect it, but unless we have discovered the thrill of life as it is, we will soon twist the most dramatic happenings into escapes rather than enjoyment.

We will be bored until we find a purpose and passion in life which will be thrilling in spite of the drab surroundings, the dull people, and the deadly routine of life. Only Jesus Christ can make life thrilling in a consistent, lasting, and vibrant way.

Here again, one of the "I am" declarations meets our need. Jesus summed up his whole ministry with the startling statement, "I am the way, and the truth, and the life" (John 14:6). As we have seen in the two previous chapters, he is the way to God, to ourselves, and to other people. He is the ultimate truth about God and what we're meant to be. But the climax of this statement is found in the word *life*. *"Egō eimi,"* Yahweh, God with us is *the* life. He revealed how life was intended to be lived. He called his followers into an exciting quality of life in fellowship with him and gave them a commission which would banish boredom from their lives forever. Jesus Christ came to make life thrilling. The key word which describes the new life Jesus imparted is *joy*—joy which is independent of people, places, positions, or pleasantries. The joy of life in Christ, and Christ in us, is the only lasting antidote to boredom.

Let's look at the deeper causes of boredom and see how Christ, the life, can heal us:

First of all, boredom is symptomatic. It tells us that something deeper is wrong. Like pain, it can be viewed as a sign that there is an inner sickness which needs healing. Boredom is the antithesis of everything God created us to know and experience. When life degenerates into sameness, we have missed the "many splendored thing"—the love of life. Boredom is sin; it's separation from the wonder of life God created us to experience.

Second, boredom is self-inflicted. It is the result of self-devaluation. It comes from accepting the fact that the life we have is all we deserve. Boredom is self-induced spiritual sickness. It's being inverted on a person who has not become very interesting—ourselves. If we don't enjoy ourselves, who else will? Healthy self-appreciation is assertive. It demands that life offer more than it has. Boredom is settling for sameness because we refuse to take responsibility for ourselves. It is an outward expression of a cowardly feeling of impotence about changing the routines and obligations of life.

Third, boredom is blaming people when we should bless them. We will never break out of the self-inflicted incarceration of boredom as long as we try to make other people responsible for our happiness. How often we hear ourselves or other people say, "If I only had more or different friends. If I had a different mate, or boss, or fellow workers." That's a game we all play at times. But no one, not even our families, is responsible to make us happy and cure our boredom.

Boredom is seeking to find meaning in the relationships and responsibilities of life, rather than bringing meaning to them. The most attractive and interesting person will become boring unless we bring vitality and vigor to our relationship with him or her. The reason people become boring is that we expect them to do or be something to make life exciting for us. Who hasn't looked at someone else's wife, husband, pastor, friend, or associate and mused, "I'll bet life is exciting for him"? No job is meant to be our ultimate meaning. When we demand that it become the source of all our purpose or passion, eventually it will cause us to miss the reason we were born.

Fourth, boredom is the trapped feeling of having no place to go, no new worlds to conquer. When your purpose in life is getting ahead, what do you do when you've arrived? If financial security is your thing, how much is enough? If recognition is the lust of your life, when will you be satisfied? What number of significant people or groups or clubs do you need for your trophy chest? And so it goes. It's an alarming experience to meet people who have what we've been pressing frantically to acquire and find that they are still bored. Be sure of this: there are no heights to which we can climb, no achievements we can acquire, no recognition we can be given, no friends we can make that will cure our boredom. The Lord made it so. He alone is meant to be our reason for being.

The apostle Paul discovered this. I believe that one of the reasons he persecuted the Church prior to his conversion was that he was bored. That may astound you, but look at his own confession. He had achieved all that could be acquired to make his life significant, according to his community. He was a Hebrew of Hebrews, born of the tribe of Benjamin, a distinguished Pharisee, a member of the powerful Sanhedrin. What further honors could he be given? What new words were there to conquer? Could it be that wiping out the followers of the Way became a distraction from boredom with a career that had crested before its time?

Then, through the witness of Stephen, whose passion for Christ made him radiant with joy even as he was being stoned to death, the Pharisee was deeply shaken and prepared for his encounter with Christ on the road to Damascus. After his conversion and years of companionship with the Lord, he was able to say the only words which can finally banish boredom: "For me to live is Christ!" (Phil. 1:21). For Paul, life really became exciting "in Christ." Then he could say triumphantly, "But whatever gain I had, I counted as loss for the sake of Christ. Indeed I count everything as loss because of the surpassing worth of knowing Christ Jesus my Lord. For his sake I have suffered the loss of all things, and count them as refuse, in order that I may gain Christ and be found in him, not having a righteousness of my own . . . but that which is through faith in Christ" (Phil. 3:7–9). He went on to express excitement about pressing ahead in the upward call of Christ.

The Lord's "I am" affirmation that he was "the life" is vividly portrayed in what happened to Paul. In Christ, Paul found what he called "fullness of life." And so can we. Life in Christ is the thrilling alternative to boredom.

It must begin with an intimate companionship with the Lord himself. We will be bored until that exciting friendship is begun. This should not be confused with religion or churchmanship, both of which can be boring without a personal relationship with Christ. I know too many bored church members and clergy to mislead you in believing that more theology, rituals, or church organizations will cure boredom. Something deeper is needed. We will become bored with the most elaborate buildings, music, and activities unless we've experienced a liberating fellowship with *the* life himself.

In Trinity Church, Boston, there is a remarkable statue of Phillips Brooks by Saint-Gaudens. The spiritual giant stands at a pulpit with an open Bible. Behind him stands Jesus with his hand on the preacher's shoulder. The reason for Brooks's greatness is preserved for posterity. In a letter to a friend he wrote, "All experience comes to be but more and more the pressure of Christ's life upon ours. I cannot tell how personal this grows to me. He is here. He knows me and I know Him. It is no figure of speech; it is the realest thing in the world." No wonder that one of Brooks's biographers says, "He conversed with Christ as his most intimate friend. He loved his earthly friends and enjoyed their companionship, but for none of them had he such attachment as for Christ." An echo of Paul's "For me to live is Christ." Or as the verse can be translated, "Life for me is Christ!"

The experience of joy is the sure test that we have begun this new life. Jesus said, "These things I have spoken to you that my joy may be in you, and that your joy may be full" (John: 15:11). The antithesis of boredom is joy. It is constant, regardless of where we are or what we have. Joy is unassailable, undiminishable by circumstances. It's the special gift of union with Christ, *the* life. With his joy we can face difficulties, deal with impossible situations, and endure the most drab, uninspiring, mundane circumstances of life. Press on in the Christian life until you experience the joy!

But that joy of intimate friendship with Christ must be renewed each day. We will drift back into boredom unless we experience a freshness for each day's needs and opportunities. Jeremiah discovered the secret in very difficult times. "This I call to mind, and therefore I have hope: The steadfast love of the Lord never ceases, his mercies never come to an end; they are new every morning; great is thy faithfulness" (Lam. 3:21–23). Repeat that every day, especially on the plateaus of boredom, and joy will burst forth in us.

The Lord has created us so that life will become boring without consistent companionship from him. Solomon discovered this. He battled boredom when he finally confronted the vanity of life. There's no better explanation of boredom than the first three chapters of Ecclesiastes. "All things are full of weariness; a man cannot utter it; the eye is not satisfied with seeing, nor the ear filled with hearing. What has been is what will be, and what has been done is what will be done; and there is nothing new under the sun. Is there a thing of which it is said, 'See, this is new'? It has been already, in the ages before us" (Eccles. 1:8–10.)

But read on. Solomon's experience of boredom finally forced him to realize that there is no enjoyment or lasting delight in life's accumulations or accomplishments. "God has made it so, in order that men should fear before him" (Eccles. 3:14). That awe and wonder are the beginning of the wisdom that nothing satisfies our quest for a thrilling life except the Lord himself. Boredom alarms us with the realization that we have drifted from our only source of joy. But when we know the joy of the indwelling Christ, there's an impelling urge to celebrate.

Therefore, the next step in overcoming boredom is to become a celebrant. Because of the Lord's joy in us, we can celebrate ourselves, other people, the wonder of life, and the magnificence of the world around us. A joyous celebrant is one whom Christ has liberated to take sheer delight in being a very special, loved, forgiven, accepted, and cherished person, one who can enjoy the person he or she is and can become. We will not be bored if we are fascinated with what Christ is doing with the potential of our lives.

That leads to the ability to celebrate people. Boredom usually comes from expecting people to excite us rather than helping people discover what an exciting miracle each is. To celebrate a person is to admire, affirm, listen, and express delight over his or her uniqueness and possibilities. People are not means to an end, but ends to be enjoyed for themselves. Even the most impossible people unfold the fascinating inner person locked up inside when they are assured that we will not misuse them.

The celebration of life involves us in praise for the most mundane of circumstances. Years of experimentation have convinced me that when we ask Christ to take control of our daily rounds he invades the most drab and dull responsibilities with his glory. The surprises of his interventions astound me. The unexpected always happens.

And the natural world? Who can be bored when there is a different sunrise and sunset to be admired each day? There's no place in the world that is naturally ugly. Some places have been made so by man's misuse, but walk or drive or fly on—inexpressible beauty awaits us at the seashore, at the mountains, in the desert. Stop and smell the roses. Listen to the birds. Contemplate the magnificent symmetry of the Lord's signature in the natural world. Who can be bored on a spring morning or a crisp winter's night with snow crunching under your feet?

But press on. The Lord has more to heal our boredom. It is an undeniable part of his plan for us that we will be bored until we are involved with him in his central work in history. He created us to know him and love him. Once we do, other people become our purpose and passion. People are the action for the Lord. He lived, died, and was resurrected that all people might know his love and forgiveness, might experience eternal life now in abundance and forever in heaven.

There is nothing more exciting than helping people find a soul-satisfying relationship with Christ. No hobby can match it; no job can rival its satisfaction; no sport can equal its excitement. In fact, I'm ready to say that it's a law of the kingdom of God that we are destined to boredom, sooner or later, if we do not discover the adventure of caring about people. We were meant to lose ourselves in people and their needs. I am convinced that is what Christ meant when he said, "He who finds his life will lose it, and he who loses his life for my sake will find it" (Matt. 10:39). The evidence that we have found life in Christ is that we constantly lose it in caring for others. We lose it not in the sense that it's lost, but that it's given away and thus increases in joy and power.

I talked to a leading church officer in the East some time ago. He was bored with his job, his wife, his church responsibilities, and mostly himself. I decided to go for the jugular vein. "When's the last time you listened to, cared about, became involved with a person who needs Christ and helped him or her find the joy of the abundant life?" His reply was classic: "The last time? I've never done that!" No wonder he was bored.

The same was true of a clergyman who was bored with the institutional church. "Budgets and buildings, meetings where no one meets, endless programs and planning. I'm bored with being the entertainer of an equally bored congregation." My response was a question and a challenge. "Are you willing to pray for one member of your church who wants to know Christ personally and start the adventure of discipleship? If you are, God will give you that person. Dare to tell the old story of what Christ can do to transform a person's life. Tell him or her about the cross, forgiveness, and grace, and help that person to make a full surrender of his or her will to our Lord."

He agreed to take my dare. And God was faithful. The next week a church officer came to him with more than complaints. He expressed his boredom with playing musical chairs in the congregation's organizational life. So the pastor pulled out all the stops. He led his friend through the wondrous story of the cross and how much God loves him. They ended up on their knees in the pastor's study, both praying for the power of the Holy Spirit. Just before the man left, he turned and looked my friend in the eye: "Pastor, what I needed all our members and 90 percent of the people in this town need. Why not preach that on Sunday?" He did, and the revival which started that Sunday has not stopped. The pastor's boredom was

caused by neglect of his central calling. The congregation's boredom was healed as members became
involved in caring for people in order to lead them to the
Savior.

Losing ourselves in people also means daring to become
involved in a stretching challenge to alleviate the causes of
human suffering. We will suffer boredom until we are
involved headlong in some cause to help people with their
social, physical, and emotional needs. This cause should
demand our time and keep us in touch with people. The
sure test is that whatever we promote will become a
vehicle of people meeting, knowing, and growing in the
Savior. If it doesn't, it will distract us from our central
calling and eventually we will be as bored as before.

All this leads to the final thing I want to say. Boredom
comes from living on our own strength within the confines of our own capacities. There needs to be some area
or relationship in our lives in which we are attempting the
humanly impossible. Robert Browning was right: "A
man's reach must exceed his grasp,/ Or what's a heaven
for?" What are you reaching for that exceeds your grasp?
What are you attempting that cannot be pulled off
without a mighty intervention and invasion of the Holy
Spirit's power? We all need a bit of danger, a careless
daring, if we are to battle boredom and win. What have we
got to lose?

Passion is a misused, distorted word in our time. It's so
much more than sexual desire. The word has been used to
describe Christ's death for a sinful, suffering world. Good
thing. This denotation preserves the word's meaning as a
strong, indomitable feeling, born out of conviction, which
enables people to attempt the impossible, knowing that
God has the final, resurrection word. Every courageous
Christian who would escape the boredom of the traditional and the drabness of the mundane needs a stretching commitment to do the impossible for Christ in some
problem in society or with a problem person in his or her
life.

We can easily discover what needs doing or saying if we

will listen to our complaints about people, churches, or government. "What are you going to do about it?" silences a lot of fruitless and futile theorizing. To confront, attack, and become involved (in Christ's name and by his Spirit's power) in the solution of a problem heals the boredom that no new job, spouse, or environment will ever cure.

A personal word of witness. I was bored until I turned my life over to the adventuresome management of Jesus Christ. My settled conviction after thirty years of living with the Savior as Lord and leader into mind-boggling, soul-stretching, spirit-enlightened challenges is that I have never been bored. He replaced my human ambition with spiritual adventure. My passion has been, and ever will be, to care for people and introduce them to the Savior. Edna St. Vincent Millay expressed my commitment to live all the years of my life:

> My candle burns at both ends;
> It will not last the night;
> But ah, my foes, and oh, my friends—
> It gives a lovely light.![1]

There's so much to do, so much left unsaid, so much that's ambiguous or untrue that needs to be challenged. There are so many people who may expire without the opportunity to decide whether they want to live forever. How could life ever be boring with an impelling challenge like that?

Moss Hart gives us a motto for a thrilling life in his play, *Light Up The Sky*. One of the characters called "Sidney" talks about his excitement and expectation for a show about to open: "We're sticking a Roman candle into the tired face of show business tonight . . . and the sparks that fly are going to light up the theater like an old-fashioned Fourth of July."

That's what we should be about—lighting the darkness, sticking a Roman candle into the tired face of boredom

---

1. "First Fig," from Collected Poems, Harper & Row. Copyright 1922, 1950 by Edna St. Vincent Millay.

whenever and in whomever we find it. Boredom will be a thing of the past if we spend ourselves being sure no one around us is bored.

You may have resisted the idea that your life is boring. It may never have occurred to you that the blandness, dullness, and sameness of your life—the ruts of routine—are really boredom. But if life is not exciting, if you don't feel a sense of adventure, if you are not delighted by the possibilities of tomorrow, if you've given up to the eventuality of sameness, then you are bored. And this could be the last day of boredom for you. Discover the joy of an intimate relationship with Christ; become a celebrant of yourself, other people, and life; lose yourself in people and their needs. Dare the impossible; expect the surprising infusion of the Holy Spirit—and I can assure you that you will never be bored again. Then you can rejoice with Christ, *the* life, and say with Paul, "For me to live is Christ!" Your experience of the adventure will be as Jeremiah expressed it—fresh every morning, and all through the day and night.

Allow me to reword the travel agency advertisement: "Escape the ordinary, the usual, the predictable, the boring. Take an eternal journey with Christ!" It will be a thrilling life—all the way up.

16

Hope in the Midst of Discouragement

Resurrection Living

"I am the resurrection and the life."
John 11:25

RECENTLY, WHEN I CHECKED in late at an airline counter
for a flight I was in danger of missing, I was waited on by
an agent who turned out to be quite a philosophical sage.
He tried unsuccessfully to get my itinerary displayed on
his computer screen. After pressing all the right buttons
repeatedly, he said apologetically, "I'm sorry, sir, the
computer is down and I can't find out where you're
going!" I eyed the clock anxiously, not at that moment
interested in reflecting on the direction of my life. Sensing
my urgency, the agent waxed eloquent: "Listen friend,
computers are like life—when they're down, they're
down, and there's nothing you can do about it but wait."

As I waited impatiently, the words of this prophet of
realism suddenly hit me. He was right and wrong, all at
the same time. Life does have its down times, its periods
of discouragement. But we can do more than wait!
There's something to receive when life goes bump on the
bottom. What to do in the down times of life is the good
news I want to share.

The old spiritual explains our life aptly and accurately:
"Sometimes I'm up and sometimes I'm down. O yes,

Lord!" We all know life has up times and down times. All too often, it's the latter. The biographer of Audubon said that the naturalist "always pursued a zigzag course between high elevation and dark spirits." How to get more zig and less zag is our problem.

The popular song of a few years ago could be our theme song: "Blues, blues, twentieth-century blues; nothing to win and nothing to lose." But we would like to win courage and lose the down times. Booker T. Washington often spoke of the "advantage of disadvantage." I want to talk about the courage we can find in discouragement.

You can find a victorious faith that defies discouragement! I have learned that from my own battles with the blue mood. Emerson said that preaching is "life pressed through the fires of thought." What I want to communicate in this chapter is just the opposite; it's a liberating thought pressed through the fires of life—my own life and the lives of countless others.

The secret of how to turn the struggle with discouragement into a stepping stone of victory is given in Jesus' most hopeful "I am" promise: "I am the resurrection and the life" (John 11:25). This dynamic remedy for discouragement is set in the most dramatic context imaginable. John 11 exposes discouragement as we all know it in life's down times, and it gives us the lift we need when life has let us down. Read the chapter from John's Gospel straight through, and then skip over to John 20:26–29. Now get inside the skin of Jesus' disciple, Thomas. We are going to look through his eyes, feel the discouragement he felt, and experience the hope he found. He made five momentous discoveries which lifted him out of discouragement and made him one of history's most courageous people.

When I contemplate what happened to Thomas, his discoveries seem to fall into five verses of a poem. I'm no poet, as you will see, but what I've composed has helped me to remember where I'm going when the computer is down. Consider first:

Discouragement is expectation wed to exasperation,
Giving birth to the illegitimate child of desperation.

The Thomas in me reaches out to the Thomas in you. Who wouldn't have reacted the way he did? The news arrived that Jesus' friend, Lazarus, was ill. Thomas feared what Jesus would do. The gathering storm of hostility from the leaders of Israel against the Master was now flashing with the lightning of hatred. The last time Thomas had been in Jerusalem, Jesus had been stoned. They had barely escaped with their lives. The last thing Thomas wanted his beloved friend and teacher to do was go to Bethany where Lazarus lived. Two miles outside Jerusalem would be too close for comfort—and safety.

No wonder Thomas sighed relief when the Lord did not rush to the bedside of his dear friend. The disciple had to admit, however, that he was also puzzled. The Lord did not seem perturbed. When he learned that Lazarus was ill, he leisurely continued his ministry for two days. Thomas and the other disciples waited anxiously, wondering what their Lord would do. Then he announced his decision: "Let us go into Judea again." "Madness!" Thomas thought. He led the other disciples in a chorus of consternation: "Rabbi, the Jews were but now seeking to stone you, and you are going there again?" But the Lord was resolute and could not be dissuaded.

Thomas felt the downward pull of discouragement that was all too familiar to him. History has called him Doubting Thomas. Discouraged Thomas would be more accurate. He had followed Jesus in search of hope. The Lord's message and miracles had infused him with excitement and expectation. But the conflict and discord of the past weeks had brought all the old feelings of discouragement back in hurricane force. When Jesus announced that Lazarus had died, Thomas was not surprised. "That's always the way it goes: trouble, disease, sickness, and death," Thomas murmured to himself. He didn't know what to make of Jesus' statement, "Lazarus is dead; and for your sake I am glad that I was not there, so that you may believe. But let us go to him." "Why go now?" Thomas questioned himself. "What's the use of risking everything to attend a funeral? What did the Lord mean, 'So that you may believe'? Believe what? That life ends in death and that discouragement is the stuff of broken dreams?"

But discouraged Thomas followed. There was nothing else to do. The Lord had won his heart; he could not imagine life without Jesus. He'd rather die with the Lord than live without him. It was immense loyalty and love that motivated his blurted commitment, "Let us also go, that we may die with him." Thomas was a man who faced the facts. His problem was that he didn't have all the facts. That is the malignant malady of the mood of discouragement.

Thomas has given us a classic profile of discouragement. It's the illegitimate child of expectation and exasperation. We are engulfed in the murky funk of discouragement when our dreams are dashed and our hopes are helpless. Discouragement means seeing things as they are without hope of any change.

What in your life has the power to discourage you? What is discouraging you now? In what areas of your life have the ineptitude of people and your own impatience to do anything sucked you down into discouragement? Where have you tried to be an effective agent of change or advancement and been defeated?

We all have expectations which are dashed by people, circumstances, or situations. There are times when we have tried and are exasperated at trying again, when our capacity to hope is exhausted. Discouragement is a horizontal hopelessness with no vertical viability—life as it is in raw realism without the possibility of the miracle of God's intervention or interpretation.

When Jesus and the disciples arrived at Bethany, they confronted discouragement in the quiet desperation of grief. Thomas's discouragement echoed by Martha and Mary when they gave vent to this strange mixture of expectation and exasperation: "Lord, if you had been here, [our] brother would not have died." There's a bite of criticism in that expression of discouragement. Did it cut into Jesus' heart? (How often we have thought, but we did not dare to say, "Lord, where were you when I needed you?")

Thomas's discouragement was based in his lack of faith that anything could change the seemingly irrevocable course of life's events. Martha's and Mary's was deeper still. They had hoped and lost—or so they thought. Jesus had not come in time. Lazarus was dead!

That leads to my second verse:

> *But when life is filled with disappointment*
> *Expect the hour of the Lord's appointment.*

Jesus came to Bethany according to his own timing, not the urgency of people's plans. He did not respond to panic. He knew that all power in heaven and earth was available to him, but he lingered so that he could teach by action a truth we all desperately need to learn in life's down times. Disappointment is the prelude to discouragement. But more than that, disappointment is the occasion of the Lord's appointment. The test for us right now is whether we can surrender the disappointment which bred our discouragement. Can we thank God that he will keep his appointment to meet our needs—on time and in time? Take whatever it is that is discouraging you right now. Expect a miracle. That's one expectation that will not be exhausted! All of this is true because, third:

> *For discouragement's darkest hour*
> *There's promise of resurrection power.*

The Lord strode into the discouragement of Bethany with a bold promise, "Your brother will rise again." Martha missed the point. "I know that he will rise again in the resurrection at the last day." It was a vague belief in her day that at a great future time all the dead would rise.

Jesus responds to her pious but powerless attestation with an "I am" assurance. Who but Immanuel, "God with us," could say it? "I am the resurrection and the life; he who believes in me, though he die, yet shall he live, and whoever lives and believes in me shall never die."

Martha's response to that was a gift of the Spirit of God. Just as Peter, in response to Jesus' question, "Who do you say that I am?", had been able to say, "You are the Christ, the Son of the living God," so too Martha was given the gift of faith to believe that all things are possible—even life for the dead. The gift of the "I am" in the down times of discouragement is to liberate us to say with Martha, "Yes, Lord; I believe that you are the Christ, the Son of God, he who is coming into the world." Just as disappointment is the prelude to discouragement, so too belief in the unlimited power of the "I am" is the preface to power for our discouragement.

Jesus was faithful to his promise. He moved straightway to Lazarus's tomb, recklessly casting aside the doubt-infected protestation that Lazarus had been dead for four days. "Lord . . . there will be an odor!"

"Take away the stone!" Jesus commanded. From inside Thomas's skin, we can feel the wonder and excitement of it all. We, too, put our shoulder to the gigantic rock to roll it away. What will Jesus do? We do not have to wonder for long. His voice pierces our ears and rumbles with earthquake proportions in our souls. "Lazarus, come out!" We watch stupified as the dead man emerges slowly from the tomb, walking in measured steps, bound by the tightly wrapped graveclothes.

Jesus' next command is equally astounding. "Unbind him, and let him go!" Slowly the grave wrappings are unwound, and we are able to look Lazarus in the eye. He's alive!

That should have done it for Thomas. He had witnessed a miracle of resurrection. Jesus had claimed to be the resurrection and the life. How could the disciple ever be discouraged again?

But that's not the end of the story. In the following

days, Thomas faced discouragement that was unmatched by anything he had ever known before. It's a terrible thing to experience hope, only to have it dashed by a greater disappointment than you can stand. When the Lord was tried and crucified, Thomas gave up hope forever. That's why he defected from the disciples' vigil of grief in the Upper Room. He had had all he could take. He wandered aimlessly about Jerusalem with the remorse that he had failed his Lord, mingled with the wish that he'd had the courage to die with him. When the other disciples found him, he was catatonic with despair.

Their excited words pierced his stupor. "He is risen! Christ is risen!" The unbelievable news did not register at first. Christ alive? Could it be true? Then the discouraged disciple responded with measured words of anger and grief. "Unless I see in his hands the print of the nails, and place my finger in the mark . . . and place my hand in his side, I will not believe" (John 20:25).

The resurrected Lord met the Thomas test. He appeared in the Upper Room just for Thomas. Imagine it from inside discouraged Thomas when the Lord entered the room and went directly to him. "Put your finger here, and see my hands; and put out your hand, and place it in my side; do not be faithless, but believing" (John 20:27). Thomas was shocked and stunned, and then a power began to surge in his troubled heart. Discouragement was pressed out of his soul with the inrushing of a mighty river of assurance and courage. "My Lord and my God!" he exclaimed in faith. What happened to Thomas then and afterward moves us on to our next vital thought pressed through experience.

The resurrection was then and is now
We need not worry when or how.

It was not long before Thomas was discouraged again. The Lord was alive, but a few days afterwards, he left them. Now Thomas had a promise without power, a hope with no help. Jesus told him and the others to wait in

Jerusalem until they received power from the Holy Spirit. Thomas remembered the Lord's teaching that he would come to them and be with them always. He had said that he would be in them and that they would be empowered to do the things that he had done. The discouraged disciple pondered that as he sat praying with the others in the Upper Room. There was no way he could live the life Jesus had called him to without the indwelling power he had been promised. Thomas remembered the question he had asked on the night before Jesus was crucified. "Lord, we do not know where you are going; how can we know the way?" (John 14:5). Jesus had said that he was the way, the truth, and the life. But the hours of waiting in the Upper Room stretched into days. Impatience bred discouragement.

Then it happened. On the day of Pentecost, the Holy Spirit the Lord had promised came upon the disciples. First there was a mighty wind, then fire over each apostle's head, and finally fire in each heart. Thomas felt a surge of power flowing into the emptiness of his discouragement. He was filled with the Holy Spirit. The same God who had created the universe, who had come as the great "I am," Immanuel, had returned in liberating, energizing power—not around Thomas but in him! His beloved Lord was now immanent and intimate. After Pentecost, Thomas knew more of the Lord than he had known after three years of following him along the roads of Palestine. He knew the reality of the second part of Jesus' "I am" promise made that day in Bethany: "He who believes in me, though he die, yet shall he live, and whoever lives and believes in me shall never die. Do you believe this?" Now Thomas believed!

During the days which followed Pentecost, Thomas discovered a strange and wondrous thing was happening to him. Filled with the living Christ, he had a new purpose, passion, and power. An impelling intimacy with Christ was transforming his personality. His battle with discouragement was over; he realized the resurrection— not only Christ's, but his own! Thomas had been raised from the tomb of discouragement as surely as Lazarus had been raised from the tomb in Bethany. A vigorous resilience pulsated in him. He was fully alive, as Christ had promised. Fear of death was over. Discouragement over other people, the power of evil, and tragic eventualities was replaced by an indefatigable, courageous zest. Eventually, when the Church was persecuted, he pressed on to new frontiers. Some say he ministered in Persia, others say India. Little matter—discouraged Thomas had become triumphant Thomas.

The central message of the early Church was the resurrection. Because of the realization of Christ's resurrection in them, Christians preached the joyous news of how the Lord could transform a living death into a deathless life. That accounts for the spectacular growth of the early Church. The miracle of Christ's resurrection, coupled by the undeniable experience of their own regeneration, unleashed an expectancy that banished the impossible.

Paul later explained what had happened. The apostles had died to themselves, and the Lord had raised them up to a new level of life filled with himself. (Romans 6 is a splendid explanation of the miracle of the transformation which we experience.)

What does all this mean to us? Magnificently this! Belief in Christ's resurrection must be combined with the infilling of his Spirit. Easter and Pentecost are one. Three great words leap from the pages of the New Testament—*fullness, full,* and *filled.* Paul tells us that in Christ, "all the fulness of God was pleased to dwell, and through him to reconcile to himself all things" (Col. 1:19–20). "For in him the whole fulness of deity dwells bodily, and you have come to fulness of life in him . . ." (Col. 2:9–10).

That fullness is offered to us in the presence of the Holy Spirit. Acts speaks of the Christian being full of the Holy Spirit and being filled with the Holy Spirit. The first is a permanent endowment; the second is a special infusion of power and gifts for a particular opportunity or challenge. Discouragement is turned into bold courage only when we experience both being full of and filled with the Spirit—"Christ in you, the hope of glory" (Col. 1:27). Imagine it: the fullness of our Lord filling our hollow discouragement! And here's what results:

> *The power that raised Jesus from the grave*
> *Is ours also for the hope we crave.*

The resurrection of Jesus began a new age of miracles. A miracle is an intervention of God from beyond the levels and limitations of the natural world. A miracle does not contradict the laws of nature; it reveals a higher law at work—the law of God's love. Immense power exists beyond our sight, experience, and understanding. Just as electricity existed before we captured its potential, or atomic energy was in the atom before we split it, so too there is unlimited spiritual power available in Jesus' name to heal, liberate, and transform human personality.

Where do you need that power right now? The age of miracles has not passed. Discouragement presses us out onto the edge of a miracle.

> The measure of His love is more than I can comprehend,
> That God so mighty is so willing, broken lives to mend.
> Then when I touch His healing hand and faith comes
>   pouring through,
> I just expect a miracle, for nothing less will do.[1]

All of this leads to my last point and the final verse of my poem. It summarizes all the rest:

> *When you least expect it, the Lord breaks through*
> *And makes the resurrection miracle of you.*

Thomas became a resurrection miracle—and so can we. Resurrection faith is to be coupled with resurrection power. The ancient Gaelic saying challenges us: "Belong

---

1. "I Expect a Miracle," by Ralph Carmichael. © Copyright 1968 by Lexicon Music, Inc. ASCAP. All Rights Reserved. International copyright secured. Used by special permission.

to God and become a wonder to yourself." Allow me to add, "and to everyone else." Our discouragements are raw material for the miracles of our Lord. Our only task is to trust him completely with whatever causes us to be discouraged.

Discouragement saps our courage; it cripples our confidence and diminishes our capacity to hope. But when we are at the end of our tethers, we can expect a breakthrough. Remember that a miracle is an intervention by which God releases power from beyond us. The miracle needed most for our discouraged world is to see what God can do with a person totally dedicated to and filled with his Spirit. And that miracle is you!

17

Don't Miss the Joy

The Antidote
To Grimness

"I am the true vine."
John 15:1

I HAVE A SUPER FRIEND who, after a good visit, shakes my hand, looks me squarely in the eye, and leaves me with this parting shot: "Whatever you do, don't miss the joy!"

Last year, I shared my friend's benedictory blessing with a group of people at a conference where I was speaking. They picked it up immediately, and it became the slogan of the conference. When people passed one another on the conference grounds, they would say, "Don't miss the joy!"

Robert Louis Stevenson would have been pleased. Though he had faced many difficulties and physical disability, at the end of his life he said, "To miss the joy is to miss everything!"

And yet many people miss the joy. There's a grimness that pervades life today. Everywhere we look we see grim, "white-knuckled" people who are desperately hanging on, enduring life rather than enjoying it.

There are those who miss the joy of life in a grim determination to be responsible. To them, life is a serious business; there is little time for joy in the pressure of meeting life's demands. Others are in such frantic search for happiness that they miss the joy. Happiness is so much less than joy; it is dependent on circumstances, people, or success. Joy is deeper. It is a condition of the soul which is utterly unassailable by life's ups and downs.

Still others feel unworthy of joy and miss its delight. Many people think of joy as a reward for perfection, performance, pertinacity. And who ever measures up to one's own standards? We say, "What right do I have to enjoy the luxury of joy with all that I've done or left undone?" The self-negation leads to incrimination of others who are feeling the first stirrings of joy. "How do you feel joyful in a world like this?" we ask drably, missing the fact that joy is the gift God gives when things are the worst.

There's a great need for joy today. It should be the identifiable mark of the Christian and the impelling ingredient of his contagion. The church should be the fellowship of uncontainable joy. New Testament scholar William Barclay was right: "A gloomy Christian is a contradiction of terms, and nothing in all religious history has done Christianity more harm than its connection with black clothes and long faces."

Grimness comes both from taking ourselves too seriously and failing to take our Lord and his promises seriously enough. It's the grayness which pervades our characters and countenances when we try to live on our own resources and face difficulties with our own cleverness, when we confront tragedies as further evidence of a blind fate that we think directs our movements on the stage of life.

Do you ever get grim? What or who can do it to you? What makes life fall in for you? What set of circumstances can throw you into an inner panic which shows in a tense grip on life? Are you feeling grim right now? When was the last time you had that feeling? And what assurance do you have that, when the world around you blows up, grimness will not be your inadvertent, clutching response?

The antidote to grimness is grace. And the outward expression of experiencing that giving and forgiving, unmerited and unmotivated love is joy. Jesus Christ can turn our struggle with grimness into a stepping stone of joy. The gift of joy is the legacy of the Lord.

At the conclusion of one of the most crucial messages Jesus gave to his disciples on the night before he was crucified, he said, "These things I have spoken to you, that my joy may be in you, and that your joy may be full" (John 15:11). What a promise—his joy, fullness of joy! Not a partial intimation but a full infusion. Jesus offers us the ecstasy of sheer joy!

But note and linger on the words, "These things I have spoken to you . . ." His joy in fullness is dependent on what he has said previously. The total sweep of John 15:1–11 moves to the climax of verse 11. This is one of those passages in Jesus' message which must be interpreted from the bottom up. Everything he said in the first ten verses reveals the conditions of authentic joy. If we want joy, his joy, full joy, we need to prayerfully consider and receive the stirring implications of one of Jesus' most personal and penetrating "I am" pronouncements. This *egō eimi* assertion and the explanation which precedes it in the first ten verses of the chapter give us the source of joy, the secret of receiving joy and of sustaining an unlimited joy—all rooted in the "I am," Yahweh, God with us.

Jesus said, "I am the true vine, and my Father is the vinedresser. Every branch of mine that bears no fruit, he takes away, and every branch that does bear fruit he prunes, that it may bear more fruit. You are already made clean by the word which I have spoken to you."

Contemplate the context of this astounding "I am" source of joy. Jesus and the disciples had just left the Upper Room, where the Lord had celebrated the Passover Feast. He had opened his heart to them and taught them about his love for them and the amazing life of power they would be able to live when he would return in the power of the Holy Spirit. A brief review of John 14 stirs us deeply. The disciples need not be troubled or afraid. Jesus' death and resurrection would prepare a place for them, now and forever. The Lord would enable them to do the things that he had done and greater things in quantity through his power. He pressed them to the edge of impossibility and assured them that they would be able to do mighty works in his name. They would never be alone. He would come to them. He alone would be the source of their joy.

How this would happen was the content of Jesus' conversation with his frightened disciples as they made their way secretly through Jerusalem, and passed the Temple on the way to Gethsemane, where Jesus would pray before he was arrested. I imagine that it was as they passed the Temple precincts that Jesus said, "I am the vine, you are the branches. He who abides in me, and I in him, he it is that bears much fruit, for apart from me you can do nothing."

Astounding! Remember that Israel prided itself in being the vine of God. Over the main entrance to the Temple was the exquisitely carved, gold-leafed symbol of the vine, branches, and grapes. No expense had been spared in creating this magnificent reminder to the people of their heritage and special calling. It was firmly rooted in Scripture and tradition. The Psalmist had prayed, "Thou didst bring a vine out of Egypt; thou didst drive out the nations and plant it. Thou didst clear the ground for it; it took deep root and filled the land" (Ps. 80:8–9). Isaiah had heightened the theme: "The vineyard of the Lord of hosts is the house of Israel" (Isa. 5:7; note vv. 1–6 also). Jeremiah spoke of Israel as the Lord's "choice vine" (Jer. 2:21). And Ezekiel deepened the imagery in the context of judgment and suffering.

Now we can sense the wonderment the disciples must have had when Jesus, with *egō eimi* authority, said, "I am the vine." He boldly took the place of Israel. Now faith in him, not Hebrew blood, was the source of salvation. In substance he was saying, "The only thing that can give you life and joy is a love relationship with me. Your hope is not your heritage, but intimate, living fellowship with me!"

This is the first of the "these things I have spoken to you" which Jesus meant when he offered fullness of joy.

He is the vine; we are the branches. Love is the flowing, life-giving sap which surges from the vine to the branch. And the fruit of that dynamic energy is joy. The delineation of the fruit of the Spirit is given by Paul in Galatians 5:22–23. Keep your finger on that passage as we consider the meaning of fruit in Jesus' promise. The Holy Spirit flows from vine to branch. It is the Lord's life himself, giving us the profound experience of a nurturing, satisfying love which is expressed outwardly in the fruit—joy.

Throughout the New Testament, joy and the Holy Spirit are closely related. Acts 13:52 says that "the disciples were filled with joy and with the Holy Spirit." Paul speaks of "joy in the Holy Spirit" (Rom. 14:17), and of "joy inspired by the Holy Spirit" (1 Thess. 1:6). The Holy Spirit, the living Lord, indwelling us, is the source of joy.

The key word describing our dependence on the vine for our source of love and joy is *abide*. The Lord's explanation is in the aorist active imperative: "Abide in me and I in you." It means, "Keep on abiding in me and you will be sure that I will keep on abiding in you." That's the only lasting source of limitless, free-flowing joy. *Abide,* in this passage, means "an unbroken connection," rather than "repose," as the word *abide* would suggest in our parlance. It implies the necessity of a constant, active relationship between us and the Lord if we are to experience the fruit, joy.

The Lord drives home the salient thrust, "Apart from me you can do nothing." There's no joy without Jesus' abiding in us. There's more here than the idea that knowing about or even knowing Jesus gives us joy. Jesus *is* joy. If we want joy, we must have him indwelling us.

This is how joy is engendered. The Lord, living within us, fills us with an abiding experience of his changeless love. When we deserve it least, he stirs within us a fresh experience and realization that we are sublimely loved, cherished, and valued. We can take anything if we know that! And it's from that unlimited source of grace, rooted in what he did on the cross for our forgiveness, reconciliation, and assurance, that we know we are loved to the uttermost. "Love so amazing, so divine"—indeed! Joy springs from that.

But press on. Jesus said, "Every branch of mine that bears no fruit, he takes away" (John 15:1); and "If a man does not abide in me, he is cast forth as a branch and withers; and the branches are gathered, thrown into the fire and burned" (15:6). That is the judgment for resisting the life-giving sap of the Holy Spirit, Christ's own presence. A branch becomes "deadwood" when the life-giving sap no longer infuses it. We can become dead branches—still connected to the vine but fruitless. And the Lord's incisive word is that if this happens we will be cut off. The health of the vine and the other branches demand it.

If we have no inner experience of the Lord's flow of love, and no discernible expression of joy, we can be cut off. Frightening? Yes! The reason it is so crucial for us to receive love and show joy is that the true sign of a Christian is reproductivity.

Throughout his message, the Lord clearly related our experience of joy with reproducing our faith in others and being involved with him in the multiplication of his resources in the lives of others. Joy is the dominant note in the parables of the lost son, sheep, coin, and the parable of the talents. The joy of heaven is shared by the father when his son returns from the far country, but the elder brother is a dry, dead branch who cannot express either love for his brother or joy at his return. The Good Shepherd feels the surge of pulsating love for his sheep and says, "Rejoice with me, for I have found my sheep which was lost." And Jesus underlines the experience of joy: "Just so, I tell you, there will be more joy in heaven over one sinner who repents than over ninety-nine righteous persons who need no repentance" (Luke 15:6–7).

The same note is sounded in the parable of the lost coin. The woman's joy in finding the cherished coin lost from her frontlet (a symbol of betrothal to her husband) is

like the joy of heaven. Jesus leaves nothing to misunderstanding. "Just so, I tell you, there is joy before the angels
of God over one sinner who repents" (v. 10).

The imagery of the fruit of the branch is now undeniably clear. The sap from the vine must flow through the
branch and bear fruit. The fruit of·joy is inseparably
related to effective communication of the faith to others.
A joyless Christian is not only a contradiction in terms but
a negation of what Christ can do in us and others. A grim,
graceless Christian will have little effectiveness in winning
others to Christ. The world will observe his or her
grimness and justifiably respond, "Who needs it?"

Be careful! If we are not engaged in loving people and
exemplifying the joy they can know, the sap of the Spirit
may be cut off. Our branches will wither. The Lord is
forgiving of our many and varied sins, except one—
fruitlessness.

The reason many of us have little joy is that we are
confused about how the Lord loves us. We have little
difficulty understanding and accepting his love as our
Lord and Savior through his ministry long ago and his
death for us on Calvary. Our impediment is with how he
loves us today. We are still hung up with the idea that his
love will always mean easy sailing and smooth waters. We
think that tranquility is a sign of blessedness. We miss the
biblical witness that those who are called and chosen are
the subjects not only of reconciliation but of renovation.
That leads us to the secret of joy.

Joy is related to the pruning process of the Lord. "Every
branch that does bear fruit he prunes, that it may bear
more fruit." A hard word! I have seen vineyards in the
Holy Land in spring; they're not a beautiful sight at all.
The vineyard is a collection of barren, cut-back stumps;
they have been drastically pruned. Then by fall a transformation has taken place. The branches have grown back
and are laden with luxuriant, purple fruit.

We must be careful in our interpretation of what love's
pruning means for us. I do not want to say more nor less

than Jesus intended; there is a danger in either alternative. What I think Jesus meant was that a fruitful branch is cherished by the Lord and deserves his special care. The pruning can be painful, but it results in greater joy and productivity. It means several things to us.

The Lord prunes out of our lives anything which will keep us from him or effectiveness for him. He does not want the energies of his Spirit running into branches or offshoots which are capable of depleting us for his service.

The Lord wants to conserve the energy of the branch for its special purpose. Whenever we become overinvolved in minor matters, he prunes us back. Thank the Lord that he knows what he is doing with us. It's a great experience of joy to trust the arrangement of our affairs and the setting of our priorities to him.

Now we are at the center of the secret of joy. The Lord does more than simply prune the irrelevant or distracting; he gives us the gift of being able to perceive our difficulties and troubles as occasions of his pruning providence. He does not send the rough places, people, or perplexities, but he surely uses them! He gives us the power to choose what our attitudes toward them will be. That's the immense challenge of Jesus' words, "Let not your hearts be troubled, neither let them be afraid" (John 14:27). Trouble can do many things to us, but it cannot rob us of our freedom of will to choose what attitude we will have toward them.

The key is surrender. The Lord can utilize everything, wasting nothing, to help us experience joy in our difficulties and life's tragedies. The peace Jesus promised, which, you will note, follows love and joy as a fruit of the Spirit in Paul's delineation (Gal. 5:22–23), is the tandem companion of the joy of relinquishment.

That's what James meant when he counseled his friends, "Count it all joy, my brethren, when you meet various trials, for you know that the testing of your faith produces steadfastness. And let steadfastness have its full effect, that you may be perfect and complete, lacking in nothing" (James 1:2–4). Especially joy!

Annie Johnson Flint expresses the pain and ultimate joy of the pruning process:

> It is the branch that bears the fruit
>   That feels the knife
> To prune it for a larger growth,
>   A fuller life.
>
> Though every budding thing be lopped,
>   And every grace
> Of swaying tendril, springing leaf,
>   Be lost a space.
>
> O thou whose life of joy seems reft,
>   Of beauty shorn;
> Whose aspirations lie in dust,
>   All bruised and torn,
>
> Rejoice, tho' each desire, each dream
>   Each hope of thine
> Shall fall and fade; it is the hand
>   Of Love Divine
>
> That holds the knife, that cuts and breaks
>   With tenderest touch,
> That thou, whose life has borne some fruit
>   May'st now bear much.[1]

Let's recap for clarity. We can look at life's hard places as either judgment, condemnation, fate, or opportunities for learning what the Lord longs to teach us. Life seldom works out as we had hoped or planned. When we are distressed physically, emotionally, or relationally (with people we love), the Lord can use the interruption in our happiness to give us joy. Joy is his special gift to people whose suffering has been submitted to him for his

---

1. Quoted in Paul E. Billheimer, *Don't Waste Your Sorrows* (Fort Washington, PA: Christian Literature Crusade, 1977), p. 49.

intervention and inspiration. We are pruned back, but the subsequent growth is worth the pain.

I know this is true. Life's complexities present me with two alternatives—bitterness or blessing. I can be hardened or softened as supple clay for the Lord's creative molding. As I am writing this, I feel a mixture of the problems and concerns any husband, parent, leader, or sensitive friend feels if he is at all vulnerable to life. The deepest conviction of my heart is that each of the unresolved decisions or distressing disappointments with people and institutional Christianity, any of the worries that are the stuff of life, can be accepted as pruning, and sources of fresh joy.

True joy, which is the fruit of the Lord's Spirit when we abide in him and he abides in us, seldom comes when things are easy and tranquil. During difficult periods of our lives it blossoms with the realization that nothing can happen to us that the Lord cannot use for an experience of fresh grace and new growth. Also, in these times we become the special targets of the Lord's intervention. Joy leaps in us when we know that the Lord knows and cares about our concerns. We are delighted anew each time we feel the release of new dependence on him and the warmth of his presence with us in the testing time. Then, when we receive an answer or a miraculous resolution of the problem that only he could have accomplished, we feel a fresh burst of joy.

The same secret of joy is expressed in that marvelous verse in 2 Chronicles 29:27: "And when the burnt offering began, the song of the Lord began also, and the trumpets. . . ." King Hezekiah brought sanity and sacredness back to Israel after the apostasy of King Ahaz. The temple was cleaned of abominations and the people admonished to repent. The king gathered the people to sacrifice the he-goats for a sin offering. He also stationed the Levites in the house of the Lord with cymbals, harps, and lyres to be ready to burst into song when the sacrifice was made. The people knew the symbolism: the sacrifice upon the altar was representative of their lives as a sacrifice of surrender and trust to God. When the whole assembly was silent, the priest went forward and with a burning torch lighted the sacrifice. When it was consumed, the song of the Lord began—with trumpets.

Whenever I think of that, I remember Paul's words in Romans 12:1–2: "I appeal to you therefore, brethren, by the mercies of God, to present your bodies as a living sacrifice, holy and acceptable to God, which is your spiritual worship. Do not be conformed to this world but be transformed by the renewal of your mind, that you may prove what is the will of God, what is good and acceptable and perfect."

It is when we place our frustrations, which make us grim, on the altar that they become a sacrifice. We can choose to accept them as vessels to contain a new experience of joy. When the sacrifice begins, the song of the Lord begins with trumpets. A song of joy springs forth.

That's the same note of victory found in the Acts account of Paul's imprisonment in the Philippian dungeon. He was in chains, and yet he and Silas began singing psalms of joy! That's the irrepressible viability of Christianity—with each human setback, a new advance for the Lord.

Where in your life is there a need to sacrifice a present perplexity? When you do, the song of the Lord will begin with trumpets of joy. Years of watching the Lord's pruning of people and feeling it in my own life have led me to a firm conviction: our difficulties will break us until completely trusting them to the Lord breaks their bind.

Now we can consider what sustains a continuous flow of joy in us, who are the branches of the vine. We are given the power of prayer as a channel for the flow of joy. Communion with our Lord in prayer is the daily and moment-by-moment release of joy. "If you abide in me, and my words abide in you, ask whatever you will, and it shall be done for you" (John 15:7). It is a ceaseless source of joy to abide in Jesus' words and commandments. He has a word for all seasons. When we attempt to obey his commandments to love God, ourselves, and others, the floodgates of the rivers of power are opened.

Prayer is intimate communion Person to person. When we abide in God, listening receptively, we experience the ecstasy of joy. Let the word stand—*ecstasy*. It is the intense emotion which bursts within us when the Lord breaks through. Then we can say with Pascal, "Joy! Joy! Unspeakable joy!"

It was this spiritual ecstasy that Peter affirmed in the early church: "Without having seen him you love him; though you do not now see him [with eye perception] you believe in him [heart and mind perception through prayer] and rejoice with unutterable and exalted joy" (1 Pet. 1:8).

In a much deeper way, we can express about Christ what Montaigne said of a friend: "How is it that we were so much to one another, you and I? It was because you were you and I was I." Grim people like us need the joy only a Savior can give. And only the great "I am" can meet our needs. We can echo Charles Kingsley's simple assurance when asked how he took the pressure in his life. "I had a friend" was his only reply. Jesus, the vine, draws the joy from the reservoir of the Eternal and sends it into our thirsty branches.

My friend's parting benedictory encouragement is now my deepest prayer for you. I pray it in the context of Jesus' triumphant "I am" promise: "I am the vine, you are the branches." "Abide in me, and I in you . . . that my joy may be in you, and that your joy may be full."

Whatever you do, don't miss the joy!

18

For Things Too Broke to Mend

Broken Relationships and Christ's Reconciliation

"I am the true vine . . . love one another."
John 15:1, 12

A WELDING COMPANY displayed a slogan on its sign: "We weld everything—except a broken heart!" That's a bold promise and an honest admission, one that's true of most of us. We can do almost anything with human skill and inventive genius, but we can't heal a broken heart—our own, or anyone else's.

Every one of us either has had a broken heart, has one now, or knows someone who is suffering the anguish of one. What can we do when life, loss, people, or circumstances break our hearts? Does the Lord know or care? Can he do anything to heal the wounds of life? Yes!

John Masefield gives us the answer:

> And God who gives beginnings
>   Gives the end;
> A place for broken things
>   Too broke to mend.

That's quite an assurance! The heart of God is the place for broken things that are too broke to mend. And Jesus

Christ, the "I am," is God's forgiving, loving heart with us. His assertion that he is the vine and we are the branches involves us in experiencing and expressing the quality of love that mends the broken things of life.

The entire fifteenth chapter of John spells out the implications. Verses twelve through seventeen tell us how to be communicators of love flowing through us from the vine: "This is my commandment, that you love one another as I have loved you. Greater love has no man than this, that a man lay down his life for his friends." Love is what we do because we are connected to the vine. Because he has called, chosen, and appointed us to abide in his love and allow his love to abide in us, we are given power through his Spirit to become initiative healers of broken things, broken people, broken relationships. We can ask to receive his love and know that we will be supplied abundantly for our ministry of reconciliation. We are born again to bear fruit. "I chose you," says Jesus, ". . . that you should go and bear fruit and that your fruit should abide; so that whatever you ask the Father in my name, he may give it to you."

It's when we have experienced the Lord's love for the broken things in us that we become healers of the broken hearts of the world. We are to do and say the loving thing: "This I command you, to love one another." We do not have a choice. To be attached to the vine means to be actively involved with the Lord in mending the broken things in the world. And what he guides, he provides!

But if we are to abide in the place for things too broke to mend, we must experience a deeper level of loving. Disturbing questions ache for answers. How has he loved us? If he loves us, why does he allow our hearts to be broken?

> Does Jesus care when my heart is pained
> Too deeply for mirth or song?
>
> . . .
>
> When for my deep grief I find no relief
> Though my tears flow all the night long?
> Frank E. Graess

We can sing, "The love of Jesus, who can know? None but his loved ones know." But why do his loved ones suffer the wounds of life like others? Are there no privileges, no residuals, no exemptions? He can tell us that we should love one another as he has loved us, but what does loving mean when the people we need to love often have contributed to our fractured hearts?

Suddenly a song which we have heard and repeated glibly takes on a much more profound implication. If we are to learn to love as he has loved us, our training must be done in the crucible of life's crises. It's facile to sing, "Jesus loves me, this I know!" until that love has reached us in life's extremities, when we can no longer separate our pious platitudes of assurance from the realities of things too broke to mend.

It follows that the reason we are so inept in loving people is that we lack the toughened spiritual muscle developed through allowing him to love us when we hurt and things seem hopeless. Jesus' new commandment, "to love one another as I have loved you," has more to it than what we would surmise on the surface. Remember that it was given to the disciples just before the crucifixion, when their broken hearts would cry, "Where is God in all of this?" It was during that night and the next day of crisis that they learned how much God loved them. It was at Gethsemane and Calvary that they discovered what it would mean to love as he had loved them.

In order to get to the deeper recesses of what Jesus means about loving as we have been loved, let's divide our investigation into three aspects of a progression of thought. First, what are the things too broke to mend in which we need his love? Second, how does the Lord love us when our hearts are broken? Last, how can we love others as he has loved us when they too are brokenhearted?

Consider first the broken things of life. For some of us they are broken dreams which fracture our hearts. Our hearts' desire has the vulnerable potential of causing a broken heart. At one time or the other, we are all pulled along by the expectation that some passionate hope will be fulfilled. Plans for the future let us endure things as they are. We wait for an anticipated breakthrough—some longed-for relationship, some person we've longed to love or whose love is life's prize, some position or promotion or possession.

Now what can we do with the frustration of waiting or the poignant ache of the dawning realization that our dream may never be? How can we handle the decision that dashes our dream? What about that rejection or reversal of circumstances which tolls the doom of all our hope?

A woman whose husband of twenty years fell in love with another woman wrote me after seeing our television program, "I had no warning, no sign that we had drifted apart. All my dreams for our life have been shattered. What do I do with the anguish, the resentment, the terrifying fear of the future? I feel like my heart is irreparably broken."

A young writer staked his whole life on selling a movie script on which he had worked for ten years. He came to see me with the rejection slip in hand. "What do I do now? I feel like such a failure, like it's all over for me as a writer."

A famous Hollywood singer lost her fame and fortune when her vocal cords became paralyzed and she could not perform. Life hit bottom with a jarring bump, because her whole identity had been wrapped up in her career.

An older couple faced financial reversals and had to give up plans for retirement and travel. The collapse of an enterprise in which they had invested their life's savings broke all their cherished dreams. What now?

All these are examples of people whose hearts' desires ended in heart despair. For others of us, the broken things too broke to mend all have the personal names of people we love. The splintered pieces are made up of what people we love do to themselves or what life does to them. Our hearts split wide open in the desire to take away the pain that difficult or tragic circumstances have dished out on the platter of experience. Ever feel the wound of worry over others? We feel helpless. We wish we could wave a magic wand, suffer for them, or heal the hurt. Concern mingles with impotent anguish.

Still others of us find that physical pain is capable of breaking our weary hearts. Persistent pain can wilt the capacity to hope. It dulls expectation and surrenders us to despair. Impaired health sets us on the shelf. Plans and pleasures gurgle down the drain.

And what about those broken ties when death takes someone we love? I will never forget the one word on a floral wreath placed on a casket of a young man dead before his time through careless tragedy. "Why?" The wreath had been placed there by his young wife who now had to raise three small children. A thing too broke to mend?

A character in Dickens's *Gin-Shops,* observing a funeral procession, gives little comfort. His advice is too glib: "Grief never mended no broken bones, and as good people's very scarce, what I says is, make the most on 'em."[1] But grief is often just that: not having made the most of life while someone we loved was alive. Time? Does it heal a broken heart? To some, it's only submerged or sublimated.

Tennyson, in *In Memoriam,* speaks for all of us whose hearts ache with grief:

> That loss is common would not make
> My own less bitter, rather more:
> Too common! Never morning wore
> To evening, but some heart did break.

Finally, we are all experts when it comes to relationships which seem too broke to mend. We all have loved ones, friends, and associates who have hurt us deeply, or whom we have hurt. We can write them off, but can't get them out of our memories. Wounds are nursed, sometimes

---

1. "Scenes," Chapter 2, *Gin-Shops*

cherished; forgiveness is withheld. And in the meantime, the only things that are hurt are our hearts.

A one-hundred-year-old man boasted that he had no enemies. "What's your secret?" someone asked. "I've outlived them all!" he said. No such luck for most of us. Nor do we have the power to take life into our own hands like Harvaez, the Spanish patriot who, when asked by his confessor about his enemies, responded, "Father, I don't have any enemies; I've killed them all!" We wish we could say, like Lincoln, "You know, I must be crazy, but I just don't have the time or energy in this life to hold that kind of resentment." But any Lincoln scholar can tell us that even that exemplary man lived a life beset by political conflict, vested interests, and an unfulfilling marriage! Very few of us escape the painful reality of broken relationships.

Reconciliation is never easy. To be the initiator in the healing of relationships requires more strength and vulnerability than many can muster. Most of us carry an inner ledger of carefully tabulated slanders, slights, and over-sights. It's a painful thing to live with the disappointment of seemingly irreconcilable relationships, but it's even harder to get them reconciled.

In this listing, I may have missed your particular brand of a broken heart. But no matter how we shift the terms, the anguish of heartbreak is hard to bear. Now we are ready to ask, where is this place for broken things too broke to mend? What does Jesus' "even as I have loved you" mean in the abject reality of life?

The Psalmist made a promise that Jesus the "I Am" kept, and keeps for us: "The Lord is near to the brokenhearted, and saves the crushed in spirit" (Ps. 34:18). Could it be that he is near to us all the time but that the broken things make us ready to receive what has been ours all along? He does what the Psalmist knew from life's bittersweet experiences; "he heals the brokenhearted, and binds up their wounds" (Ps. 147:3). Jesus declared why he had come when he quoted Isaiah 61:1: "He has sent me to bind up the brokenhearted."

But Jesus' cure for broken hearts was a costly affair. It broke his own heart, and the Father's heart that beat in him. Calvary—that's the place for things too broke to mend. And that's how much he loves you and me. The cross is our historical evidence of the love that beats eternally in the heart of God.

We can talk to the Lord about our broken hearts. He's an eternal authority; he knows what it's like. And yet the healing balm which flows from Calvary is not cheap grace. That's the mystery and wonder of it all.

Hang on now for the hard truth. The only cure for a broken heart is brokenness! The breezes of assuring compassion from the Lord stiffen into a wind to fill our depleted, flapping sails. The Lord loves us so much that he will use the broken things of life to break the bind of our self-willed determinism.

David found that out in the self-pity of remorse. His breakthrough to a new beginning came when he could say, "The sacrifice acceptable to God is a broken spirit; a broken and contrite heart, O God, thou wilt not despise" (Ps. 51:17). There is a mysterious, miraculous moment in every experience of a broken heart when we must ask for God's perspective, peace, and power. That comes when we move beyond cynicism, despair, rebellion, self-pity, self-blame, or thrashing accusations, and into sublime surrender. When we can pray, "Lord, I know you did not send this but I know you can use it," we are on the hallowed place for broken things too broke to mend.

This too involves the cross. Calvary is not only an assurance of the Lord's love and forgiveness, but the healing of our broken dreams and wishes. The cross is not only the death of Christ for us, it is the summons to our death to ourselves. To be crucified with Christ means that we say with him, "Not my will but thine be done." Mending begins with that.

I have never known a broken heart that was not healed when the person unreservedly surrendered the hurt to our Lord. As a man said to me recently, "If my heart had not been broken, my pride would never have been shattered, and I would never have discovered the deeper levels of the Lord's love when we have a contrite heart."

Go back over the broken things and see if the truth holds. Broken dreams force us either to cynical despair or a new trust in God and for his strategy for us. Broken hopes for loved ones force us to let go, to stop playing God either as their strength or their comfort, and to release them to the Lord's amazing capacity to bring good out of evil. Our concern over health must finally bring us to the brokenness of praying, "Whether I live or die, I am the Lord's. Here, Lord, is my body. Heal me according to your plan for now and eternity. I praise you that I belong to you. I am more than this frail body which I relinquish to your complete control." The same is true in grief. There comes a time when we must give the broken pieces of our shattered emotions to him. He is the Lord of the living—here and in heaven. The brokenness of grief can open us up to the Lord as never before. And when our hearts are broken by other people, there's no place to go but to the Lord to ask for the power to forgive and to be an agent of reconciliation.

> Down beneath the shame and loss
> Sinks the plummet of the cross
> Never yet abyss was found
> Deeper than Thy love can sound.

In all the varied experiences of a broken heart, the Lord is most concerned with our healing. The brokenness of a contrite heart is our gift to him out of our suffering; a new heart filled with confidence and hope is his gift to us. Oscar Wilde was right when he wrote, in "The Ballad of Reading Gaol," "How else but through a broken heart/ May Lord Christ enter in?" My teacher and friend James Stewart of Edinburgh puts it this way: "It is when a man strikes rock bottom . . . that he suddenly finds he has struck the Rock of Ages."

Allow me to recap the basic elements of how Jesus heals a broken heart. A broken heart must lead us to a point at

which we surrender to our Lord the cause of the shattering experience. Our disappointment with ourselves, other
people, life itself, or even God must be *relinquished* to him.
Until we are broken of our tendency to try to heal
ourselves, he cannot help. Next, accept his *reconciling* love
for the bitterness of what you have done or others have
done to you. *Receive* the Lord's indwelling Spirit as a
constant companion. Then thank the Lord for the *rebirth*
of hope and the desire to live again. He heals the memory
of the pain and focuses our attention on what he is going
to give us—a new beginning.

Now Jesus' commission flashes with new light of
wisdom. If we are to love others as he has loved us, the
brokenhearted are the focus of our concern. As he came
to bind up the brokenhearted, so must we—by his power
and not our own. But how he ministers to us in our
broken things gives us the key to understanding how we
are to love others. Here again presence, perspective,
peace, and power give us our strategy. As he has been
with us, so we are to be with people who are hurting—not
sympathetically aloof, but empathically involved. Loving
as Christ loved means to identify, listen, understand, and
comfort.

But there's more, much more. Loving as Christ loved
means helping the person understand what the Lord is
saying to him or her through what is happening. It is real
love to move a person beyond, "Why did this happen to
me?" to "What can happen to me through what has
happened to me?" If we can enable a person to change the
end punctuation of "God, what's the meaning of this"
from an exclamation point to a question mark, we will
have been a channel of divine love.

The only way to communicate what God can do with the
broken things of another person's life is to tell him what
he has done with ours. It was Oswald Chambers who first
used the vivid image of the Christian being broken bread
and poured-out wine. If we have never been crushed by
life or people, there's no wine. If we have not allowed our
broken hearts to lead to a brokenness before God, we will

offer people stones instead of the bread of true and remedial comfort. Our availability to others in their times of need will be directly proportionate to our experience of the Lord's availability to us in times of need.

The most difficult task of loving is to help a person relinquish the pain of life's broken things. Loving people as Christ loved us must include the kind of accepting, forgiving, reconciling love which has qualified us to share our experience of brokenness and help them move from a broken heart to their own brokenness and then to deep healing. Someone has said that true love is your pain in my heart. That quality of grace is an irreducible maxim which prepares us to say, "My friend, I know what you're going through. It can make you either a bitter or better person. And I'm going to stick with you until your surrender of this painful thing has its full impact of bringing you into a deeper relationship with God."

The more I study and meditate on Jesus' commission in the new commandment, the more aware I am that the broken things we think are too broke to mend are what keep us from loving one another as he has loved us. Broken dreams, plans, and hopes, coupled with broken relationships harden our hearts. The painful memories of the past make us determined never to be hurt again or get into a position of being disappointed. When we have failed or life has tumbled in on us, we tend to develop cold, calculating attitudes. We build walls to protect us from further heartbreak.

When this happens to us, the Lord's challenge to love, to be to others what he's been to us, becomes lovely sentiment for someone else. The Lord cannot use us in love's service; the seed of his word cannot penetrate the hard, unplowed soul-soil. But once he "sets the coulter deep and wakes our soul from sleep" we can receive the seed of his truth and hope. It will grow in the cultivated ground of heartbreak and will be watered by the tears of repentance and joy. Then we will be indefatigable in our love for others, like the Lord. We will be able to forgive before forgiveness is asked. We will be capable of initiating reconciliation regardless of our rights or our defensive need to be justified.

That's what Jesus meant when he said, "By this all men will know that you are my disciples, if you have love for one another" (John 13:35). The world is still waiting to see that quality of authentic love. If the church of Jesus Christ ever modeled that, we could change the world! Wouldn't it be wonderful if we could offer a different slogan than the welding company? How about, "We weld relationships through the healing of broken hearts"?

That statement of purpose would require a church that preached, experienced, and shared the love of the cross. No wonder Paul exclaimed, "For I decided to know nothing among you except Jesus Christ and him crucified" (1 Cor. 2:2). The cross is the only healing place for "things too broke to mend." It's there that we find the love Jesus wanted his disciples to share—a love that will not let us go from him or from each other.

19

The One Great Need Beneath All Our Needs

The Authority of Jesus

*"The high priest asked him,
'Are you the Christ, the Son of the Blessed?'
And Jesus said, 'I am.'"*
Mark 14:62

THERE IS ONE GREAT NEED beneath all our needs, one horrendous struggle which makes all the other struggles we've talked about more difficult. It's the root of all of life's difficulties, the cause of our distorted perception of them. In fact, it's the need which makes us struggle with our struggles.

The deepest need in all of us is to accept Jesus Christ's authority over our lives. He is not only the source of strength in our struggles; he is the one who uses them to bring us to the sharp edge of realizing and accepting why he came. Sin is at the core of all our struggles and our attitude toward them. Pride, the willful determination to run our own lives, use God for our own ends, and manipulate his blessings for our own comfort is the root cause of our problems.

A disturbing question has been lurking beneath our studies of the "I am" promises of Jesus and how they relate to our struggles. It must now be confronted. Why do Christians struggle in their problems? If we believe that Christ lived, died, was raised up and is with us now as triumphant Lord of all life, why are we still unsettled by anything which happens to and around us? Why are we still anxious, lonely, afraid, pressured, guilty, frustrated, and distressed?

Much has been written and said in the last decade to free Christians to accept their humanity and admit their needs. The heavy load of pretension has been lifted. We no longer have to fake it to make it. It's okay to feel insecure, worried, and troubled. The emphasis on honesty has liberated us to be real and authentic. We can admit our struggles and experience the power of our Lord in the midst of them.

But we would "heal the wound lightly" if we did not go deeper to confront the cause of much of our distress in our difficulties. Our struggles are manifestations of our need for reconciliation. Each of the distresses of life forces us back to our Lord to recover the assurance of his love, forgiveness, and power.

In fact, for a Christian, the issue is not just the pain or anxiety we feel, but the authority of Christ over our frustrations and our willingness to trust him in spite of what happens. That's the struggle—to be reconciled in the estrangement from our Lord which we feel when we question his providence and rebel against his plan and purpose for us. It's when we cry out, "How could you have allowed this, Lord? After all I've done and been for you, don't I deserve an exemption from the things that distress others?" We try to force his hand, demanding that he act on our time schedules and according to what we have determined is best for us. All these things are indications that we are out of the stream of his Spirit, playing God over our own lives, alarming revelations that we have usurped the authority which belongs to him alone!

There are two great "I am" statements from the last hours of Jesus' ministry which assert his authority as God with us. Both statements were motivated in response to people who tried to use Jesus for their own purposes.

Each of these men resisted his authority. One was a friend and disciple, the other an enemy—Judas and Caiaphas. Both were strugglers whose manipulation put Jesus on the cross. I want to look at these two men and discover what their resistance to Jesus means for our understanding of how we react to Christ's authority. My thesis is this: in every struggle there are two levels—the problem, and our deeper problem of answering the question, "Who's in charge here?"

There's a struggling Judas in all of us. Alarming? Perhaps. But stay with me as I explain. Careful study has indicated that Judas was probably an insurrectionist who joined Jesus' band of disciples because he believed the Master would rally a revolution against Rome. He was an opportunist who wanted to use Jesus and his power. We wonder how he could have been with Jesus for three years and not have understood the very different kind of kingdom the Lord had come to establish. He had completely missed Jesus' oft-repeated explanation that he was the Messiah who would die for the sins of the world. He had refused to accept the predictions of the cross and the sacrifice Jesus would be for all people.

Judas was a petulant man who could not accept authority. He had a very different agenda than the Lord's. He burned with intense patriotism and pride. He would not surrender his dreams of political glory. That's what led to his betrayal of Jesus. And he did it out of love—or so he thought.

When Jesus entered Jerusalem triumphantly, the crowds chanted words that fired Judas's blood: "Hosanna! Blessed is he who comes in the name of the Lord, even the King of Israel!" (John 12:13). The people longed for a king as much as Judas did. Jesus had a great following. He had inspired the loyalty of the people through the years of his ministry. The signs and wonders he performed incited their expectant longing for the Messiah. But it was the raising of Lazarus that had ignited uncontainable excitement. "When the great crowd of the Jews learned that he was there, they came, not only on account of Jesus but also to see Lazarus, whom he had raised from the dead" (John 12:9).

An analysis of mob psychology would suggest that Judas's fellow insurrectionists had had a hand in staging the demonstration. I am convinced that they started the frenzied chant of the ancient words from Zechariah and Psalm 118:26. Messianic fervor, indeed!

We can imagine the disappointment Judas and his precipitous rebels felt when Jesus did not grasp the ready-made opportunity to lead the people in a revolution. With his power and the fierce loyalty of the people, they could have won! A movement powerful enough to defeat Pilate's legions in Jerusalem could have been started. Victory was within their grasp. But Jesus wouldn't cooperate.

Hope for insurrection was revived again when the Lord cleansed the temple and drove the moneychangers out. But why did he trifle with the Temple authorities? It was Rome that was the enemy; Israel must be liberated. Again, Jesus did not meet Judas's expectations.

As the week wore on, the disciple knew that he had to precipitate a confrontation. Jesus must be forced to act! That's what prompted the betrayal. I am convinced that Judas firmly believed that, when pressed by arrest, Jesus would finally declare himself and lead a revolution. Judas went to the chief priests when all else had failed. He did not see his act as betrayal at all, but as the staging of events to enable the Lord to perform according to his own twisted understanding of what the Lord should be and do.

But Jesus knew! For a long time he had been able to see through Judas's ambivalence about him and his message. He knew that Judas would make his move soon. With the perception of God, Jesus sensed the subtle signs of denial on the disciple's face before the betrayal was evident in his actions. Judas did not have to explain to Jesus. His body language shouted that he had made a secret arrangement with the chief priests to betray the Lord.

During the Last Supper (John 13:21–30), the Lord

brought it all out into the open. "One of you will betray me." The other disciples responded with consternation, "Lord who is it?" Jesus answered, "It is he to whom I shall give this morsel when I have dipped it." Then he dipped the morsel and gave it to Judas. Imagine what passed between the two of them when Jesus looked his beloved Judas in the eye. "What you are going to do, do quickly." And Judas went out into the night, but the darkness was in his soul.

After the Passover meal, Jesus led his disciples over the Kidron Valley to a wooded place called Gethsemane. (The word means olive press.) The area was owned by wealthy Jews who lived in large estates on the slopes of the Mount of Olives. One of those had been a secret benefactor of the Lord and had made his garden available to him and his disciples as a secret retreat and hiding place in the tumult of that last week in Jerusalem. Luke carefully records this detail: "And every day he was teaching in the temple, but at night he went out and lodged on the mount called Olivet" (Luke 21:37). Only the disciples knew the place, and one of them would reveal the secret to the chief priests for thirty pieces of silver—the price of Judas's own soul.

While Judas was negotiating the betrayal, Jesus prayed. The hour of anguish had come. The cross for which he was born was imminent. But it was not for himself and his fear of the cruel execution of the cross that he prayed. He knew what was ahead. The sin of the world then, before, and afterward would be laid on him. Isaiah's prophecy would finally come true. He would be the Lamb of God sacrificed in substitution for the sins of all people. More than being an act of love for his friends, the death on the cross would be a battle with Satan. All of the power of evil would be focused on him. He would be sin, though he knew no sin. It had to be done. Nothing less would suffice to reconcile the world and provide an eternal basis of forgiveness, righteousness, and expiation for man's sin against God.

No wonder Jesus prayed, "Father, if thou art willing,

remove this cup from me; nevertheless not my will, but thine, be done" (Luke 22:42). He was in agony. He prayed even more earnestly. The anguish was so profound that he sweat drops of blood. The medical term is *hematidrosis;* the intensity of the Lord's excruciating spiritual trauma actually broke some of his blood vessels, causing the blood to ooze out through his sweat glands. That's how much he loved you and me! He accepted the awesome task of suffering for us. Grapple with the immensity of it: every rebellion, evasion, sin—large and small, would be internalized in him as he died.

It was the last thing Satan wanted. That was the reason for the anguish of Gethsemane. The tempter who confronted Jesus in the wilderness and then departed for a more opportune time was there seeking to prevent the reconciliation of the world. But Jesus won and, faithful to the will of God, gave himself up completely to be the Savior of the world. He would be the Lamb of God! It was with resoluteness that he arose from his prayer of complete submission.

Looking down into the Kidron Valley, Jesus could see soldiers and Temple police making their way toward the garden. The ominous clanking of swords and armor echoed up the Mount of Olives. Torches blazed in the hands of an angry mob.

Why the torches? There was a full Passover moon, making the night as day. Did they think they would have to search for him in the caves or in the shadows of the dark hiding places of the garden? He was ready; they would not have to hunt him down as an escaping criminal.

And why the swords and spears? All the legions of heaven were available to him if military warfare had been God's will. I wonder if Jesus did not smile; it was a ludicrous moment in the midst of his agony. Look at the number of soldiers sent to arrest a carpenter of Galilee! John's Gospel tells us that a band of soldiers and some of the officers from the chief priests and the Pharisees were sent as the arresting dispatch. The word for band is *speira,* meaning 1,240 cavalry and 760 infantry. Sometimes the word is used for a maniple, which numbered 200 soldiers.

Whichever was the case, quite an expedition was sent out to capture an unarmed Rabbi! They feared that he might perform another miracle or, as Judas hoped, that he would incite the beginning of an insurrection. When they reached the garden, Jesus stepped out from among the olive trees, defenseless and unafraid. He had just done battle with Satan and won. What could any man do to him now? Knowing full well why they had come and what was ahead of him, Jesus asked, "Whom do you seek?" (John 18:4). The answer was, "Jesus of Nazareth."

Jesus' response was more than a self-identification as the man from Nazareth. With all the intensity of his prayer of submission to be the sacrifice for the sins of the world, and with all the power of the incarnate Messiah, he thundered, "I am." *Egō eimi* again—never spoken more forcefully than here. All the sovereignty and omnipotence of God himself was in his voice. No simple declaration of human identity, this. It carried the unmistakable authority of the voice of God!

No wonder Judas and the soldiers drew back and fell to the ground! The original words imply that they were knocked down by the impact of his two-word reply. This was more than the determined resoluteness of a man who knew who he was because he knew what he was destined to do. This was the regal sound of a King, the Lord of all creation. It was the Word of God.

No consideration of the "I am" statements of Jesus is complete without this most majestic one. The English translations miss the awe and wonder when *egō eimi* is translated as a gentle "I am he." Jesus' response was "Yahweh!" He answered as the one who makes things happen, the all-powerful "I am."

Once again, now to the frightened and prostrate arresting band, he asked, more concerned for their trepidation than for his safety, "Whom do you seek?" Meekly one replied, "Jesus of Nazareth." This time, his response was filled with wistful longing. He had his age, God's people, his followers in mind when he said, "I told you I am." It was an utterance filled with tears too deep to weep.

But then his mind turned to his disciples. They must be kept safe at all costs. The future of the New Israel, the Church, had been invested in them. After the crucifixion and the resurrection, they would be entrusted with no less of an agenda than joining him as ambassadors in his adventure of reconciliation. And so, out of grave concern for them and not himself, the Lord said, "If you seek me, let these men go." That is sublime love; not for a moment was he without primary concern for others!

We can imagine that the Lord's eyes met Judas's as the soldiers seized and bound him. There was nothing but forgiveness and love in those eyes of the Lord—forgiveness and acceptance. He could not meet Judas's terms; he had not come to be a conqueror, but a Savior. And Judas, of all men, needed what he was about to accomplish on the cross.

The other Gospels add a telling dimension to the Judas portrait. To identify Jesus, Judas drew near to kiss him. Jesus' response is very revealing, "Judas, would you betray the Son of man with a kiss?" The words brought into focus the central conflict between what Judas wanted Jesus to be and what Jesus had told him he had come to be. They set us wondering how often the two may have discussed the real meaning of the mission of the Son of man.

Jesus had constantly tried to clarify what the Old Testament designation of the Messiah meant. Was it that Judas was not listening, or that he heard and would not accept what the Lord said he came to do? The clamoring voices in Judas were too loud to really hear the Lord. His own agenda for the Lord was too firmly set to be altered. Judas wanted Jesus for what the Lord could do to fulfill his own dreams of glory.

Luke records another telling statement, said to the soldiers but meant for Judas. "Have you come out as against a robber, with swords and clubs? When I was with you day after day in the temple, you did not lay hands on me. But this is your hour, and the power of darkness." What does that mean? I suspect that Jesus knew that Judas had offered to do more than identify him. Pointing out Jesus would not really have been necessary. Surely the chief priests and their secret service knew about his place of retreat on the Mount of Olives. And if they had wanted to arrest him, he had been available any day, teaching in the Temple. Could it be that Judas had agreed to be a witness against Jesus in a trial, thinking that things would never go that far before Jesus would act with military might?

I believe that when Judas heard Jesus' commanding *egō eimi* that night, he knew that he was truly the Son of God. But instead of confessing and repenting, the willful man did what he had always done. He took his punishment into his own hands and, in one final self-justifying act, committed suicide. If he had only waited seventy-two hours, he could have been among the disciples who were astonished with the wonder of the Resurrection. Along with Thomas, his longing to be part of a movement would have been satisfied. Think of what Judas could have been after Pentecost, filled with the Holy Spirit, his zeal guided and empowered for a truly new Israel and a liberation that would last. He misjudged the Master. The Lord would be the only creative revolutionary the world would know.

The final "I am" of Jesus' earthly ministry is set in the context of the tragic irony of his trial before Caiaphas, the high priest. Mark records it for us. In his own way, cunning Caiaphas had as much difficulty with the authority of Jesus as Judas did. He had watched Jesus with alarm for a long time, and when Jesus raised Lazarus from the dead, he had known something would have to be done. In a meeting of the Sanhedrin called to discuss the matter, the Pharisees had voiced their fear: "If we let him go on thus, every one will believe in him, and the Romans will come and destroy both our holy place and our nation" (John 11:48). The very people who said they longed for the Messiah feared the one who displayed Messianic power, because it might threaten their position and authority.

It was then that Caiaphas had committed an ultimate blasphemy. The Jews believed that God spoke through whomever was the high priest. He was considered a channel of God's word to the nation. Caiaphas had feigned a prophecy: "It is expedient for you that one man should die for the people, and that the whole nation should not perish" (John 11:50). He had used his sacred office to protect his authority and power. The words he had spoken, though rooted in jealousy, had been indeed close to the heart of Jesus' mission—one *would* die for all. From that day on, the plot to execute Jesus thickened.

The cleansing of the Temple a few days later had doubled Caiaphas's determination to get rid of Jesus. His vested interests had been threatened when Jesus had driven out from the Temple the moneychangers and sellers of sacrificial animals. Caiaphas and his father-in-law Annas had made a great fortune by extortion and exploitation of the Temple trade.

When Jesus was brought before Caiaphas after Judas's betrayal, the high priest was ready for him. Witnesses were necessary to convict a person of blasphemy. And Hebrew law required that no criminal be asked a question which would incriminate him. But when Caiaphas's staged witnesses could not agree, he threw aside the law and asked Jesus the direct, incriminating question, "Are you the Christ, the Son of the Blessed?" Jesus' reply echoed throughout the sacred chambers and reverberated in the souls of the chief priests. *Egō eimi*. "I am!" (Mark 14:61–62).

Ignorance could be no excuse. One who healed, proclaimed the kingdom of God, did undeniable miracles, and raised the dead had clearly said that he was God with them—Immanuel, their Messiah. But the threat to their authority made the religious leaders both blind and deaf to who he was and what he said. In a final act of imperious blasphemy, Caiaphas, knowing full well what answer he would get, said, "You have heard his blasphemy. What is your decision?" The chief priests, elders, scribes, Pharisees, and Sadducees called for Jesus' death. They spit on him and struck him. But they had to cover his face! What must have been the expression on *Egō eimi*'s face that they could not look at him? Did some of them suspect that he was who he said he was, and then condemn him in spite of what they perceived, because he threatened their authority?

When Jesus was turned over to Pilate, we see a very different kind of equivocation. Pilate had had very embarrassing confrontations with the Jewish leaders and had lost each time. He was under tremendous pressure when he tried Jesus. His wife had warned him to have nothing to do with the trial because of a dream she had had about Jesus. "Have nothing to do with that righteous man, for I have suffered much over him today in a dream" (Matt. 27:19). His own instincts told him Jesus was innocent. He was drawn to the magnetism of Jesus. And yet the voice of Caiaphas and the Jewish leaders pressed him into an impossible sitation. When he questioned Jesus about the charge that he claimed to be a king, the Lord's reply was, "You say that I am a king. For this reason . . . I have come into the world, to bear witness to the truth. Every one who is of the truth hears my voice" (John 18:37).

In answer to his question, Pilate got a yes and a no. Yes, Jesus was a king. No, he was not a king in Pilate's terms; his kingdom was the Kingdom of God. J. B. Phillips's translation of Jesus' answer to Pilate about being a king is, "Indeed, I am!" (Mark 14:62).

Pilate is representative of those who refuse to accept the authority of Jesus because they fear the opinions and approval of others. He had lost his credibility long before that dawn when Jesus was brought before him. A series of rash acts had made his position with Rome very tenuous. To avoid further conflict, he allowed himself to be a participant in Caiaphas's plot. How sad!

What does all this mean for our struggles? These "I am" statements force us to question the extent of our acceptance of the authority of Jesus for our own daily and eternal lives. Christ is the ultimate authority about the nature of God. Have we accepted his ministry and message as our only rule for faith and practice? He is also authority over who we are and what our deepest need is.

Paul accepted that authority. His classic statement to Timothy settles the matter. "The saying is sure and worthy of full acceptance, that Christ Jesus came into the world to save sinners. And I am the foremost of sinners" (1 Tim. 1:15). Acceptance of our Lord's authority begins by acknowledging our basic need for forgiveness and reconciliation and his cross as our only hope. But then, the Master must be given complete control over our daily decisions and the evolution of our destinies.

All through Jesus' ministry, the basic issue was the acceptance of his authority. When he healed the paralytic, he first forgave the man's sins, saying, "[I do this] that you may know that the Son of man has authority on earth to forgive sins" (Mark 2:10). His "I am" authority is recognized by Matthew in 7:29: "He taught them as one who had authority; and not as their scribes." The leaders of Israel constantly asked, "By what authority are you doing these things, or who gave you this authority to do them?" (Mark 11:28). He had told them; they were not listening. He had said again and again "I am!" His authority was the entrusted power of God.

The Greek word for authority is *exousia,* meaning the delegated power to carry out the will of another. Jesus was the authority of God on earth. That authority was displayed in his message, ministry, reconciling death, and resurrection. The same authority was then given to those who believed in him as Savior and Lord. "All authority in heaven and on earth has been given to me. Go therefore and make disciples of all nations, baptizing them in the name of the Father and of the Son and of the Holy Spirit, teaching them to *observe* all that I have commanded you; and lo, I am with you always, to the close of the age" (Matt. 28:18–20).

The meaning of the word *authority* is rooted in its first

two syllables, *author*. Christ's authority is that of the creative logos. He is the "Author of life" (Acts 3:15), the uncreated creator, the verb of God who makes things happen. "For in him the whole fulness of deity dwells bodily, and you have come to fulness of life in him, who is the head of all rule and authority" (Col. 2:9–10). The fullness Paul affirmed is meant for us in the frustration of our struggles, but only if we accept the Lord's authority to call the shots.

Hebrews gives us the key to the resolution of our struggles. "Looking to Jesus the pioneer and perfecter of our faith" (Heb. 12:2). The word *pioneer* is *archēgon* which also means author, beginner, originator, initiator—the one furnishing the first cause. Christ is the author of our life, and the one we must trust to write each new chapter day by day.

One of the major causes of emotional sickness is the inability to accept and live with authority. We either acquiesce or rebel. Or, what's worse, we give lip service to Christ's authority and still insist on running our own lives. At this very moment, while I write this and you read it, we are all struggling with the central issue of life: will we yield to our Lord's will and way? Who's going to be in charge? Who is the ultimate Lord of our lives?

Let's be very specific. Focus on the particular struggle which is frustrating you today. Then look beneath the circumstances to your inner condition. Can you commit the deeper struggle to our Lord? That's the inner secret of turning our struggles into stepping stones. The Lord knows all about what we're going through and knows what is best for us. He will bring grace and growth out of the pain. The author of life knows what he's doing. Trust him!

20

The Gift of Disillusionment

Nothing Is
Impossible Now

"I am the first and the last and the living one."
Revelation 1:17

"I AM DISILLUSIONED," a woman confided. "Wonderful!"
I replied. "I don't think you heard me. I said that I am
really very disillusioned." "Congratulations!" I exclaimed.
The woman was becoming perturbed.

I hastened to explain. The real meaning of the word
disillusion is to be set free of illusions. No one wants to live
with illusions about life, people, or situations. An illusion
is an impression which misrepresents reality. It is a false
impression or delusion. The Latin, *illusio,* means mocking
or deceit. It's a blessing to be liberated from illusions.
Disillusionment is a gift.

The word *disillusionment* is one of our most misunderstood and misused words. I knew what the woman
meant. She had been disappointed to discover that she
had been living with expectations and wish dreams about
people. She had been confronted with reality. But how
much better to live in the real world!

All the struggles we have dealt with in this book are
rooted in some illusion about the Lord's power or our
potential to utilize it. Consider these illusions we live with
that distort our perception, those untruths which confuse

and limit our vision of what *Egō eimi* can make happen. Our fears, heartaches, self-condemnation, anxiety, worry, insecurity, loneliness, inhibition, boredom, impotence, discouragement, grimness, and grief are all caused by some misunderstanding, some twisted idea that we are supposed to be adequate on our own. They are all distortions of God and what he intended life to be, deadly misrepresentations of ourselves or people. Each struggle eventually leads us to the necessity of facing some illusion which has dominated our reactions, and to an encounter with *Egō eimi*, who uses impossibilities as raw material for miracles. Praise God for struggles; they bring us to confront our twisted perception of reality and to experience creative disillusionment.

One of the most disillusioning "I am" statements of Jesus was spoken decades after his earthly ministry, death, resurrection, and return as indwelling power at Pentecost. That's why it has so much significance for us. It was spoken to the apostle John long after the exciting years with Jesus in the flesh, and it proves to us that the same Lord who spoke the liberating "I am" promises during the incarnation is alive and available today. It assures us that the darkest time of difficulty is always an occasion for a fresh "I am" intervention. Whatever happens to us, we can return to the vision of the living Christ given to John in his most discouraged, anxious hour.

Alone and depleted on Patmos, a prisoner of Domitian, John received a new "I am" hope that banished his illusions. Distance has its own dynamics—and difficulties. Years after John had heard with his own ears the "I am" affirmations we have studied, he needed a fresh reminder that the One who makes things happen was still in charge of history. His illusions about death, the power of Rome, his aloneness, his feelings of impotence, and his fear needed to be disillusioned by the Lord himself.

If the Lord could come to John, he can come to us in our times of need. The "I am" power is not limited to what he said during the brief years of the Palestinian ministry. There can be fresh disillusioning encounters today, right now. What the living Lord said to John, he comes to each of us to say and be: "Fear not, I am the first and the last, and the living one; I died, and behold I am alive for evermore, and I have the keys of Death and Hades" (Rev. 1:17–18).

That's what John needed to hear as he sat alone in a cave on the isle of Patmos. He had been banished there by Rome for his belief in Jesus Christ as Lord and his leadership of the infant church which would not honor Caesar as God. Removed from the heat of the conflict, there was nothing John could do but wait and wonder. His heart was broken over what the persecution was doing to his beloved fellow Christians, many of whom had been introduced to Christ by him. Sick with worry, he peered across the Aegean Sea and imagined what was happening to his loved ones in Roman Asia. Uncertainties and questions played havoc with his vigilant faith. He reflected on the joyous days of following the Master, the excruciating experience of the crucifixion, the victory of the resurrection, and the miraculous days of power that followed the infilling by the Lord's Spirit at Pentecost. The years since had been high adventure. John had followed the Spirit's guidance in missionary advances, winning thousands to belief in the gospel and establishing new churches. He was not a man to be put on the shelf of inactivity. Illusions of Domitian's power and the persistence of Satan's influence, discouragement over setbacks in the expansion of the Way—all needed the disillusioning intervention of the living Lord. And that's exactly what the "I am" came to do in John that day when he felt acutely, "the tribulation and the kingdom and the patient endurance" (Rev. 1:9). Each aspect of this "I am" promise dispelled an illusion and gave John new hope to communicate to the churches.

When the Lord appeared to John, the apostle fell at his feet "as though dead." No wonder. The magnificence and majesty of his presence were awesome. But the Lord had come to bless, and not to blame. He laid his right hand upon the prostrate John. The hand of the Lord in

Scripture represents his power; the touch of assurance, the communication of love. A feeling of the Presence broke the illusion of aloneness. A sublime companionship is the context of realizing any of the "I am" truths the Master has to speak to us in our struggles. Our deepest struggle is facing life alone on our own strength and perception of reality. More than concepts or ideas, we need the Lord himself!

During the weeks that I studied and grappled with this passage of scripture from Revelation in preparation for this book, I was also wrestling with a crucial decision in my work. A tough personnel problem confronted me, in which none of the alternatives was easy. What should I do? The lives of people I loved hung in balance. I tried to penetrate the veil of uncertainty. Then I realized that, more than the Lord's guidance, I needed the Lord himself. I longed for the assurance of his presence.

Then it happened. The long days and restless nights culminated. Then *Egō eimi* came. He had been there all along. But he knew that I needed the undeniable experience of his hand upon me right then. And then all of the anguish suddenly paid off. I knew what I must do! Whatever the results, I would be able to return to that moment of divine breakthrough for fresh conviction to follow the guidance I received in the midnight hour.

I share that personal illustration, not because it in any way matches the momentous issues on John's heart, but because it conveys my urgent belief that, more than the promises of the "I am" statements, we all need the power of the "I am"'s presence. And this is not the special, esoteric gift of a privileged few. Be sure of this: the Lord will find a way to bring us to a place in which we want *him* more than we want his guidance or the resolution of some problem.

Leadership is lonely. Most decisions are not simplistic. The more we grow in Christ, the more we long to know his will and do it. Crossroads are inevitable. We must make difficult choices. Problems are persistent if our lives count at all in the battle for truth and the expansion of the kingdom. The "I am" promises and presence are given to those who really care. If John had been able to accept the persecution of the church with a trite, "Well, that's the way it goes!" kind of glibness, he would not have needed nor received the touch of the Lord's hand.

That touch of intimacy was accompanied by the courage-infusing words, "Fear not." Those are the watchwords of the Master for those times when we entertain the illusion that we are alone and must face the struggle on our own strength. Over fifty times throughout Scripture the Lord admonishes us not to fear.

The admonition must always be coupled with a fresh realization of who is speaking it. In this instance, the Lord's "I am" assurance to John was, "I am the first and the last." It is the origin and ultimate end of all creation who tells us not to be afraid. The same words were spoken to Isaiah: "I am the first and I am the last; besides me there is no god" (Isa. 44:6). "Hearken to me, O Jacob, and Israel, whom I called! I am He, I am the first, and I am the last. My hand laid the foundation of the earth, and my right hand spread out the heavens; when I call to them, they stand forth together" (Isa. 48:12–13).

The creator God recreates us in the midst of our struggles. He knows us and knows what's best for us. He can speak with authority when he tells us that our fear is based on the illusion that we are facing something which is too big for the creator, sustainer, and redeemer of the world.

That day on Patmos, the living, resurrected Lord spoke with the authority of God, using terms which only Yahweh could use. This has been a consistent theme all through our study of the "I am" affirmations of Jesus. The same God who had come to Isaiah, who had come in flesh as Jesus of Nazareth, the Messiah, was now speaking with one voice. In verse eight of the first chapter of Revelation, John quotes the Lord God, "I am the Alpha and the Omega. . . ."—the first and last letters of the Greek alphabet. The Apocalypse concluded with the Lord Christ saying, "Behold, I am coming soon. . . . I am the

Alpha and the Omega, the first and the last, the beginning and the end" (Rev. 22:12–13).

But press on. The Lord also said that he was "the living one." That is another epithet for God found in his Old Testament self-disclosures (Deut. 32:40; Isa. 49:18, for example). Christ's powerful identification of himself to John in this way is consistent with his own explanation recorded in the apostle's Gospel: "For as the Father has life in himself, so he has granted the Son also to have life in himself, and has given him authority to execute judgment, because he is the Son of man" (John 5:26–27).

The impact for us is that the Creator God, who came in Jesus, comes to us. The Father, Son, and Holy Spirit are one. That dispels our illusions about who it is who comes to us in our struggles. The Yahweh who made things happen makes them happen today. John needed to know that, and so do we.

That's why, in his Revelation to John, the Lord further underlined his identity. "I died" is a definite reference to Calvary. John was not only battling with the Emperor's claim to be a god, but with the Gnostic distortion that Jesus never endured the physical suffering and pain of the cross. The false philosophers asserted that God, who was spirit and all good, could not enter into evil flesh. Some of them said that the spirit of God entered Jesus at the time of his baptism and left before the crucifixion. The Lord knew what John and his beloved followers were facing in these beguiling illusions. He disillusioned them all with the reminder, "I died."

The cross is always basic to the Lord's creative disillusionment. It brings us back to the basic hope of the gospel—that Christ died for you and me. Each day, we need the assurance it gives us that we are loved and cherished. The sacrifice of Calvary is our confidence that we have been forgiven, and therefore we can forgive ourselves and others. That's our courage for confident living in the midst of pressure. All the illusions that we must do or be something in order to be loved by God are exposed and healed. And, as we have seen in previous chapters, most of our struggles are projections of our inability to love ourselves as we are loved utterly by God.

After setting straight the matter of Calvary, the "living one" led John on to a reminder of the source of victory. Illusions about death's power were wrenched from the Apostle's heart by the triumphantly disillusioning words, "And behold I am alive for evermore." We know from our own experience why the Lord had to remind John of the power of the resurrection. We tend to slip back into the illusion that if we are to survive our struggles, we must do something on our own strength.

It's a comforting assurance that the Lord had to bring John back to the Easter hope, and then to the realization that resurrection is the key to daily rediscovery that possibilities we never dared imagine are raised out of the ashes of our dead dreams. We cannot have the overcoming vitality the Lord wants to give without a constant return to the power of the resurrection. At the core of each of our struggles is the need for surrender and an experience of the uplifting hope that God's best follows the worst than can happen to us. Surely, this is the reason John could write later to his troubled friends what had become freshly real to him: "He who is in you is greater than he who is in the world. . . . For whatever is born of God overcomes the world; and this is the victory that overcomes the world, our faith. Who is it that overcomes the world but he who believes that Jesus is the Son of God?" (1 John 4:4 and 5:4–5).

I want to share a personal word. Today, as I write this, I have had an Easter reassurance. (I should not be amazed; the Lord so often gives me a personal experience of the very things I am attempting to write.) The phone just rang. My business administrator Ted Behr told me that funds were now available to go ahead with a new series of television programs next fall.

Because of my conviction that we should not produce programs until monies are in hand, I had set today as the deadline to determine whether we could move ahead. Last night, when I said my prayers, we were still a distance from our goal of adequate production funds. Ted had refigured the gifts received thus far and needed several thousand dollars more to give me the okay. I came to that excruciating "death to self" experience which punctuates my adventure with the Lord.

But the morning mail brought exactly what was needed. "Why did the Lord wait until today?" I wondered. The answer sounded in my soul. It was so that I could give up the vision and experience it as a new gift from the Lord. In all of the most strategic projects and missions I have ever attempted, the Lord has never allowed me to get out ahead of daily dependence. Never a surplus that would encourage the illusion that I had pulled off a miracle for the Lord. Rather, he gives just enough—so that I would never drift into independence. As I write, Bill Gaither's song rings in my heart: "Because He lives, I can face tomorrow!" And so can you.

Note that the Lord says, "I am alive *forevermore*." That word has special meaning to us now, centuries after John's Patmos disillusionment. It means "unto the ages of ages"—your age and mine. We do not know when God will draw the curtain on history. The signs of our times indicate it's closer than ever. But that is not our concern. We have the "evermore" assurance for our Patmos perplexities. The Lord says to us what he said to John. We have the choice as to whether we will live in the context of that victory or the illusion of a defeat in our circumstances.

One final disillusionment awaits us. The Lord says, "And I have the keys of Death and Hades." That means everything for us personally and for our calling to be emancipators of others. The keys are a symbol of Christ's authority, just as the gift of the keys of a city to someone is symbolic of opening the city to him. We all live forever; death is not an ending. The gift of Jesus Christ, who has authority over death, is eternal life, a quality of relationship which begins with him now and continues in heaven after we die physically.

The word *Hades* was a neutral word in New Testament

times. It comes from the Greek, *Haidēs,* a rendering of the Hebrew *Sheol.* It means the unseen place of the dead. The conception of its nature was vague and undefined. The Hebrews thought of it as beneath the earth (Num. 16:30-33; Ezek. 31:17; Amos 9:2), and envisioned its entrance through gates (Isa, 38:10). There was no distinction made as to who would go to Hades. But once there, some would endure the punishment of what was called Gehenna, and others would enjoy the rewards of what was referred to as Paradise.

Jesus had very salient things to say about Hades. His parable of Dives and Lazarus (Luke 16:19–31) shocks us with a vivid picture of the great gulf between the serenity and peace of Paradise and the torturous, burning fires of Gehenna. Paradise was called Abraham's bosom, a realm of blessed assurance with the patriarch and all the faithful people who were sharing the reward of beatific bliss. Gehenna, however, was like the burning refuse heap outside of Jerusalem, which burned but was not consumed. In his parable, Jesus depicts Dives in Gehenna and Lazarus in Paradise. The uncrossable gulf divides. Neither can cross over to the other's realm.

The parable, along with the total impact of Jesus' message, sets us free from illusion. Death is not final. Nor will there be a second chance to accept in Hades what we refused during this life. The positive side of it is that Jesus holds the keys. Our goodness, performance, or character development does not determine our eternal destiny. Only Christ can give us the confidence of eternal life—a paradise of unrestrained joy and peace in his presence forever. The promise made to the repentant thief on the cross is made to us: "Today you will be with me in Paradise" (Luke 23:43). And indeed we are—long before our physical deaths. We have a taste now of what will be multiplied in delight beyond human words of explanation.

Why did the Lord include this promise in his "I am" comfort to John and to the early Christians suffering persecution? He wanted them to remember that this eternal status was theirs because he had chosen and called them. A faith that endures in life's struggles is one that is built on the sure foundation of the Lord's election, which nothing could change. "You did not choose me, but I chose you and appointed you that you should go and bear fruit and that your fruit should abide; so that whatever you ask the Father in my name, he may give it to you" (John 15:16). The Lord who holds the keys of death and Hades had predestined John and his beloved friends. They were eternally alive. The judgment and destiny of their persecutors were in the Lord's hands.

But that eternal election became the basis of profound love and authentic evangelism in the church. The Lord who holds the keys also entrusts them to those who belong to him. The powers of Hades shall not prevail against the church. The Lord had promised, "I will give you the keys of the kingdom of heaven, and whatever you bind on earth shall be bound in heaven, and whatever you loose on earth shall be loosed in heaven" (Matt. 16:19).

The keys of the kingdom are ours! That changes our attitude toward the people who distress and disturb us. They are not enemies, but bound-up people who need to be liberated. Our challenge is to live and share the gospel. The early church needed to be reminded that the deepest need the Roman oppressors or the confused Gnostic philosophers had was to meet Christ. The power to unlock them had been given by Christ himself.

There is nothing which changes the illusion of our impotence in the struggles of life more than a recall to our basic purpose of communicating the love of Christ to the very people we blame for our struggles. Often our depression over our struggles is lifted the moment we thank the Lord for the opportunity we have to model what he can mean in tragedy and discouragement. People cannot rob us of our relationship with the Lord. That confidence makes their relationship with him our deepest concern. Suddenly, our own struggles are secondary.

The disillusionment of Paul's conviction exposes our

illusions about the power of people to hurt us:

> If God is for us, who is against us? He who did not spare his
> own Son but gave him up for us all, will he not also give us all
> things with him? Who shall bring any charge against God's
> elect? It is God who justifies; who is to condemn? . . . Who
> shall separate us from the love of Christ? Shall tribulation, or
> distress, or persecution, or famine, or nakedness, or peril, or
> sword? . . . No, in all these things we are more than con-
> querors through him who loved us.
> Romans 8:31–34, 35, 37

We are left to examine our own private set of illusions.
What false perception of reality and the power of the
Lord cripples you? I know mine. *Egō eimi* wants to give us
the glorious gift of disillusionment. Then we can respond
in a way very different from the response of the woman
described at the beginning of this chapter. Our thankful
expression will be, "I have been disillusioned. Thank the
Lord!"

21

When It's Time to Say Good-bye

Good Grief

"I am the bright morning star."
Revelation 22:16

MY FATHER USED TO HAVE a favorite expression of
consternation when something or someone raised his ire
and indignation. "Good grief!" he would exclaim with
startled alarm. I can remember wondering where that
very ambiguous exclamation came from. All that I had
ever known or seen of grief was that it was not something
I would call good!

Grief is an intense state of emotional shock. We feel it
whenever life levels a blow to our security through the loss
of a loved one or a traumatic reversal in our plans and
hopes. Most often we associate grief with bereavement at
the death of someone we love. The longer I live, however,
the more I realize that the same emotions of grief are
experienced when a profound disappointment comes our
way or when we have to face the fracturing of a cherished
relationship. It invades us when something we've planned
and yearned for becomes impossible. Grief is a universal
emotion; we all feel it when we stand in the midst of life's
shattered dreams.

We experience grief whenever we have to say "good-
bye" with finality—good-bye at death's door, good-bye at
the collapse of something we've worked for, good-bye to

247

the past and memories; good-bye to the what-might-have-beens of life. Grief is essentially our response to separation from anything or anyone we wanted, loved, anticipated. It is the pain of final separation from a person, a relationship, a place, a comfortable surrounding. We experience similar emotions of grief after a funeral, a divorce, a broken friendship, a loss of a beloved leader, or the collapse of a venture in which we have invested our ego and future fulfillment.

How can this be called good? Look at it this way. Grief is the healing process given to us as a gift of God. If I had received a severe blow to my head, I would become dizzy, see stars, or become unconscious. The more serious the blow, the longer it would take for my brain and nervous system to return to normal. There would be a physical cause and effect. Similarly, if I broke my leg, I would expect the bone to knit through a healing process. I would not curse the wonder of healing, but would be amazed at the body's resiliency when infused with the healing power of God.

The same is true for our emotions. When a loved one dies or when dreams and hopes are shattered, we experience excruciating reactions. We may tremble, shiver, become faint. But most of all we will ache emotionally. When we feel intense grief, we may know a time of inertia or hyperactivity. There may be tantrums or outbursts, or we may withdraw, become unexpressive or hostile. Most of all, we will want to find some vent for our anguish. Grief is not wrong; it is a natural part of the healing process.

I want to consider grief and how to deal with it in the light of Jesus' final "I am" statement in the New Testament. It's found in the last sentences of the Book of Revelation. As we discussed in the previous chapter, the resurrected, living Lord Jesus appeared to the grief-stricken apostle John on the island of Patmos. John had been filled with deep grief for the churches and what seemed to be happening to the cause of Christ in the world. To him, the reigning Christ revealed his supremacy over life and death, frustration and pain, loss and loneliness. He gave John a vision of the ultimate plan of God and the culmination of history. Then he gave the secret for enduring grief in the interim between now and God's final victory.

Into the dark night of John's turbulent heart came the shaft of light in the words, "I am the root and the offspring of David, the bright morning star" (Rev. 22:16). *Egō eimi,* the Word of God, is the creator of all life. He was in the heart of God in the calling and anointing of David, and in the birth and glory of the Davidic kingdom. He shared in the broken heart of God over the fracture of his purpose for his people. Through the checkered history of Israel, the Lord blessed the lineage of the house of David.

The prophets longed to see the day when the Messiah, who would be born of the lineage of David and be called the Son of David, would come. Jeremiah quotes the Lord in affirmation of the promise: "Behold, the days are coming, says the Lord, when I will fulfil the promise I made to the house of Israel and the house of Judah. In those days and at that time I will cause a righteous Branch to spring forth for David; and he shall execute justice and righteousness in the land" (33:14–15).

In this "I am" assertion, Jesus was again saying that he was and is the Messiah. But the significance for us in our consideration of grief is that he knows the beginning and the end. He is Lord of all life!

That gives us background for the grief-healing assurance that the "I am" is also the bright morning star. Just as the evening star signals the end of day, the morning star promises a new day. It is the star that appears and shines brilliantly just before the dawn. Christ is that to us in our grief. In the dark night of our emotional turmoil over the varied causes of grief, he comes to us with the promise of a new beginning. We can endure the dark, murky hour of grief. The morning star, shining with hope, shall rise in our hearts.

The only other time the "I am" had referred to the powerful image of the morning star was in his promise to

the church at Thyatira in Revelation 2:28: "And I will give
. . . the morning star." This climaxed the Lord's message
to the troubled, pressured, and persecuted church. Secu-
lar morals, eroticism, idol worship, and a sacrifice of the
lordship of Christ for success in the commercial city were
a constant threat; pressure was never off the Christians to
compromise. They knew a very intense kind of grief from
rejection and hostility. To them the Lord's word was to
"Hold fast what you have, until I come. He who conquers
and who keeps my works until the end, I will give him
power. . . . and I will give him the morning star" (Rev.
2:25–26, 28). There's a triumphant motto when grief
stalks through our emotions and our hearts burst with
pain: Hold fast! The morning star is rising in the black,
worry-filled sky.

Peter tells us that the morning star rises not only in the
firmament of history but in the regions of our hearts. He
encourages the early Christians to endure suffering "until
the day dawns and the morning star rises in your hearts"
(2 Pet. 1:19). The Second Coming of the Lord is anticipated in this verse, but the liberating word is also for his
coming into our grief today.

On the night before Jesus was crucified, he gave his
disciples a morning-star kind of assurance for the grief
they would experience at his death, a promise of what
they could expect to heal the ache in their troubled hearts.
Here indeed, is an explanation of good grief: "Truly,
truly, I say to you, you will weep and lament, but the
world will rejoice; you will be sorrowful, but your sorrow
will turn into joy. When a woman is in travail she has
sorrow, because her hour has come; but when she is
delivered of the child, she no longer remembers the
anguish, for joy that a child is born into the world. So you
have sorrow now, but I will see you again and your hearts
will rejoice, and no one will take your joy from you" (John
16:20–22).

Jesus indicated that the greatest tragedy in that time
would be that the disciples would not ask for help (v. 23).
They would try to endure it alone, nursing their own

feelings with guilt and self-condemnation. Then the Lord gave the secret for working through and triumphing over grief: "Hitherto you have asked nothing in my name; ask, and you will receive, that your joy may be full" (John 16:24).

In the context of these scriptures, we can take a new and more healthy look at grief. What I want to say is for all who know the grief of a loss of love. The faces of people with whom I have stood at gravesides flash before my mind's eye. I can feel the convulsing bodies of people I've held as they've cried out in anguish, "How can I ever live without him?" I can recapture the feelings I have had when I've talked with those for whom life has tumbled in because of a diminished dream. And then, I think of those who have suffered the tumult of divorce, or the seemingly irreparable break with a child, a friend, or an admired fellow believer when the acids of misunderstanding smart in the emotional wounds caused by lack of communication. My sharing in this chapter is in an empathic salute to sufferers of all kinds who struggle with grief. I believe, from my own experience, that we can turn the struggle with grief into a stepping stone of greatness. Here's how.

First, we need to embrace grief as a friend. It is no more an enemy than sleep, rest, or the healing processes of the body. Grief is a gift of God for the cleansing and healing of the emotions. And good grief is an evidence of the capacity to love; lack of authentic grief is a sign of shallow love. A man came to me after the death of his wife. "I am shattered and in terrible pain over my wife's death. Am I defaming her memory by grieving?" My reply was, "My friend, you are honoring her. You would defame your years together if you did not care." There would be no grief if we did not care. Loss is real and we feel pain. But good grief is absolutely necessary if we are to live again after a heart-racking loss of someone or something dear to us.

It's not easy to befriend grief and go through it creatively. What others say to us and we say to ourselves can rob us of its healing power. Some people can deny us our grief with admonitions which imprison our feelings.

Some suggest that if we believed more we would grieve less. I remember a new Christian who lost a child. Her Christian friends told her that now that she was a Christian she would not feel the grief others feel. They sandbagged her with image of a victorious Christian who would be impervious to grief. But when I talked with her years later, her submerged grief had taken eccentric expressions. Her friends had denied her the healing process of grief.

Other people may deny us the healing of grief by making comparisons. "How fortunate you are to have the rest of your family alive to care for," some may admonish. "Your tragedy is nothing in comparison to what others have faced," others may say. "Don't spend your energies feeling sorry. Remember all the good things life has offered you." And so it goes.

The most serious of all the distorted advice we may get is to be admonished because we are only grieving for ourselves. What's wrong with that? We're worth it! The blow we have felt is our own. We have been denied something crucial to us. Why shouldn't we feel the loss? How can we ask God to help us if we feel we are unworthy of his comfort? Of course, grief is self-concern, and that's okay!

Then consider the shallow shibboleths people thoughtlessly dish out: "It's God's will! Just accept it!" Or "The Lord must have wanted it this way, so don't grieve." Or "Death is not an ending. Your loved one is better off now." Only after we have been allowed to express our grief and receive the comforting power of God can we begin to think clearly about the benefits of eternal life and the dawn of a new day for those we have lost. Only after Jesus acknowledged the sorrow his disciples would go through did he talk about the hope that would be theirs.

Equally as devastating as the things others say to deny us the healing of grief are the things we say to ourselves. All our evasions of the genuine feeling of grief over a sorrow deny us the possibility of working through our losses and making a new beginning. When we try to tell ourselves that we should be stronger, less vulnerable, and more Christian, we side-step the healing process.

There is no such thing as unexpressed grief. If repressed, it only comes out in another form. When we feel grief, we need to acknowledge it, to let it out, to talk about the way we feel. We need to let grief flow; it will boomerang if we don't.

This leads to the second thing I want to say about overcoming grief. It's closely related to the first: don't embarrass God by trying to be more adequate than he is. The Scriptures are full of expressions about God's grief over his people. I've often wondered why there is always a period of time between his judgment of and his reconciliation with the people of Israel throughout the Old Testament. God did not trifle with sin and rebellion. It broke his heart; he really cared. Old Testament passages tell us of the repentance of God, his turning from his anger, and the gracious reversal of his righteous judgments. We read about the vulnerability of God to what we do and to our honest repentance.

The Messiah was "a man of sorrows, and acquainted with grief" (Isa. 53:3). The great "I am" can be epitomized in the shortest sentence in the Bible, "Jesus wept" (John 11:35). Jesus' grief over Lazarus was real, although it did not end there. He went on to claim the power of God in raising Lazarus from the tomb, but first he gave honest expression to his grief. We dare not try to be greater than the Lord himself. He knew the anguish of rejection, broken dreams, and disappointing friends.

So let's join the human race! Grief is a part of living if we are at all sensitive. It is an emotion experienced by our Lord himself, a prelude to his healing power.

The next insight I want to communicate is: Don't waste your grief! It can be a time of growth that prepares us for new maturity. Often we waste our grief in self-condemnation; the "if onlys" flood our minds. "If I had only done this or that!" we say, "my loved one would not have died," or "I would not have failed in this venture." If there is something we could or should have done, we need to tell God about it and accept his forgiveness and grace.

Self-pity is also a waste of good grief. "What did I do to deserve this?" we often ask. "Why is life treating me so badly?" "Why did this happen to me after all the good I've done and the responsible life I've tried to live?" Resentment can be equally cancerous; we feel that someone must be blamed for our loss. But of all the misuses of grief, self-will is the most dangerous. Many of us have never had to deal with "No!" in our lives; we have never been denied anything we wanted. Then when death takes a loved one, or something we've planned and worked for does not work out, what looks like a grief reaction on our part is little less than a childish tantrum, a refusal to accept the reality of our loss.

Grief can be one of the most creative times in our lives. Since it's a profound emotion, grief can help us experience the love of God for us in depth. Amy Carmichael, the missionary to India and devotional writer, was right: "The eternal essence of a thing is not in the thing itself but in one's reaction to it. The distressing situation will pass, but one's reaction toward it will leave a moral and spiritual deposit in his character which is eternal."

Paul knew what that meant, and counseled the Corinthians in their difficulties, "For this slight momentary affliction is preparing us for an eternal weight of glory beyond all comparison, because we look not to the things that are seen . . . for the things that are seen are transient, but the things that are unseen are eternal" (2 Cor. 4:17–18). It's what happens to our characters through the sorrows of life that is most crucial in the preparation of the person in us who will live forever.

Finally, grief as a healing process prepares us for the moment when we can really say "good-bye." If we have owned and befriended grief, have felt through the very human reactions, and have grown in open trust of God with our feelings, there will come that wonderful moment of release.

Many of us have never been able to say good-bye to a loved one who's died. Because we have not alowed God's gift of good grief to cleanse us, we keep trying to recapture the past and clutch onto a person's memory— good or bad—for our security. I'll never forget a steel executive who lived with a strange mixture of anger and adoration for his father. He had never been able to free himself of his powerful parent's script for his life. When his father had died, the executive had not allowed himself the freedom to grieve for his loss nor deal with his unresolved feelings. In a bit of role-playing, I took the part of his father and forced him to talk out both his gratitude and his frustration. Then I said, "It's time to say good-bye." It was not easy, but finally he said it. That day was the beginning of new health and a new life of self-esteem.

I knew a woman who refused to enjoy life because she had lost her husband years before. She had never said good-bye. He was a Christian, and she had no doubt of his eternal life, but she had given up living when he died. Good grief would have helped her. It would have brought her to the place of healing where the artesian wells of God's Spirit would begin to flow again in a new zest for living.

The necessity of eventually saying good-bye is equally true for our shattered dreams. When things do not work out as we've hoped when doors are closed forever, when we've done our best and it has not changed a situation, the grief process has its full fruition in helping us accept the reality and move on to the future.

I meet people everywhere who are living in the past's unfulfilled expectations. Their lives are built around the memories of what might have been or was—the good and the bad, the glorious and the grim.

Some time ago, I visited a church whose pastor had moved to another congregation. He had been deeply loved, and the impact of his ministry was obvious in hundreds of lives. The new pastor who had invited me to speak was having a difficult time. The grief spasms in the congregation were identifiable. The people had never said good-bye to their previous pastor.

I remember a cherished project I felt destined to do but never was able to pull off. I felt genuine grief over the failure of the venture. My friends were sensitive to my need to talk about it and helped me feel the smarting disappointment. Finally, I felt free to accept that it could never be. The Lord gave me the freedom to say good-bye.

A man in his twenties fell deeply in love with a woman who eventually married his best friend. When this happened, he was shattered. Friends were glib with advice and no one let him feel free to express his grief. As a result, he's never said good-bye to what cannot be. He muses over his own hurt and says he will never marry. How tragic!

A young single woman had a prolonged relationship with a married man. Her need and his loneliness in his marriage formed a symbiotic relationship that was difficult to break. Then one day it became obvious to the young woman that the man would never leave his wife. Years later, I talked with her in a counseling session. She was still a burning caldron of regret, recrimination, and hostility. Because of the guilt she felt, she had never told anyone about the affair. Her grim, joyless face was a mirror of her memories. She had never been able to accept the closed door and say good-bye.

The healthy grief process after life's losses and disappointments neutralizes the toxins of bitterness and cynicism. Joshua Loth Liegman called it the "slow wisdom of grief." When Jesus said, "Blessed are those who mourn, for they shall be comforted" (Matt. 5:4), I think he had the many things which cause us grief in mind. But he also meant that those who experience the cleansing of grief have a God-inspired blessedness, a joyousness, a closeness to God. Those who mourn the losses of life are the ones who are open to be comforted.

Grief is good, but it also has its God-ordained duration. His comfort helps us to work through our feelings, but it also signals the time of the end of the night. Jesus did not deny the night of grief, but he also promised the morning star—himself, *egō eimi.* He is the one who has all power in heaven and earth to heal us and give us new beginnings. When we've been given the courage to say good-bye to what has been and can never be again, we are ready to experience what we never dared dream was possible for the future.

Then we can pray triumphantly:

> From prayer that asks that I may be
> Sheltered from winds that beat on Thee,
> From fearing when I should aspire,
> From faltering when I should climb higher,
> From silken self, O Captain, free,
> Thy soldier who would follow Thee.
>
> From subtle love of softening things,
> From easy choices, weakenings,
> Not thus are spirits fortified,
> Not this way went the Crucified,
> From all that dims Thy Calvary,
> O Lamb of God, deliver me.
>
> Give me the love that leads the way,
> The faith that nothing can dismay,
> The hope no disappointments tire,
> The passion that will burn like fire,
> Let me not sink to be a clod:
> Make me Thy fuel, Flame of God.[1]

---

1. Amy Carmichael, "Make Me Thy Fuel," *Toward Jerusalem* (1936; reprint ed., London: Society For Promoting Christian Knowledge, 1950), p. 94.

How to Use This Book

This study guide is designed to be used either by an individual reader or by a small group. *The Bush Is Still Burning* contains twenty-one chapters, enough for three weeks of daily individual study or five months (plus one week) of weekly small group meetings.

If you are planning to study this book on your own, find a quiet, comfortable place where you are alone and not likely to be disturbed. It will be helpful to have on hand a Bible and a spiral-bound or looseleaf notebook to use as a journal when following the study guide. Begin your study time by reading the chapter and any Scripture references not reproduced in the pages of the book. Then begin the questions, taking time to think each one through carefully and slowly. It's important actually to write down your responses; don't just do them "in your head." The action of writing will stimulate further ideas as well as help you organize and clarify your thoughts. Then, when you have completed the study, you will also have a record of your growth.

If your study will be a group study, it is recommended that the size of the group be limited to eight people or fewer; this will assure that everyone has time during the hour to share with the group. If more than eight people wish to participate, it is best to divide them into two smaller groups. The groups can meet the same night and share a coffee-visiting time, then break up into separate rooms for the study course. Participants should remain in the same group throughout the entire five-month study period; this will improve continuity from week to week as the group members get to know each other.

The discussion questions after each chapter can be covered in a meeting time of about an hour. Before the discussion each member should have read the chapter and through the study questions, writing down his or her thoughts in a journal or notebook. (This can be a "homework" assignment.) Then each person will have an opportunity to share out loud what he or she has written. The option to decline is always available, however; no one should be made to feel that he or she *must* share everything with the group.

Since *The Bush Is Still Burning* and this study course focus on our deepest human needs and how God can meet them, we suggest that the group make a decision to keep confidential anything shared in the group study. The fear that what is shared will be discussed all around the church or neighborhood can inhibit open sharing.

The leader of the group can be any person in the group who will accept the responsibility. It need not be someone who is normally in a "leadership" role; in fact, group members may be more likely to share openly in the presence of someone not usually perceived as an "authority" figure. What is most important is that the leader should be a person who is also on the quest to discover how to live his or her whole life for Christ and is willing to be open to a certain degree about this quest. The group leader does not have to have special training or do extra work, but he or she does need to commit to certain special responsibilities:

a. Be present at every meeting or arrange for a substitute.
b. Be willing (if necessary) to be the first person to answer a question. This means being prepared by studying the chapter and thinking through the questions ahead of time.
c. Discuss with group members the matter of confidentiality and commitment at the beginning of the study.
d. Be sure each person has an equal amount of time to respond to the questions with the group. (The leader should avoid the temptation to dominate the discussion and should be prepared to step in if another group member threatens to dominate the meeting.)
e. Read aloud or assign occasional passages from the study guide.

It is not necessary for the same person to lead the entire study. Your group may prefer to rotate leadership among the members. This can be decided the first meeting and responsibilities assigned.

Since *The Bush Is Still Burning* is such a personal book, we suggest setting aside some time at the first meeting for individual group members to introduce themselves and share a little about their personal pilgrimage of faith. And if one of the purposes of your group meeting is to create a caring community, it is helpful to set aside some time at each meeting for sharing personal concerns and needs and praying for one another. This can take the form of both silent and spoken petitions and praise.

Study Guide

The overall theme of *The Bush Is Still Burning* is that in the New Testament Jesus made several "I am" statements that tell us who he is and what he can do in our lives today. Some of these statements may surprise you! Our information about who God is and what his place should be in our lives sometimes comes from sources other than the Lord himself, and such misinformation can dilute the biblical excitement of the great power of healing, love, and forgiveness God wants us to have.

The book relates the "I am" statements of Jesus to twenty-one of the deepest needs people experience—needs that were revealed in a survey Dr. Ogilvie took among men and women nationwide. The questions in this study guide are designed to help readers identify needs in their own lives and to pinpoint concrete and specific ways Jesus Christ can satisfy these needs and offer us the opportunity to live joyful, free lives.

Chapter 1: A New God for Our Old Struggles

1. What was your mental image of God before reading this chapter? In a journal or notebook, write down four or five words which describe him (for example, judgmental, loving, etc.).

2. Identify at least one of your most difficult struggles today. It may be an internal struggle (anxiety over an impending visit to the doctor, irritability about a child's behavior, feelings of low self-worth because of a certain incident, etc.) or an external one (dislike of one's job, conflict with another person, etc.). In your notebook, describe this struggle in a sentence or two and give your feelings about it.

3. On page 17 is the statement that "most of the struggles of our lives come because we have painted ourselves into a corner of impossi-

bility. We can't imagine that things will change. Our own efforts seem futile." List two or three efforts you have made that have not helped your situation (or perhaps have worsened it).

4. This chapter gives at least four kinds of distorted thinking which can block our ability to see what God can do today. They are listed below. Read each one and compare it with your own thinking, looking for similar kinds of distortions. In your notebook, write out any thoughts you have during this process.

   a. I should be able to handle life myself without asking for help.
   b. God is more interested in judging my failures than in loving me in spite of what I've done or been.
   c. How can the Lord care about me when there are millions of people with greater needs?
   d. I think of God more as a historical figure than as a Person who can and will do things today in my life.

5. Keeping in mind the struggle you identified in question 2, imagine how Christ would have dealt with someone in the New Testament who had the same problem. What do you imagine that person would tell Jesus about it, and what would he or she ask Jesus to do? Write out what you imagine.

6. Can you think of a time in your own life or the life of someone near to you when God apparently did help you out of a seemingly impossible situation? Describe the situation. (If you can think of examples from both your own and someone else's life, give only the example from your own.)

7. Consider Moses' forty years in the desert—his wondering if God were aware of the struggles of his people, if he cared, and why he didn't do something. This time was spent by God to "hammer out" in Moses the kind of person whose only strength would be in God (p. 16). What changes in your own personality, if any, have you noticed as time has gone by in this struggle?

Chapter 2: Someone Knows and Understands

1. The two realms in which we live are the *personal* (private) region— our minds and emotions—and the *interpersonal* area—what we

want people to think and assume we are (see p. 26). Think back to your childhood, a time when you were at or near the ages of Lloyd and Arthur when they had the fight with some other boys after school. Was there something that happened to you or that you did which you chose not to tell your parents? Describe the incident in your notebook.

2. Dr. Ogilvie states that although keeping a private sanctuary of the inner self can be good in many ways, there are also dangers. Below are some of the dangers he has outlined in this chapter. Write a description of incidents in your own life which illustrate as many as you can of the dangers listed below. (Can you think of other dangers?)

   a. Feeling that I alone have this problem
   b. Feeling more and more unwilling to talk about my inner feelings as the years go by
   c. Having people put up fronts with me that match the fronts I put up with them
   d. Developing personality tics and compulsive behavior which reveal my inner life in ways I don't intend

3. The Lord knows what's inside us, even though we have the freedom to hold him at arm's length and choose our own actions. And yet, Dr. Ogilvie says, "the twist of our self-deception is that we assume we can think and act without his knowledge" (because we can do so without his intervention). Try to remember one or two incidents in which you thought or acted as if God wasn't aware of what you were thinking or doing. Describe the incident.

4. The Lord can forgive us and reconcile us to God *and* to ourselves, and he has the authority to release us from self-condemnation. Are there any actions in your past for which you feel guilt today— whether it be only a small twinge or a big, keep-you-awake-at-night anxiety trip? List it or them. (Of course, you are free to share at whatever level you choose.)

5. The Lord can forgive us and release us from self-condemnation only to the extent that we are honest with him and ourselves about the things for which we feel guilt. Now that you have answered the question above, you may be in a place where you can really feel the Lord's forgiveness. One sign that you have received it will be a

fading and disappearance of the guilt feeling. If this doesn't happen, it might be helpful to talk about it more with a trusted person (spouse, pastor, friend from this group, etc.) who understands this principle, and to pray together with that friend.

6. Spend a few moments in prayer about discovering the potential person that is within yourself: If you are studying this book on your own, sit quietly, focus your mind on an imaginary place within yourself that has a door like a safe, with a combination dial on the front. Imagine that you turn the lock to the first number, then the second. Now remove your hand and imagine the hand of God turning the dial to the third and final number. You hear the lock click and then the door swings open. Inside is the potential you, the you that is greater than the difficulties. Now write down any images, thoughts, phrases, or ideas that came to your mind as you looked into the imaginary safe.

   If you are meeting in a group, use this procedure: Each group member should sit comfortably and close his or her eyes. The group leader or someone the leader has appointed reads the scene aloud. After the imaginary scene has been read, each group member opens his or her eyes and writes down what was imagined. This can be shared with the group or not, depending on each individual's desire.

7. Jesus Christ is the only reliable diagnostician of our real needs. Whatever we may choose as our block toward growth may only be a sign or symptom of our real sickness. We can ask the Lord to tell us what our aching need really is. On page 35, Dr. Ogilvie suggests a prayer, which is printed below. If you are ready to face that thing which debilitates you, read this prayer to yourself as you pray. (If it doesn't feel like the right time to do this, offer your uncertainty to God in a prayer using your own words.)

   Lord, help me to know the one thing in me that debilitates me, that keeps me from being whole. Heal me at that level so that I can get on with the adventure of living.

8. When we become aware of receiving the power of the Holy Spirit, we can begin to become on the outside the person we are on the inside. Try to think of at least one thing of which you've dreamed of being able to do (affirm someone, confront someone, discipline a child, etc.), but have not done. Describe in your notebook how you would do it now, with a new awareness of this power in your life.

Chapter 3: I Don't Need My Fears Any More

1. Dr. Ogilvie suggests that identifying our own personal fears is a necessary first step toward becoming free of them by letting God have them. Major or minor, they all affect our lives. Take a few minutes to think about any fears you may have. Below is a list taken from this chapter to prompt your own examination. Write down in your notebook any that apply to you, and add any others that are in your life but omitted from this list:

   a. Fear of the unknown
   b. Fear stemming from bad memories
   c. Fear of being in pain or ill health
   d. Financial worries
   e. Fear from relationships (risk of loving, pain of loneliness)
   f. Fear of demands from others (commitment)

2. There are several kinds of fear. One is fear of things that are really happening, like the disciples' fear of the storm as they crossed the sea of Galilee. Another is fear or dread about things that might happen. A third category is the fear of things we don't understand, such as the disciples' fear when they saw Jesus actually walking on the water. Review the list you made for question 1 and divide them into the appropriate categories under the following headings:

   | *Things that* | *Things that* | *Things I don't* |
   | *are happening* | *might happen* | *understand* |

   (If a fear is about something that really happened in the past, consider the possibility that it might actually belong in the second category, since your fear could be that it might happen *again*.)

For the rest of the questions in this chapter, choose the most bothersome fear from any of the lists you have just made. Go through the questions with this fear in mind. Then, if you wish, choose another fear and repeat the process.

3. Dr. Ogilvie believes that fear is most often caused by previous hurts or defeats. Therefore, he says, the second step in becoming free of a fear is to dissect that fear, or analyze the root cause of it. Think more deeply about the fear you chose in question 2. Has something happened in your past which you feel justifies or explains your fear? Write out your thoughts in your journal.

4. Consider how long you have had this fear. Since God is willing to let us keep on clinging to our fears as long as we need to, it is possible to go all through life with them, as if we were holding on to the fear rather than the fear gripping us. Does your fear go back to your childhood? Teens? Young adulthood? Roughly how many years has this fear been in your life?

5. If someone were to ask you, "What is the worst thing that could happen with regard to this fear?" how would you answer? (Write your response in your notebook.) The move toward *disowning* the fear is a risk in itself, because it means giving up something habitual and familiar for a new, unfamiliar response to the situation. Now ask yourself, "If that worst thing happens, can I handle it with God's help?" If you find the answer is "Yes!" or even "I *think so*," then you are moving toward disowning that fear.

6. Displacing a fear with a love relationship with God means it is possible to remember and call upon the fact that God loves you and wants to be in charge of the fearful circumstances. This seems difficult at first, but with practice the habit can be strengthened, as a muscle improves with gradually increased repetitions of exercise. This doesn't mean that one day we have fear and the next day it's gone—any more than one day we can't do one pushup and the next day we can do a hundred. Take a few minutes to begin the practice of calling on God by meditating on God's love. Imagine God reaching out to you in whatever way means "love" to you. Below are several images to help you get started:

   a. A warm hug
   b. A comforting arm around my shoulders
   c. A special look
   d. Stepping between me and whatever is causing my fear and taking away the brunt of the pain

   In your notebook, write any other images that occur to you.

Chapter 4: When Your Heart Aches

1. There are many specific things that can cause heartache. The bottom paragraph of page 49 lists some general categories of

events which can create heartache. Write in your notebook the specific thing or things that are causing your heart to ache in the sense described in this chapter.

2. One page 51 is the statement, "We always think there is something we should *do* rather than something we desperately need to *receive*" in order to overcome a specific heartache. Yet Jesus said, "This is the work of God, that you believe in him whom he has sent." With this in mind, try to think of (and write down) some of the things you have thought about doing, or have actually tried to do, to get over your particular heartache(s). (We'll talk about "receiving" later.)

3. Try to open your mind to God as you pray about what you might need to receive from God with regard to the heartache. Take a few moments now to ask God what it is, then "listen" for two or three minutes, being aware of any thoughts or ideas that come into your mind during this time of silence. Afterward, write these thoughts or ideas in your notebook. (Do not interrupt the two-to-three-minute silent period to write. To avoid interrupting the communication between you and God, write everything down *after* the entire time has elapsed.) If no ideas come at all, make note of that instead.

4. Dr. Ogilvie says the basic cause underlying each of our heartaches is a separation from God; the pain we feel is an indication that our hearts are hungry for spiritual nourishment. He lists three ways Jesus feeds our hungering hearts with the bread of life: saving, satisfying, and strengthening. Keeping your specific heartaches in mind, try to decide whether it is a saving, a satisfying, or a strengthening you need. The chart below might help you decide. If you like, reread the section from the bottom of page 52 to the end of the chapter.

What is needed	*Cause*
Saving	Loss, disappointment, feeling of helplessness
Satisfying	Stifled needs, love, money, material possessions, etc.
Strengthening	Weakness in the face of a difficult task, illness, etc.

5. Question for silent reflection: Dr. Ogilvie shares five examples of people with heartaches who cut themselves off from healing by trying to deal with the situation themselves in ways Dr. Ogilvie describes as "self-justification" (pp. 54–55). All the people had good intentions, yet a subtle form of arrogance had crept into their lives, causing them to believe they were correct in their various approaches. Some of them received side benefits, such as sympathy or preferential treatment, because of their emotional pain. Try to honestly evaluate your own heartache, looking for side benefits you may be receiving because of it. Also, try to become aware of other signs that you may have taken charge of a problem which should be trusted to God. One way of thinking which indicates this may have happened is, "Since I can't solve the problem or undo what has caused the heartache, I will just have to go on aching like this." Write any thoughts you have in your notebook.

6. If your journey inward to examine your emotional pain has revealed any signs that you may have inadvertently taken over a problem which belongs to God, you are now in the exciting position of being able to decide whether you can let go of the side benefits (if any) and turn the problem over to God once again. If you were to decide to release the problem, what is at least one thing you would change about your behavior in relation to this heartache?

Chapter 5: Lord, What Is It You Want Me To Do?

1. Think back over your life to a time in which you felt clearly that you received guidance from the Lord about a course of action. If there was such a time, briefly describe it, using this outline as much as possible. (Group time: 2 minutes for each person.)

   a. State the situation (conflicting choices, etc.).
   b. Describe your search (prayer, talking to people, asking for a specific sign from God, waiting patiently or impatiently, etc.).
   c. Describe the moment you "knew" God's will. (Was it before you acted or after? Did you see evidence of God's guidance yourself or did someone else point it out? etc.)

2. Is there some specific issue in your life now about which you are seeking God's will? If so, describe the issue and alternatives in your notebook.

3. Are you seeking priorities around which to organize your life in general? Describe your search in your notebook.

   (If you answered yes to questions 2 and 3 above, choose one or the other on which to work for the rest of these questions. Afterward, if you like, come back and work through the questions with the other one.)

4. Dr. Ogilvie points out that *Jesus is the source of guidance.* So the process for finding his will begins with asking him for clarity both in our intellects and in our attitudes and emotions. Let's examine these areas with regard to the issue you have chosen:

   a. Are there missing facts? For example, is someone angry at you for reasons not clear to you? Or is a possible job opportunity not clearly defined? Gathering the missing information is an important step. Write in your notebook what additional information you may need that would help clarify this issue. Then write down whom to ask and when you will go to them with your questions. Ask God for guidance in these areas as you plan.

   b. Are you sure you understand the facts you do have? If you have any uncertainty about these facts, write down what facts you are unclear about and what your questions are. Decide how to clarify these issues and write down your chosen procedure.

   c. Misunderstandings sometimes come from distortions of the facts about how God can guide us. These distortions can weaken our desire to know and do God's will. Reread the last two paragraphs on page 65, which pertain to misunderstandings about God's nature and his attitude toward us. Then take a few minutes to write out any questions you may have about God's ability to give us guidance. Try to be honest about your doubts, no matter how "silly" or minor you may think they are. Bringing them out in the open can make it possible to remove them from your mind, specifically and deliberately, by discussing them with other people and with God through prayer.

5. Paul points out that the purpose of the life of a Christian is to "walk in the light" of truth about ourselves—our sins, attitudes,

feelings. Turn to the list of questions on page 68. With your specific issue and its alternatives in mind, go through these questions. When you have finished, look at your answers for clues to God's guidance. Write down any new insights you had after completing these questions.

6. At times some issues do not seem much clearer even after taking inventory of all the alternatives. The next step in the process, in this case, is to turn to the three resources Dr. Ogilvie says are available to us. *One resource is the Bible.* The Bible can give you guidance through passages which deal with people who faced similar decisions or through verses which flash a truth. Jot down several words which summarize the issue for which you are seeking guidance. Later, when you have access to a concordance, look these words up to find Scriptures that apply to your situation. (If you are not familiar with how to use a concordance, ask someone who has used one.) You may also wish to ask your pastor, counselor, Sunday school teacher, or Bible study leader to suggest appropriate passages for further Bible study.

7. *Another resource is other people.* Be alert as you talk with people. Think back to recent conversations you've had about this issue. Is there something someone has said that seems to be sent by the Lord to indicate what he wants you to do? Try to think of a person (or people) on this same Christian journey whom you could ask how they have faced this issue you are facing (perhaps someone in your group, if you are doing this study with others).

8. *A third resource is prayer.* Daily times of prayer, plus moment-by-moment "flash" prayers, can prepare us to know what to do. Turn to the closing paragraph of page 71, which is a prayer for guidance. If you are studying this book on your own, take a few moments to close your study period with prayer, first by reading this prayer aloud (even if you are alone) and then by "listening" for a few minutes for any thoughts, phrases, ideas, or suggestions that may come to you. (Write these down.) Continue to do this daily as you search for guidance until the issue seems resolved.

If you are meeting in a group, close the meeting by doing whatever your usual closing procedure has been with regard to praying for individual concerns. Then read together the prayer on page 71. Following the reading, pray silently for two minutes (the group leader keeps track of the time). At the end of that time, the group leader closes by saying, "Amen."

Chapter 6: Love Is Not Blind

1. Being sensitive is a valued quality among Christians because it is by recognizing the pain or needs of others that we can know how to love them. In this chapter, being *insensitive* is compared to being "blind." Think back to your childhood, when you were between the ages of seven and twelve. Was there a time when someone unintentionally hurt you by being "blind" to your needs or feelings (for example, a teacher, parent, friend, etc.?) Describe the incident.

2. Describe in your own words the meaning of the healing of the blind man as described by Dr. Ogilvie in this chapter.

3. To help clarify whether you need healing of the "heart-eyes" in any area of your life, turn to pages 81–83. Ask yourself the questions listed on these pages. If your answer is yes to any of them, list one or two examples beside the number of the question. If your answer is no, just write "no" beside the number.

4. The first step to having our "heart-eyes" healed and restored from blindness is to come to a place where we can admit that we are in need of healing. Think back over your past to a time when something painful or hurtful was happening in which you could not see God's presence or influence and you wondered, "Why is God letting this happen to me (or to them or him or her)?" Describe such a time.

5. The result of the healing is that we can see things from God's perspective—with the spirit of wisdom and revelation. We can see:

   a. Hope in the situation
   b. The legacy of unlimited grace
   c. The power we can receive for each challenge in the future

   Write in your notebook examples of hope, grace, and/or power you can see in the situation you described above.

6. Dr. Ogilvie says that one indication we have become more sensitive (or have been healed of the "blindness" of our "heart-eyes") is we will feel a new love for people. We'll be interested in touching someone with this love. Think of someone whose "blindness" (or insensitivity) hurts you or others. Try to imagine one way you

might begin to love that person in a healing manner. Without revealing the identity of the person, write out the loving action you have imagined.

Chapter 7: How Do You Take The Pressure?

1. In this chapter, Dr. Ogilvie says that "we are either under pressure, the cause of pressure, or conduits of pressure—sometimes all three at the same time" (p. 86). Turn to the list of questions on page 87 and write the answers in your notebook. If a question describes your tendency or response in general, answer yes; if it describes something you rarely or never do, answer no. Then count the number of times you wrote "yes." If the number is eight or more, it is probable that you qualify for membership in the Order of Pressured Americans.

2. Scan your overall schedule for the coming week and pick out the point at which you believe there will be the most pressure. Describe it in your journal.

3. Dr. Ogilvie suggests that the first step in finding the Lord's answer for how to live with pressure is to *know who you are*. There are often many "selves" in us vying for control. List the various "selves" (roles, needs, desires, etc.) that may be pulling on you at the pressure point you listed in question 2 (for example, mother vs. wife, employee vs. friend, etc.).

4. A second aspect of creatively living with pressure is to *know whom you are trying to please*. List the various people you are trying to please in this pressure point (including yourself and God).

5. Reconsider the pressure point in the light of (a) belonging to God and (b) trying to please God first, ahead of other people and yourself. Describe what you would do if you could be free to please only God. This is the key to the third aspect of living with pressure: *know what you are to do*.

6. On page 96 is the statement, "Because we do not expose who we are and where we are going, we often communicate an outer com-

pliance with the direction or plans of others." Honestly evaluate *what you want to do* in the situation. Describe it in your notebook, whether or not it is different from your answer to question 5.

7. When we know who we are, whom we want to please, what the overall purpose of our life is, and what we want (because we know what the Lord wants), then we can receive the indwelling power of his Spirit to combat pressure. He can come into our lives and give us a feeling of peace and serenity in the midst of pressure. To get a feel for what this is like, sit comfortably and close your eyes. Take a deep breath, then exhale through your nose slowly and completely. Visualize a cold, windy day. There is a long, warm robe wrapping you and soothing you in its folds. If you like, after a few minutes of enjoying the warmth of being wrapped in this robe, use this time of relaxation to pray about peaceful feelings, surrendering to God's timing, and wanting to please God.

If you are meeting in a group, use this procedure: Each group member should sit comfortably and close his or her eyes. The group leader reads the scene aloud, then leaves a few minutes of silence in which the group can pray silently. At the end of the silence, the leader says "Amen" and the meeting is adjourned.

Chapter 8: I've Decided to Live!

1. Living a Christian life is usually thought to involve keeping the commandments, following Christian principles, and performing certain Christian acts such as attending church, reading the Bible, praying, and making a financial contribution to the church. Consider the difference between living this way and being born into a new relationship with God through Jesus Christ. If someone were to ask you what the specific differences are, what would you tell them after reading this chapter? Write down your answers in your notebook.

2. The "I am" statement discussed in this chapter is thought by Dr. Ogilvie to be one of Jesus' most awesome and dynamic self-disclosures: "You will die in your sins unless you believe that I am"

(p. 102). Dr. Ogilvie defines sin as separation from God. By this definition, when we keep areas of our life separate from God, either by assuming we can handle them ourselves or by ignoring them altogether, we are in effect sinning.

a. Try to think of an area (or areas) of your life which you tend to think aren't important to God. Write it (or them) down and tell why you tend to think that way.

b. Try to think of an area (or areas) of your life with which you don't feel it is necessary to have God's help because you feel you should be able to handle it (them) yourself. Write it (or them) down, and tell why you tend to think that way.

3. According to Dr. Ogilvie, the plight of human nature is that there are two basic instincts in all of us: creativity and destruction. The destructive instinct is sometimes hard to recognize because its outlets are subtle, as illustrated in this chapter. For example, being ill is often an indication of the urge to destroy because sickness is an "acceptable" expression of it. What, in your opinion, are some of the ways the destructive instinct expresses itself in your life?

4. The promise of Jesus Christ is that, if we believe, we can live a life that is free from this destructive urge. What is your answer to the question on page 111: "Have you ever made a complete and unreserved surrender of your negative instinct of destruction?"? Perhaps you have never thought of it in quite these terms. Take a few moments of silence to consider what it might mean to do this, to choose to live as described in this chapter. If you have not done so before and would like to do it now, make that surrender. If you have made this kind of surrender before and would like to renew it, do so.

5. After a surrender of our *general* instinct of destruction, we can then have new eyes to see *specific* ways this instinct is expressing itself in our own lives. These specific expressions can then be surrendered one at a time, as we gradually become aware of them. Look back at your answers to questions 2 and 3. If you were to surrender any one of these specific areas to Jesus Christ now, what would you change about your life in that area? Write your answers in your notebook.

Chapter 9: Freedom from Guilt

1. Describe your ideal self below in a few sentences or with a short list of attributes.

2. Describe ways your performing self does not live up to your ideal self.

3. In what ways does your punitive self nag your performing self, trying to "whip it in shape"? What makes you feel most guilty?

4. On page 115 is the statement, "The same fears we had as children influence our adult lives." Think back to a time when you were between the ages of seven and twelve. What were some of the things you did to win approval from your parents? List a few of them.

5. Think about the ways your performing self goes about winning approval today from those you love. Are there any similarities with the things you did as a child?

6. Think about the rules and regulations often associated with organized religion. Are there any of these rules that you find yourself not living up to?

   a. What are some of the rules that seem the most difficult to you?
   b. Do you have trouble receiving forgiveness or forgiving yourself when you fail to keep the expected church do's and don'ts? Describe your feelings in your notebook.

7. If you are studying this book on your own, imagine this scene: Your ideal self is sitting on a chair on a small raised platform in the room. Your performing self is sitting in a chair on the floor near the platform. Your punitive self is giving the standard lecture, pointing to your ideal self and telling you all the ways you have failed to be like this ideal person.

   a. Now "freeze" the scene, as if you had stopped the camera from rolling a movie.
   b. Next, consider this statement: Because of Calvary, God relates to us as if we had never done or said the things that expressed

our loveless separation from him. And we will never be able to do anything that God can't use to bring us closer to him.

c. Keeping this in mind, resume your imaginary scene. Now imagine that Jesus Christ has walked into the room. Your punitive self becomes silent and moves back. What do you imagine Jesus Christ says to your performing self?

If you are meeting in a group, use this procedure: Each group member should sit comfortably and close his or her eyes. The group leader reads aloud the scene described above. After the instructions have been read, each group member opens his or her eyes and writes down the words Jesus said in his or her fantasy. This can be shared with the group or not, depending on the individual's desire.

Chapter 10: How to Deal with Anxiety

1. An important first step in dealing with anxiety is to identify its cause. Describe the anxiety-producing situation(s) with which you are currently living.

2. There are two kinds of anxiety described on page 128: *objective* (a response to real danger) and *neurotic* (an intense and pervading dread that persists with no apparent cause). Divide your list of anxieties into two groups under the appropriate headings:

       Objective   *Neurotic*

Use the items you listed under the heading "Objective" to answer questions 3–6.

3. Ask yourself if it is possible that you have put the anxiety-producing object, situation, or person first in your life, ahead of God. Dr. Ogilvie suggests that if you are anxious about it, you probably have.

4. Think about your daily schedule and write down a specific time each day during which you can begin consistently, day by day, to ask for God's will for everything you do and say, regarding this specific situation as well as your life in general. Record this time in your notebook.

5. Visualize God (or Jesus Christ) walking into this situation. If he were to ask you to describe your anxiety and to tell him what would relieve that anxiety for you, what would you say?

6. Review in your mind the feelings that accompany your anxiety about the person, situation, or object. Write down any that come to mind (for example, fear, anger, helplessness). Now imagine that these feelings are written on individual index cards, and that God has prepared a different set for you. You and God exchange cards. When you read your new set of cards (written from God's perspective), what do you think you will find? Write your answer(s) in your notebook.

For the remaining questions, refer to any items you may have written under the heading, "Neurotic."

7. Think back in your life to a time when you were between the ages of seven and twelve. When you were angry and expressed it, what was the response of the other people in your family?

8. Think about a person in your life now whom you love very much. Imagine that person has done something to hurt you but comes to you to confess and ask your forgiveness. What do you say to them and how do you feel?

9. Think about a specific anxiety in your list. On page 134 is the statement that "anxiety is spelled a-n-g-e-r." What is your answer to the question asked on that page: "What are my unhealthy ways of suppressing my hostility?"? Do these ways relate to the situation about which you are anxious? What connections come to you as you follow this train of thought?

10. This "I Am" statement is "I am the door of the sheep. . . . If anyone enters by me, he will be saved, and will go in and out and find the pasture" (p. 125). Imagine a sheepfold like the one described at the beginning of this chapter. Jesus is the shepherd at the door and you, a person, enter into this sheepfold. It is furnished like the most comfortable room in any house in which you've ever lived or visited. In it you find safety, security, and serenity. While you are in this room, begin to sort out these three things about your anxiety:

a. What needs forgiveness?
b. What must be expressed to others?
c. How can I pray about my painful negative feelings?

In your journal, write out any answers that come to you.

Chapter 11: What Are You Worried About?

1. Below is a series of "worry is" statements made in this chapter. In
   your notebook, write down examples (situations) from your own
   life for any with which you identify:

   a. "Worry is thinking turned toxic, the imagination used to pic-
      ture the worst" (p. 139). In what specific ways does your
      imagination tend to picture the worst?
   b. "Worry is a lurking form of doubt. At base it's rooted in a
      question about the adequacy of God to meet our own and
      others' needs" (p. 140). What is your true feeling about God's
      adequacy in the situation(s) that cause you the most worry.
   c. "Worry is a form of loneliness. It entails facing life's eventual-
      ities all by ourselves, on our meager strength" (p. 140). How
      do you tend to cut yourself off from available help (from God
      and/or other people)?
   d. "Worry is really a distortion of our capacity to care. If we
      were thoughtless, irresponsible, impervious people, we would
      not worry" (p. 140). What things about which you care tend
      to cause you worry?

2. Take a few minutes to review the specific things about which you
   worry and list them in the appropriate categories below. (Note:
   Some worries might fit in more than one category.)

   The Past   The Future   People   Health   Finances

3. The "I am" statement for this chapter is "I am the good shepherd." On page 141 is the suggestion to picture in your mind
   Jesus, like a shepherd guarding his sheep from a wolf, standing
   between you and whatever causes you worry—"physical danger,
   people who would use or misuse you, a hostile fate which would

disturb or destroy you, or powers of evil." As you visualize this image, how does it appear to you? Describe the scene.

4. *Worry about the past* tends to involve either feelings of inadequacy or guilt because of a past failure or feelings of fear that this past failure will be exposed and become open for all to see (bringing shame). If you listed any specific worries in this category, analyze which of these two aspects applies to each worry (or worries).

   a. Worry that involves feelings of inadequacy or guilt (or any kind of pain) because of a past failure may be evidence that we have determined to atone for our own failures instead of accepting the gift of forgiveness. If Christ were to put in words his unreserved forgiveness to you for this past failure, what can you imagine he would say? Write it out below.

   b. If a fear of exposure applies to your worry about the past, consider that after we seek forgiveness, Jesus Christ by his loving intervention can keep our secrets *when the exposure would not help us or his cause.* The following exercise may help you become consciously aware of it:

   Imagine that Jesus is holding a file folder containing a report that describes in detail your past sin or failure. He takes the file and places it in a wall safe in his office, closes the safe door, and spins the knob. As the knob is spinning, it fades from view and disappears so that no one can open the safe ever again. Is there some opportunity in your life you've been afraid to take because of the fear that this past failure will be exposed? If so, describe in your notebook how a possible exposure of something from your past could thwart it. With this concept of Jesus' ability to keep secrets (or make a positive outcome of the exposure), you can begin to pray in a new way about whether to take the opportunity or not.

5. On page 144 Dr. Ogilvie suggests that when we have *worries about the future,* we are misusing our imaginations by envisioning what might happen *without* the intervention and blessing of our Lord. Take time now to begin to practice the cure suggested here—habitually practicing the presence of Christ. Do so at this time by closing your eyes and envisioning him commanding, controlling, and conditioning every situation you can imagine. Review your answer to question 1-a for some specific situations.

6. On page 147 the late Robert LeTourneau's approach to *worry about people* is given: "Worry and trust cannot live in the same house. When worry is allowed to come in the door, trust walks out the other door; and worry stays until trust is invited in again, whereupon worry walks out." With regard to the three categories of worries about people mentioned by Dr. Ogilvie and listed below, how would you answer the question, "What have you made your honored guest—worry or trust?"?:

   a. Worries about what people might do to me
   b. Worries about what people might think of me
   c. Worries about the safety of those I love

7. Imagine yourself with the person who is involved in your worry, and also imagine that Christ is there with the two of you. In your fantasy, what does Christ say to you about this other person and the cause of your worry? Write down the words you imagine him saying.

   If you are meeting in a group, use this procedure: Each group member should sit comfortably and close his or her eyes. The group leader reads the scene aloud. After the imaginary scene has been read, each group member opens his or her eyes and writes down what was imagined. This can be shared with the group or not, depending on the individual's desire.

7. This chapter suggests that most of our *worries about our health* are shadows of the looming fear of death, whether health problems are created by actual disease or by worry itself. Take a few minutes to consider your own death. Imagine whatever it is you fear most about it, then immediately visualize Jesus entering into that situation, taking your hand, and looking into your eyes with strength and assurance. What does he say to you in this imaginary scene? Write down what you imagine he says to you.

   If you are meeting in a group, use this procedure: Each group member should sit comfortably and close his or her eyes. The group leader reads the scene aloud. After the imaginary scene has been read, each group member opens his or her eyes and everyone writes down what was imagined. This can be shared with the group or not, depending on the individual's desire.

8. *Worries about money* usually involve the fear of not getting enough or of not being able to keep what we have. This chapter suggests that the surrender of our worries over finances begins with the

tithe. Write in your notebook the approximate percentage of your income you are now contributing regularly to the church or other charitable organizations. (You do not need to share this with anyone unless you want to.) Even if you feel you cannot tithe right now, consider increasing your percentage by 1 percent over the next year. If the thought of doing this brings on feelings of fear and anxiety, honestly present them to God and ask his help in dealing with your financial worries.

9. Another antidote to financial worry, in Dr. Ogilvie's experience, is a courageous, daring faith gift. How would you go about choosing a person, organization, or cause to which you would consider giving such a gift? How much would you give? Write down some possibilities in your notebook.

10. Copy this phrase in your notebook or on an index card and use it as a prescription by repeating it each morning as suggested on the final page of this chapter:

> The Lord is my helper. I will not worry. What can life do to me that the Lord will not be able to handle for my good and his glory?

Chapter 12: How to Overcome Insecurity

1. All of us have gone through failures, hurts, and blows to our egos. These create misconceptions and incorrect ideas about ourselves which are set into our brains. And God sees these things and more as he looks at us in three different ways, listed below: Describe yourself in each area as you imagine he sees you.

   a. What has happened to me in the past which created painful wounds to my sense of worth
   b. What I am going through now that tears the scabs off these old wounds
   c. What kind of person I can be in his image

2. One area of insecurity comes from unfavorable comparisons of ourselves with other people. Is there a specific person (or persons) with whom you tend to compare yourself (and come up inad-

equate)? Write this person's name and what it is about him or her that leads to this unfavorable comparison. (If you are meeting in a group, describe the person without giving the name.)

3. Another possible source of insecurity is bad feelings about our physical selves. Do you have any physical attributes that you dislike? Describe them here. (If you are meeting in a group, sharing your answers with the group is optional—as is true of all the questions in this study guide.)

4. Dr. Ogilvie suggests that an antidote to feelings of insecurity is to find out what you can do and say to communicate esteem to other people. Is there someone you know for whom you could begin to do this? Write his or her name in your journal, along with at least one attribute or act that you appreciate about that person but have never shared with him or her.

5. Imagine that your heart is like a small, mashed, and bent box with its lid jammed in place by distorted feelings about yourself. Now imagine that God's loving touch softens the box so that it is smooth and pliable. The lid comes off in his hand, and he fills the box with wisdom, knowledge, faith, discernment, healing power, and praise—all the gifts of the Holy Spirit listed on p. 157 of this chapter. Now, describe what your heart looks like after its transformation is finished.

If you are meeting in a group, use this procedure. Each group member should sit comfortably and close his or her eyes. The group leader reads the scene aloud. After the imaginary scene has been read, each group member opens his or her eyes and everyone writes down what was imagined. This can be shared with the group or not, depending on the individual's desire.

6. The question given on page 157 is "What would you do and be if you did not worry about your self-imposed limitations?" Do you have a dream which you have never dared to attempt? Describe it in your notebook.

7. Now that we have outlined some specific details about your individual feelings of insecurity, read these words below:

   a. "Trust me to show you your special place to stand."
   b. "Your body is my temple, I love you as you are. My Spirit living in you can make you the radiant person you long to be."

c. "We can be blessed by being a blessing."

d. "I am sorry that you have been living in spiritual poverty when all of these gifts were available to you. No wonder you felt insecure!"

e. "Dare to believe that your dreams are my inspirations!"

After reading them, describe in your notebook any difference you feel about the insecurities you've described in this exercise.

If you are meeting in a group, follow this procedure. Group members close their eyes. The group leader reads the words while each member hears them. Then, after a minute of quiet, the group members open their eyes and complete the rest of the exercise.

Chapter 13: The Way Out of Loneliness

1. Describe the time or times in which you feel most lonely.

2. Below are three "loneliness is" statements from this chapter. Check off any with which you identify and write a few words about specific ways in which you identify:

   a. "Loneliness is the anxiety of unrelatedness, the disturbing realization of our separateness."

   b. "Loneliness is not isolation; it's insulation. It's the fear of knowing and being known."

   c. "Loneliness is none other than homesickness for God."

3. Dr. Ogilvie suggests that one of the tools Jesus Christ used in filling the empty space created by loneliness is solitude. In your notebook, write down the appropriate answer to the question, "How often do you experience times of solitude?" (Daily? Several times a week? Weekly? Rarely? Never?)

4. What behaviors have you used to escape solitude? Or, what keeps you from times of solitude?

5. Solitude can be difficult because it is the place in which we draw into our own inner center to allow God to do battle with the way we put ourselves down and see ourselves as unworthy and inad-

equate. Visualize a quiet place that is appealing and comfortable to you. Now imagine that Jesus Christ comes into the place, leading someone by the hand. Then he introduces you to him or her. It is the person in us whom frantic activity and overinvolvement has produced—the depleted self, spent in exhausting human relationships. How do you visualize that person? Write your description in your notebook. Now, imagine Christ's healing touch as he places his hands on the shoulders of this depleted version of yourself. Notice the changes in posture, facial expression, hairstyle, and so on. Describe the changes.

If you are meeting in a group, use this procedure. Each group member should sit comfortably and close his or her eyes. The group leader reads the scene aloud. After the imaginary scene has been read, each group member opens his or her eyes and everyone writes down what was imagined. This can be shared with the group or not, depending on the individual's desire.

6. Another antidote to loneliness suggested by Dr. Ogilvie is learning *God's way of relating to others.* Below is a list of the seven aspects of Christ's way of living with other people which will help banish loneliness. Take a few minutes to evaluate each of them, picturing people who act that way toward you. Then think back over the past week to encounters you have had with family, friends, and other people (at work, in stores, etc.). Have you always been able to respond according to this way of relating, or have you found yourself not living up to it? Describe an example. (If you like, reread Dr. Ogilvie's description of these ways of living on pages 167–169.)

   a. Nondefensiveness
   b. Acceptance
   c. Being Nonjudgmental
   d. Forgiveness
   e. Vulnerability
   f. Initiating love
   g. Being a follower of the Way

Chapter 14: Freedom from Inhibitions

1. What came to your mind as you read the question on page 175: "What keeps you bound up, uptight, restricted?" Write your thoughts in your notebook.

2. One way to determine what inhibitions we have is to examine specific areas of our lives. Below are several areas explored in this chapter. Read each one and in your notebook write out any ways with which you identify with having inhibitions in these areas. (Add any other areas that come to mind.)

   a. Hard to love people who do not meet the test of my rules and regulations (bound by legalism)
   b. Occupied by anything which threatens my material status (bound by money)
   c. Feel protective and defensive about my personal status, my identity, my adequacy, my sense of "who I am" (bound by commitment to self)

3. This chapter suggests that Christ's truth can free us *intellectually* by reorienting our thinking about God and the meaning of life. Ask yourself the following; and write down your answers in your notebook:

   a. What are the areas of confusion about God which nag at my mind? Are there areas in which my beliefs differ with almost every other Christian I know?
   b. What are my questions about the meaning of life in general or of my own life?

4. This chapter also suggests that Christ's truth can free us *emotionally* by becoming the basis of sorting out our feelings. Are there strong emotions which control and direct you at times (such as anger, despair, fear, the need to control others, etc.)? List them in your notebook. Then describe the last situation in which this feeling seemed to control your actions.

5. The third way Christ's truth can free us is *relationally*, by giving us a new way of relating to people with forgiveness and unqualified love. Is there someone in your life with whom your relationship is broken because of some painful encounter or action on either of your parts? Describe the situation which caused the break.

6. The secret of becoming a free person is to be taken captive, to give our lives to Christ and follow him in absolute obedience. Picture yourself as a free person, liberated by God's truth. If you could be this free person, what would you change about any of the situations you described in questions 1–5? (Write out what you think of, even though you may not feel ready to go out and make these

changes immediately. This is an exercise in imagining what kind of changes might make a difference, not necessarily a commitment to make them.)

Chapter 15: Our Battle with Boredom

1. In your notebook, write "always," "sometimes," or "never" as the answer to each of the following questions:

   a. Do you have the hope that some new experience will give your life excitement or purpose?
   b. Do you long for adventure to sweep you off your feet?
   c. Do you long for a new challenge, opportunity, or change of scenery to put some gusto into your life?
   d. Does the thought of life's staying as it is depress or discourage you?
   e. Is there something in you that has sort of given up and feels that life has passed you by?
   f. Could you say that life is thrilling?

2. To get a feeling for your current level of boredom, add up all the times you answered "always" to the questions in the above exercise. Multiply that number by three (3) and write the answer down in your notebook. Then, add up the times you answered "sometimes," multiply that number by two (2), and write your answer. Multiply the number of times you answered "never" by one (1) and write the answer. Now, add these three totals together to get your "Boredom Score." If your score is 6–9, your life right now is not boring. A score of 10–14 means you are bored, and a score of 15–18 indicates you are *very* bored. If you have discovered that according to the definition in this chapter you are bored or *very* bored, consider the rest of the questions in this chapter in the light of your current situation. If not, think back to a time in your life when you *were* bored and use examples from that time to answer the questions.

3. On page 179 is the statement that boredom is a sign something deeper is wrong. Try to look at your life beneath the surface level of daily schedules and responsibilities. Can you pinpoint anything

that is not quite right and that you would really rather not face and think about?

4. Boredom is self-inflicted and comes from accepting the (false) idea that the life we have is all we deserve. Do you feel powerless to change the routines and obligations of your life? Answer "yes" or "no" in your notebook and jot down any other thoughts that occur in this context.

5. This chapter also suggests that boredom can result from blaming people when we should be blessing them. Do you find yourself thinking, "If only I had different [choose one] friends, children, parents, mate, etc."? If the answer is yes, write out in what ways the relationship is not meaningful. Below that, write out the ways in which you had expected this relationship to make life exciting for you.

6. Another explanation of boredom is a trapped feeling of having no place to go, no new worlds to conquer. Are you in a position to say that you have met your previous goals financially, vocation-ally, or in relationships? (Write "yes" or "no" in your notebook.) Can you think of any new challenges available for you? Describe it or them in your notebook.

7. This chapter suggests that if one or more of the above factors or others not discussed here are the root of your boredom, the alter-native is a life in Christ. This can be approached in three steps, the first of which is *developing an intimate relationship with Jesus Christ*. After making a commitment of our lives to him, we can get to know Christ more intimately by reading the Bible or devo-tional books and by praying (talking to God and listening for God's response). Write in your notebook the things you have done that have helped you get deeper into an intimate relation-ship with Christ. Next, write out any new ideas you are willing to try.

8. The next step to a life in Christ is *learning to celebrate ourselves, other people, and life itself.*

   a. In your notebook, write down ways you can imagine to help yourself become aware and really enjoy knowing that you are a very special, loved, forgiven, accepted, and cherished person to God.

b. Think about a person in your life with whom you feel bored. In your notebook, write out ways you can admire and affirm that person. If no ways come to you, remember to listen to that person the next time you are with him or her to try to discover things to admire and affirm. You may want to "water" these "green shoots" you see by telling the person those things you admire about him or her.

c. Celebrating life means taking time to praise the most mundane circumstances. Think back to the last time you took time off for yourself to enjoy something in your world. When was that time and what did you do?

9. When both of the first two steps listed in questions 7 and 8 have been integrated into your life, it's time to move into the third, which is *becoming involved in God's central work in history.* Take a few minutes to think about ways in which you can become involved in "losing yourself in people and their needs." Turn to page 186 and review the first paragraph before writing out any ideas that come to you.

10. Boredom can come from living on our own strength within the confines of our own capacities. When was the last time you took a risk, depending on God to help you do what was beyond your capacities? Describe that time. How did you feel during the time? How did you feel afterward? If you have never taken such a risk, write down that fact.

Chapter 16: Hope in the Midst of Discouragement

1. If you did not read the eleventh chapter of John and John 20:26–29, as suggested on page 190, do so now. In your notebook, jot down any ideas you pick up from these passages as they pertain to discouragement.

2. Three statements about discouragement are listed below. Pick the one that seems to describe your own situation of discouragement best. Write it down in your notebook and describe why you feel it

applies to you. If you can think of a statement that even better describes your situation, write it down, too. (If you are not feeling particularly discouraged right now, pick a time from your past when you *were* discouraged and think of it as you answer the questions in this chapter.)

a. A situation in which I hold certain expectations has disappointed me.
b. I am stuck in an unpleasant situation for which I see little hope of change.
c. I have been waiting for developments in a certain situation (for example, waiting for a promise to be kept) for so long that I am feeling very impatient.

3. Thomas was so discouraged over the death of Christ that when he was told the Lord had risen he could only respond with "measured words of anger and grief" (p. 195). Think back over a time in which you have been discouraged. Have there been times when someone offered hope, or a suggestion, that you could respond only with similar words of anger, grief, and skepticism? What were those words?

4. In Thomas's case, Christ did what the disciple needed in order to have hope; he appeared and allowed Thomas to touch his wounds. Consider what test you are consciously or unconsciously asking Christ to meet as you struggle with discouragement. As you think of it in these terms, write out a brief summary of this test. Begin to put it specifically into your prayer time and try to listen for the Lord's answer.

5. When Christ met Thomas's test, he also said, "Blessed are they who believe without seeing and touching." Keeping in mind that God doesn't always give us the kind of proof we ask for, but only what we need to bring us to deeper faith, review the recent events in your discouraging situation. Consider the possibility that there are signs you have overlooked. Write down any ideas that come to you as you follow this train of thought.

6. On page 198 a miracle is described as "an intervention of God from beyond the levels and limitations of the natural world" which reveals the higher law of God's love. By this definition, a miracle could include either changing the situation itself or changing your

feelings of exasperation, impatience, or hopelessness into acceptance, patience, or hope. If your feelings were to be changed as you
sleep tonight, how would you change your approach to the situation? Describe one thing you would do differently.

7. The next-to-last paragraph of this chapter suggests that "our discouragements are raw material for the miracles of our Lord. Our
only task is to trust him completely with whatever causes us to be
discouraged." If Jesus Christ were to appear in your dreams tonight and ask you about your situation of discouragement, how
would you verbalize to him your feelings (exasperation, impatience, hopelessness?) and your desire to trust him? Write out your
answer in your notebook.

Chapter 17: Don't Miss the Joy

1. According to this chapter, living a life without joy is living with
grimness. On a scale of 1–10 in which 1 represents "Very Grim"
and 10 represents "Full of Joy," how do you rate your feelings
right now?

2. Grimness can come from different situations. Below are several
mentioned in this chapter. Pick the one with which you identify
most and write it in your notebook. (Write your own if none of
these fit.) Then, beside it, write out your own specific circumstances.

a. Life is serious business; there is little time for joy in the pressure
of meeting life's demands.
b. I'm searching for happiness but I don't seem to be finding joy.
I can't find the right circumstances of people or success to make
me happy.
c. I don't feel that I deserve joy, considering all I've done or left
undone.
d. How can anyone feel joyful in a world like this?

3. If you have not done so already, read John 15:1–11 and Galatians
5:22–23 before proceeding with the questions that follow.

4. If we are to be "fruitful branches" for the Lord, the passage in John indicates that from time to time we must be pruned back. Imagine in your mind the circumstances which are depriving you of joy. If someone were to ask you in what way this situation might be "pruning" you, how would you answer? Write out a brief answer in your notebook.

5. Distresses in life can be opportunities for learning what the Lord longs to teach us. Is there something your less-than-joyful circumstances might be teaching you? Write out any possibilities in your notebook, and include these in your prayer time as you ask God for guidance.

6. On page 210 is the statement that "our difficulties will break us until completely trusting them to the Lord breaks their bind." The power of prayer is given to us as a channel for giving ourselves to God and receiving the flow of his joy. Write out a brief prayer about the specific grim circumstances in your life now. Take a few minutes to talk to God about what you have written.

Chapter 18: For Things Too Broke to Mend

1. If you have not already done so, read John 15:12–17 before proceeding with the other questions in this chapter.

2. This chapter suggests several "broken things of life." With which one (or ones) do you identify? Write them down in your notebook, along with a brief explanation of how they apply to you. (Add any you can think of that are not in the list.)

   a. Broken dreams (plans for the future, a longed-for relationship, a position or promotion at work, a coveted possession, etc.)
   b. Broken lives (beloved people suffering because of what they're doing or what life has done to them)
   c. Broken health and/or persistent physical pain
   d. Broken ties due to the death of a loved one
   e. Broken relationships

3. Review the circumstances of a situation which is breaking your heart. Do you catch yourself reacting with any of the responses

listed on page 218: cynicism, despair, rebellion, self-pity, self-blame, thrashing accusations? In your notebook, write examples of such responses (things you've said, thought, or done).

4. This chapter suggests that the only cure for a broken heart is our own brokenness—being broken of our tendency to try to heal ourselves. Before Christ can help us, we must go through a phase of surrender to God. Some specific forms of surrender are listed below:

Broken Thing in Life	Surrender Phase
Broken dreams	New trust in God
Broken hopes for loved ones	Releasing that person to God
Concern for health	"Whether I live or die, I am the Lord's"
Grief	Giving broken emotions to God
Broken relationships	Asking for power for forgiveness and reconciliation

Keeping in mind the area of brokenness with which you identified in question 2, consider the appropriate surrender phase for you. If Christ were to come to you alone in the privacy of your prayers, how would you put your surrender in words? If there is an obstacle to your being able to surrender, put that into words instead. In your notebook, write out any ideas which come to you.

5. This chapter describes five steps to allowing God to heal our area of brokenness. The first is to *surrender the cause of the shattering experience,* as suggested in question 4. The next step is to try to *accept God's reconciling love.* Once you have expressed your surrender or the obstacle to it (as in question 4), what do you imagine Christ saying to you out of his love? Write it out in your notebook.

6. The third and fourth steps include *receiving the Lord's indwelling Spirit* and *thanking God for the rebirth of hope and the desire to live.* One way to do this is to begin to ask "What can happen to me through what has happened to me? How can I grow?" Write out any ideas you have about positive growth you have experienced through

your circumstances of brokenness. If none occur to you, write out what you hope can happen.

7. The fifth step to allowing God to heal our brokenness involves *helping other brokenhearted people* to find healing and to understand what the Lord is saying to them through what is happening. One way to do this is to tell what God has done with the broken things in your life. If a friend of yours confided an area of brokenness to you, how would you tell him or her (without preaching or trying to straighten them out) about what God has done in your life concerning things that were "too broke to mend"? In your notebook write out what you would say.

Chapter 19: The One Great Need Beneath All Our Needs

1. This chapter says that the one great need beneath all our needs is the willful determination to run our own lives, to use God for our own ends and manipulate his blessings for our own comfort. Before continuing, read John 12:21–30 if you have not already done so.

2. How we react to submitting to Christ's authority is a key to understanding our inner motivations. The deeper question in every struggle is "Who's in charge here?" Two examples are given in this chapter and are reviewed below. With which one do you tend to identify when you are struggling? (Write your answer in your notebook and explain why.)

Judas: He wanted the Lord to perform according to his own understanding of what the Lord should be and do. He wanted to manipulate the Lord to fulfill his own dreams of glory.

Caiaphas: He refused to accept the authority of Jesus because he feared the opinions and approval of others.

3. On the last page of this chapter is the statement, "One of the major causes of emotional sickness is the inability to accept and

live with authority. We either acquiesce or rebel." Is either of these your tendency when dealing with people in authority over you? Try to think of an example.

4. Bring to mind a particular struggle which you face today. Look beyond the surface circumstances to your inner condition as related to Christ's authority over you. Is it similar to your reaction in question 3—resentful acquiescence or rebellion? Write any parallels you may see.

5. If you were to decide to commit this deeper struggle to the Lord, what would be your feelings? Describe them in your notebook.

6. If a friend were to confide a struggle to you and ask you how to surrender it to God, what would you tell him or her?

Chapter 20: The Gift of Disillusionment

1. If you have not already done so during your initial reading of this chapter, read Revelation 1:9–18 and Luke 16:19–31.

2. Dr. Ogilvie suggests the biggest struggle is facing life with the illusion that we are alone and must deal with it on our own strength and perception of reality. Try to think of a recent example of this struggle in your own life. Describe it in your notebook.

3. This chapter presents several ways our illusions can manifest themselves to us. Read through the list below and write down in your notebook the one with which you most identify, along with an example from your own experience. (If none of the examples listed relate to your life, write your own.)

   a. The feeling of being alone in life, of having to face the struggle on my own strength

   b. The feeling that I am facing something which is too big even for God—the creator, sustainer, and redeemer of the world

   c. The feeling that I must do or be something in order to be loved by God

   d. The feeling that something I have done on my own was like pulling off a miracle for the Lord

4. In the previous chapters, we have thought about and experienced ways to find God's guidance in various situations. This chapter contains the statement (on page 239) "Be sure of this: the Lord will find a way to bring us to a place in which we want *him* more than we want his guidance or the resolution of some problem." Have you ever reached this point in a struggle in your life? If so, describe (a) the circumstances, (b) the things you tried to do about it, and (c) what happened after you surrendered it to God—both your feelings and any changes in the circumstances which may have occurred.

5. This chapter also emphasizes that our goodness, performance, or character development does not determine what happens to us after death. The fact that Christ holds "the keys of Death and Hades" means that only through having a personal relationship with Christ, dying to our own desire to run our lives ourselves, and living under his authority can we have eternal life. Imagine Christ holding in one hand a list of all your good deeds, loving attitudes, and positive character development. In the other hand is a list of your failures, unlovable character traits, and bad qualities. If the statements about Christ's unrestrained love are true, what does Christ do with these lists? Imagine the scene and describe it.

If you are meeting in a group, use this procedure. Each group member should sit comfortably and close his or her eyes. The group leader reads the scene aloud. After the imaginary scene has been read, each group member opens his or her eyes and writes down what was imagined. This can be shared with the group or not, depending on the individual's desire.

6. If you could rid yourself of one illusion after reading this chapter, which do you think would be the most important or helpful to eliminate?

Chapter 21: When It's Time to Say Goodbye

1. If you have not done so during your initial reading of this chapter, read Revelation 22:16 and John 16:20–24.

2. In this chapter, grief is associated with several kinds of experiences. Write a brief description in your notebook of your experience with

one or more of the items listed below. (If there are others in your life, write them down also.)

a. Death of someone I love
b. Deep disappointment over something I've planned for and longed for
c. The fracturing of a cherished relationship

3. When our physical bodies are injured, a time of healing is necessary before we are restored to sound health. Grief is the process by which our emotions are healed, and there are several steps in the process. The first step is *embracing grief as a friend,* letting it into our conscious lives. Yet this necessary step can be short-circuited by what others say to us and what we say to ourselves. Some Christians who do not understand the grief process, incorrectly interpret grieving as indicating a lack of faith. If you are in a time of grief, have you experienced any attempts by friends to talk you out of feeling the pain? What are some of the comments you have heard? If you are not currently in a time of grief, think back to a time when you were grieving. If you have not experienced a major grief, think about things you might have said or heard other people say to friends who were experiencing grief.

4. The second step in healthy grieving is to *be aware of the fact that both God in the Old Testament and Jesus Christ in the New Testament went through grief experiences.* Is there some way in which you have been trying to make yourself seem "more adequate" and less emotional, vulnerable, and moody? Describe some of the thoughts you have or things you have told yourself or other people about how you're feeling which seem to be an attempt to be "handling it well." If you could really be honest with your friends, what would you say instead?

5. Dr. Ogilvie lists several attitudes that can hinder growth during the grieving process: self-condemnation, self-pity, resentment, and self-will. The two paragraphs beginning at the bottom of page 253 and continuing on page 254 describe these attitudes more fully. Review these two paragraphs. Have you experienced attitudes like this from time to time? Write down some specific examples.

6. Jesus' promise in the "I am" statement explored in this chapter is that there will be an end to the pain of grief, even though going

through the pain is necessary. Imagine yourself lying in your bed in your room. It is dark, but as you turn your head toward the window you can see the first faint signs of dawn. Imagine the window covering is open and you can see the sky. There is one solitary, brightly gleaming star—a morning star. It symbolizes the hope that the day is dawning. Now imagine that your night of grief is over (even though you may not have worked through to this point in reality) and you are about to get out of bed and greet the day. Try to describe what this might be like.

a. If you are at the beginning or in the middle of the grieving process, this may be difficult. Come as close as you can but don't worry if nothing comes.
b. If your grief experience is in the past and you have experienced such a dawn, describe that moment as you recall it.
c. If you have not experienced a deep grief up to this point in your life, do you know someone who has? Do you remember noticing a change when the grief process was over? Try to describe it.

If you are meeting in a group, follow this procedure. Group members close their eyes. The group leader reads this passage aloud slowly as the group members follow the fantasy in their minds. Leave a few seconds of silence after the reading. Then the leader asks the members to open their eyes and everyone writes out what was imagined. After a few minutes, those who wish to share their fantasy with the group may do so.

This study guide was prepared by Andrea Wells Miller, a professional writer, speaker, and consultant. She is author of two complete study courses—*Faith, Intimacy, and Risk in the Single Life* (with Keith Miller) and *BodyCare*—and has written three books: *A Choir Director's Handbook, The Single Experience* (with Keith Miller), and *BodyCare.*